ORAL AND WRITTEN COMMUNICATION

WRITTEN COMMUNICATION ANNUAL
An International Survey of Research and Theory

Series Editors
Charles R. Cooper, *University of California, San Diego*
Sidney Greenbaum, *University College, London*

Written Communication Annual provides an international forum for cross-disciplinary research on written language. The **Annual** presents the best of current research and at the same time seeks to define new research possibilities. Its purpose is to increase understanding of written language and the processes of its production and comprehension. Each volume of the **Annual** focuses on a single topic and includes specially commissioned papers from several countries.

Editorial Advisory Board

Volumes in This Series

ORAL AND WRITTEN COMMUNICATION
Historical Approaches

edited by

RICHARD LEO ENOS
Carnegie Mellon University

WRITTEN COMMUNICATION ANNUAL
An International Survey of
Research and Theory

Volume 4

SAGE PUBLICATIONS
The International Professional Publishers
Newbury Park   London   New Delhi

For information address:

SAGE Publications, Inc.
2111 West Hillcrest Drive
Newbury Park, California 91320

SAGE Publications Ltd.
28 Banner Street
London EC1Y 8QE
England

SAGE Publications India Pvt. Ltd.
M-32 Market
Greater Kailash I
New Delhi 110 048 India

Printed in the United States of America

International Standard Book Number 0-8039-3107-7

International Standard Series Number 0883-9298

Library of Congress Catalog Card No. 86-655578

P
211
W74
V.4

FIRST PRINTING, 1990
Sage Production Editor: Astrid Virding

Contents

In Memoriam

Eric A. Havelock

The 'Orality Problem' as it has presented itself for investigation during the last twenty-five years, has been argued from several points of view. There is the historical dimension: What has it meant for societies and their cultures in the past to discard oral means of communication in favor of literate ones of various sorts? There is the contemporary one: What precisely is the relationship between the spoken word of today (or yesterday) and the written text? There is the linguistic one: What happens to the structure of a spoken language when it becomes a written artifact? Does anything happen? From this, one can proceed to the philosophical (or psychological) level and ask: Is oral communication the instrument of an oral state of mind, a type of consciousness quite different from the literate state of mind? (Eric A. Havelock, *The Muse Learns to Write: Reflections on Orality and Literacy from Antiquity to the Present*, p. 24)

This memorial was composed near the completion of the volume, when we learned that Eric A. Havelock had died. Our loss was much more than that of a contributing author to this volume but—as the above quotation makes apparent—to the entire enterprise of examining oral and written communication. Few would argue against the statement that Havelock's contributions to the historical examination of oral and written discourse place him within the inner circle of this century's great scholars. As he so well expressed it in his final book, *The Muse Learns to Write*, scholarship from several diverse fields—ranging from classical studies to anthropology—simultaneously but independently recognized the complex relationship between oral and written compositon (p. 25). Findings from Milman Parry and Albert B. Lord, from Claude Lévi-Strauss, from Jack Goody, from Walter Ong, and others (including Havelock himself) revolutionized our understanding of composing and reading. Rhetoric, in turn, became repositioned as a central activity so pervasive that it transcended time and culture. Yet, despite rhetoric's longevity as an enterprise for explaining the relationships between thought and expression, each period and society adapted rhetorical principles to its own needs and, in the process, created new methods of composition warranting historical inquiry. Havelock and scholars of his generation opened the door to such an inquiry, and for that we must be forever indebted. It is only as a small measure of our esteem, and the acknowledgment of our great loss, that we dedicate this volume to the memory of Eric A. Havelock.

Preface

This volume widens the scope of *Written Communication Annual* to include the history of rhetoric. The volume reminds those of us in composition studies how fortunate we are that our history is more than antiquarian: We have inherited a history that collects still unresolved issues and generates profoundly important questions. Ignoring or slighting our history, we are deprived of valuable insights into the relation of speaking and writing and of reading and writing, the influence of cognition and culture on the shift from orality to literacy, the relation of text to discourse, the social context of discourse and the roles of speaker or writer and listener or reader, and even some possibilities of pedagogy. Contributors to Richard Enos's volume take up these issues and more.

Oral and Written Communication is the fourth volume in the *Written Communication Annual* series, which began in 1986. Forthcoming volumes take up subjects as diverse as academic writing, writing in the community, and the writer-reader relationship.

—*Charles R. Cooper*
—*Sidney Greenbaum*
Series Editors

Introduction

This volume of *Written Communication Annual*, the fourth in its series, offers a continuing but different contribution to communication. As mentioned by Havelock, scholars have sought to examine communication from dimensions that are linguistic and contemporary as well as historical. The three prior volumes in the series took up precisely those topics: the first dealt with linguistic approaches to written communication, the second with cross-cultural issues, and the third with the Western tradition of academic writing. The present volume contributes from the historical dimension, offering scholarship that examines the diversity and depth of oral and written communication across time and cultures. For this and other reasons, the present volume is much more diverse than the first three in the series. Chapters in this collection span from prehistory to issues that can be easily applied to present-day communication concerns. The chapters vary not only in topic but also method and procedure, yet all studies share a concern for how oral and written communication influences—and is influenced by—culture and period. Thus, while all of the chapters address issues dealing with the relationship between thought and expression, such diversity invites a brief discussion of their roots in order to make their shared concerns and objectives evident.

The 11 chapters comprising this volume fall into several basic categories. The first two chapters provide a background for the study of oral and written communication. Denise Schmandt-Besserat, in "Symbols in the Prehistoric Middle East," introduces readers to the earliest use of symbols and, in the process, reveals those features in the development of scripts that both relate to oral communication and are distinct from it. Readers familiar with her masterful essay in *Scientific American* of 1978, "The Earliest Precursor of Writing," will recognize her ability to synthesize complex linguistic processes for readers and still provide a statement that puts forth original observations about the development of language and symbolic manipulation. Similarly, Edward P. J. Corbett introduces readers to issues; in this instance, however, Corbett draws upon his long-established scholarly career and his commitment to pedagogy. The result is a confluence of insights, personal and historical, that are presented in a synoptic format. While some of the topics may appear familiar to readers, it is his discussion of their impact and implications for reading and writing that distinguishes his chapter from overviews and lays the foundation for subsequent essays.

The next two chapters concentrate on the study of rhetoric during what has been called the first truly literate society: classical Athens. Richard Leo Enos's chapter discusses the relationship between oral and written communication and the role that sophists played in its development and in the dissemination of classical Greek script. Readers familiar with the terms and contributions of Walter J. Ong will be provided with a concrete example of the cultural, social, and political forces that shape the relationship between competing dialects, the emergence of a grapholect, and its resulting "literature." Enos's macroscopic approach to the study of rhetoric in the Hellenic world complements the chapter by Father William M. A. Grimaldi. In many respects, Father Grimaldi's brilliant chapter, "The Auditors' Role in Aristotlelian Rhetoric," is unique to the volume. While Enos's chapter emphasizes the impact of oral and written rhetoric in a public domain, Grimaldi is concerned with the relationship and impact of the reader/listener in rhetoric. Grimaldi's emphasis on *ethos* reveals how the auditor participates in the shaping, making, and ultimately the assessment of meaningful discourse between people. It is this connection "between people" that is a link not only with the assembly of meaning central to Enos's chapter, but with the volume itself. That is, all chapters are grounded in the presupposition of the making of meaning as a public activity between individuals. Grimaldi's chapter makes explicit that relationship in terms of Aristotle's notion of *ethos*. Readers familiar with Grimaldi's earlier efforts will recognize how this chapter not only complements his recently published commentary of Book II of Aristotle's *Rhetoric* but also his internationally distinguished commentary of Book I, particularly his discussion of *pisteis* in the appendix. Through Grimaldi's analysis and careful documentation, those new to classical rhetoric will have the opportunity not only to learn of the centrality of *ethos* to Aristotle's theory, but to enjoy a statement that amends long-established (but imprecise) interpretations by earlier scholars. From this perspective, while unique in its orientation, this chapter is central in establishing an understanding of the rhetorical process which later chapters presuppose.

One of the most active areas of research in the history of rhetoric is the medieval period. One reason for this activity is the recognition of the importance of rethinking assumptions about literacy and its impact during this period. The need for reassessment stems from our initial inclination to assume a univocal meaning for the term *literate* and what such basic activities as reading and writing meant during the Middle Ages. James L. Kinneavy's chapter on *ars praedicandi* provides a lucid statement on the evolution of meaning and techniques growing out of sophistic rhetoric and its impact on scholasticism. As intriguing as his findings is Kinneavy's methodology for amassing evidence. One of the most praised features of his recent volume, *Greek Rhetorical Origins of Christian Faith* (1987), was the method and taxonomical system he devised for understanding his subject and presenting proof to his readers. Here again we see Kinneavy at his best: posing an important problem and constructing a method for providing the most sensitive explanation. Readers will find that they will be as interested in how Kinneavy constructs his interpretation as with what he discovers.

Of all the chapters in our volume, Denise A. Troll's study of the medieval scribe is the most thorough example of challenging assumptions about the meaning of literacy. The religious and intellectual forces that shaped the scribal traditions of the Middle Ages produced a unique type of literacy, one which is only recently being understood. Troll's chapter, one of the most responsible efforts at carefully articulating and documenting this phenomenon, is a result of preliminary efforts leading to her dissertation. Unlike the standard history of rhetoric texts in our field, Troll's chapter directly addresses the mentality driving literacy.

John O. Ward, whose primary research concerns the history of classical rhetorical theory in the Middle Ages, looks here at the broader, sociological implications of the history of literacy and rhetoric in a period recognized as the seedbed of modern, rational mentality and culture called "the twelfth-century Renaissance." Building on work that examines the nature of power, truth, and knowledge, Ward argues that the relatively rapid advent of more wide-scale literacy promoted new opportunities for social mobility and new arenas for social conflict. Out of this lively period arose the dominant ideas, methods, and structures of modern knowledge, "truth," and education. Ward argues that "Renaissance" here reflects not a quantitative revival of knowledge as such, or even the general advent of attitudes similar to those familiar to us from classical and modern literature, but rather the advent of new groups to literacy, the collapse of social boundaries for literate people, and of firm notions of a single "truth" in society. The appearance of multiple "truths" reflecting the society—as well as efforts of different groups to rationalize, institutionalize, and profit from the new opportunities and modes that literacy promoted—make apparent the dynamism of the period. The "routinization" of the conflicts and instabilities that characterized the eleventh and first half of the twelfth centuries produced, from the second half of the twelfth century onward, the sciences, methods, and concepts of truth and knowledge, the institutions, degrees, curricula, and textbooks that lie directly behind those of today. The particular role of rhetoric in all this provides a continuous thread in the chapter.

Part of understanding oral and written communication from an historical perspective requires an understanding of history not only for our own direct knowledge but, indirectly, so that one may understand the historical assumptions that influenced a period. James J. Murphy provides an excellent illustration of precisely this point in his chapter on the impact of Quintilian in the Middle Ages and Renaissance. There is little argument that Quintilian was not only one of the Roman Empire's preeminent educators but that his impact continued (with noted absences in the descent of manuscripts) throughout the course of higher education. Murphy's chapter provides readers with a specific study of Quintilian's impact and how pervasive his views of rhetoric were in the shaping of speaking and writing.

Although the nineteenth century is often regarded as the zenith of philological research in classical rhetoric, the real understanding of rhetoric as it operates in social contexts is only being realized by this century's historians of rhetoric. One of the scholars most worthy of recognition is Robert W. Smith. His landmark study, *The Art of Rhetoric in Alexandria: Its Theory and Practice in the Ancient World* (1974), provided important historical information about a period long recognized as important in the history of rhetoric, but relatively unknown. Smith's present contribution to rhetorical education in France before 1600 performs much the same function; Smith builds on what knowledge is known about the period and then provides new, basic information so that the reader is left with a comprehensive overview of an important period. The mark of this contribution, and a measure of Smith's scholarship, is the harmony with which he integrates received scholarship with his own primary research. There is little doubt that this chapter will become standard reading for students and scholars of rhetoric.

One of the most difficult tasks of the scholar is to synthesize research—one's own and others—and make a statement that provides readers with an understanding of the implication of claims. Our last two chapters in the volume make such a contribution. Walter J. Ong, one of the pioneers in the field of oral and written communication mentioned at the start of this introduction, provides a provocative study of how mentality itself can be shaped by technology. Readers familiar with such works as Ong's *Interfaces of the Word* and *Orality and Literacy: The Technologizing of the Word* will see here also a specific topic studied in depth, in order to then provide a piece of evidence for the complex and evolving shaping of meaning prompted by technology. Our final chapter, Lynette Hunter's essay on public discourse, offers a detailed, extended analysis that captures many of the issues raised and dealt with by earlier studies. In a certain respect, her chapter complements the introductory statements of Schmandt-Besserat and Corbett by positioning and reassessing presuppositions and operating notions that influence our understanding in the shaping of meaning.

All the chapters of this volume are the result of considerable labor and cooperation far beyond the limits of reasonable expectations. For their commitment, patience, and consideration I express my heartfelt thanks to the authors. I also wish to thank Peggy Vento, Liz Weaver, and Rick Pisani for their help with preparing the format of these chapters. Sandie Danovitz, Nancy Landy, and Anna Marie Skaro will always be remembered for their encouragement and attention to special details necessary for such work to exist. A special thanks is extended to Ann West at Sage for her help and support and to series coeditor Charles R. Cooper, who had the confidence and compassion to support my efforts during this project. To all mentioned—and to those inadvertently forgotten—appreciation is extended.

1

Symbols in the Prehistoric Middle East:
Developmental Features Preceding Written Communication

DENISE SCHMANDT-BESSERAT

Historical studies of oral and written communication, particularly those of Western orientation, tend to stress relationships between verbal and literate discourse as it bears on the development of script. Yet foreshadowing—and indeed developing—the advent of writing is not only the systematization of speech techniques but an awareness of and development in the process of symbolization itself. From this perspective it is clear that the study of written communication from an historical perspective must not only be based on the study of orality but on the development of semiotics if we are to understand more completely the relationship between how individuals think and how they convey information. But what do we know about the early use of symbols and signs in prehistory? To answer this question, even in part, requires a review of evidence available for the evolution of symbolism in the prehistoric Middle East from the first appearance of man in the region to the Neolithic period; the particular emphasis here is on Paleolithic tallies, interpreted as notations, and Neolithic tokens used as symbols of goods. This chapter will discuss how these mnemonic devices paved the way for the invention of writing.

WHAT ARE SYMBOLS AND SIGNS?

Symbols are things endowed with a special meaning which allow us to conceive, express, and communicate ideas. In our society, for example, red is the symbol of blood and life; the star-spangled banner stands for the United States of America and the cross for Christianity. *Signs* are a subcategory of symbols. Like symbols, signs are things that carry meaning, but they differ in conveying narrow, precise, and unambiguous information. Compare, for example, the color red, the symbol standing for "life," with the signs "1" or "+". Red is a symbol loaded with a deep but diffuse significance, whereas 1 and + are signs which unequivocally stand for "one" and "plus". Symbols and signs are used differently; namely, symbols help us to conceive and reflect upon ideas, whereas signs are communication devices bound to action (Langer, 1960).

The use of symbols, a characteristic human behavior, is by definition as old as mankind itself (Bruner, 1966). There can be no doubt that the first human groups used symbols; in fact, symbols have encapsulated the knowledge, experience, and beliefs of all people. Also from the beginning, humans have communicated by signs. Unfortunately, symbols are ephemeral and, as a rule, do not survive the societies that create them. A first reason for the impermanence of symbols is their reliance upon evanescent phenomena. We may assume, for example, that some prehistoric societies conferred a symbolic meaning on lightning, thunder, or eclipses. These symbols are obviously lost forever, since these events do not leave any traces. The same is true for symbolic motions such as dance, or everyday life gestures of greeting or threat. Moreover, speech (which is both the most usual and most complex human symbolic system) relies on sounds that fade instantly. The only symbols from past societies that can survive the ages are items made of materials that do not disintegrate easily, such as minerals and a few organic substances, like bone or antler. Furthermore, the symbolic connotation of such objects can only be perceived when suggested by a special context. Red ochre found scattered upon human skeletons, for example, is interpreted as being a "symbol" because it cannot be explained by a mere practical reason. Symbols and signs are also ephemeral because the meaning they carry is arbitrary. For instance, the color red, which evokes life in our culture, may just as well stand for death in another. Nodding the head, which is a sign of acquiescence in our society, means negation in others. It is a fundamental characteristic of symbols that their meaning cannot be perceived either by the senses or by logic, but can only be learned from those who use them (Bruner, 1966). As a consequence, when a culture vanishes, the symbols left behind become enigmatic because there is no longer anyone initiated into their significance. For these reasons, the symbolic relics from prehistoric societies are not only extremely few, but those extant are enigmatic.

Symbols in the
Middle Paleolithic Period:
60,000-15,000 B.C.

No symbols have subsisted from the first half million years of human occupation in the Middle East. Although a number of settlements of the lower Paleolithic period dating from 600,000 to 60,000 years ago have been identified and carefully excavated, they have not revealed the symbols and signs used in these remote times (Smith, 1986). The first archaeological material attesting a symbolic tradition in the Middle East belongs to the epoch of Neanderthal man, the Mousterian period, as late as 60,000-25,000 B.C. The data are twofold: First, fragments of ochre were recovered in the cave of Qafzeh, Israel (Vandermeersch, 1972). There is no indication how the red pigment was used, but it was obvious that it was collected intentionally and carried to the settlement by the Neanderthal hunters because hematite does not belong to the geological setting of this particular area. It is also certain that the pieces of ochre were utilized, because they bear definite traces of scraping. The second set of evidence for symbolism in the Mousterian period consists of funerary paraphernalia displayed in burial sites. For example, flowers were deposited in a grave at Shanidar Cave, about 60,000

B.C. (Solecki, 1972), and at Qafzeh, Israel, a child's tomb was furnished with animal antlers (Vandermeersch, 1972). Although there will never be a chance to know the significance that ochre, flowers, and antlers had for Neanderthal man, it is generally assumed that the red pigment and the funerary deposits were symbols carrying a magico-religious connotation. As Shackley (1980) remarked, Neanderthal humans had developed the means of expressing abstract concepts.

It seems significant that European Paleolithic sites have produced the same kind of evidence for the use of symbols. The European material is, however, more substantial and more diversified, including in particular the first evidence of graphic symbols. The Abbevillian/ Acheulian site of Terra Amata, France, furnished traces of the use of red ochre by *Homo erectus*, the antecedent of Neanderthal man, as early as 300,000 B.C. (Lumley, 1969). Furthermore, heavy concentrations of pigments are attested in several European Mousterian sites, including ochre for reds, browns, or yellows and manganese for black (Bordes, 1972; Klein, 1966; Leroi-Gourhan, 1961). Neanderthal groups of Europe also provided graves with ochre or food offerings. For example, at La Chapelle aux Saints, France, a man of about 50 years of age had been buried with a few pieces of flint, several lumps of ochre, and the leg of a bison (Bouyssonie, 1908). At Teshik Tash in eastern Europe—like at Qafzeh—the body of a child was buried with animal antlers (Movius, 1953). The European Mousterian assemblages also yield animal teeth, small bones, oddly shaped or colorful stones, and shells (Leroi-Gourhan, 1955), sometimes grooved for suspension, which are assumed to have been conceived as beneficent and borne as amulets.

The Mousterian of Europe is important for this study, mostly because it produced the first known monument bearing graphic symbols. These appeared on a triangular stone, which apparently belonged to a funerary setting because it was found face down over the remains of a 6-year-old child at La Ferrassie, France (Peyrony, 1934). The slab was engraved with several shallow, round markings pecked with a stone ax. These "cup marks" are particularly significant because they do not represent an isolated and short-lived phenomenon, but constitute the point of departure for a tradition of graphic symbolism which was continued by

Homo sapiens during the Upper Paleolithic period. Cup marks sculptured on stone blocks are known to be present in several French sites, among which are Abri Castenet and Abri Cellier (Leroi-Gourhan, 1971).

To sum up the present knowledge available on symbolism during the Lower and Middle Paleolithic, we have to admit first that there is little or no information on the symbolic activity of our forefathers except for the use of pigments in their settlements and a ritual to bury the dead. The earliest evidence of graphic symbols does not come from the Middle East, but from Europe: cup marks that were apparently also linked to a funerary practice. The cup marks are important in the evolution of symbolism because they constitute the earliest examples of manmade symbols. Whereas at Terra Amata, *Homo erectus* conferred a meaning on pigments readily available in nature, Neanderthal man at La Ferrassie started modifying materials in order to translate thought. While evidence is obviously scanty, it is apparent that the intent to symbolize is present and—to this end—objects and material are utilized and even "made" for the purpose.

Symbols in the Upper Paleolithic Period: 15, 000-10,000 B.C.

The earliest artifacts bearing graphic symbols in the Middle East are bone fragments, engraved with a series of notches usually arranged in a parallel fashion. Such notched bones were recovered in the cave of Ksar Akil and the rock shelter of Jiita, both in Lebanon, and dated to the late Kebaran period (about 15,000-12,000 B.C.). Ksar Akil produced one bone awl, about 10 cm long, bearing some 170 incisions grouped along the shaft into four different columns (Tixier, 1974). The markings consist of mostly straight strokes with some instances of overlapping into V and X shapes. The incised bone of Jiita, also used as an awl, bears three irregular rows of markings arranged in a zigzag pattern (Copeland & Hours, 1977). Notched bones are also present in Europe during most of the Upper Paleolithic period (between 29,000 and 11,000 B.C.). In western Asia, as in Europe, the first notched bones coincide with the earliest occurrence of iconic symbols, mostly representing animals. The cave of Beldibi, Turkey—dated, like Ksar Akil and Jiita, to about 15,000-12,000 B.C.—produced the earliest examples of pictorial representations in the Middle East. Two kinds of examples are involved: First, the images of two animals (a bull and a deer) shown leaping were traced with a flint at the entrance of the cave (Bostanci, 1959). Second, animal designs were engraved on pebbles (Bostanci, 1964).

In the Middle East, as in Europe, the function of these two categories of symbols—iconic and linear, or naturalistic and geometric—can only be hypothesized. According to Alexander Marshack's theory, the notched bones were tallies, each notch representing one item. In fact, Marshack (1972) proposed that the notched bones were lunar calendars, each incised line recording one appearance of the moon. On the other hand, Andre Leroi-Gourhan (1971) viewed the animal images as referring to the numinous, each species representing one manifestation of a complex cosmology. If these interpretations are valid, we can for the first time identify the use of both symbols and signs. The iconic representations, according to Leroi-Gourhan, were symbols of magicoreligious significance. The animal representations were therefore loaded with a deep meaning and served as instruments of thought by which individuals conceived a common cosmology. Following Marshack, the linear markings referred to discrete and concrete entities, such as—perhaps—successive appearances of the moon. They can therefore be considered as signs which promoted to the accumulation of knowledge for specific ends.

The Paleolithic tallies were an impressive step in the evolution of technologies for the communication and manipulation of data. Their major significance was to promote abstraction:

1. The signs translated concrete information into abstract markings.
2. They removed the data from their context. For example, the sighting of the moon was abstracted from any simultaneous events such as atmospheric or social conditions. Each moon occurrence was noted by a

same stroke, whether after a rainy or scorching day, or a hungry or fulfilled day.

3. The signs separated the knowledge from the knower, presenting data—
   as expressed by Marshall McLuhan (1964)—in a "cold" and static visual form, rather than the "hot" and flexible oral medium which
   involves voice modulation and body language.

As a result, graphic signs not only brought about a new way of recording, handling, and communicating data, but an unprecedented objectivity in dealing with information.

The tallies remained, however, a rudimentary device. First, the
notches were unspecific because they could have an unlimited choice
of interpretations. Marshack (1972) hypothesized that they stood for
phases of the moon, but others have postulated that the markings kept
tallies of animal kills and it is possible that both theories are correct;
the notches representing whatever needed to be kept track of, be it
moons, animals, or any other possible item. The notched bones were
limited, in fact, to the storing of quantitative information only concerning things known by their maker, but which remained enigmatic to
anyone else. These quantities were entered according to the basic
principle of one-to-one correspondence, which consisted in matching
each unit of a group to be tallied with one notch, with seemingly no
attempt at showing sets. Finally, because tallies had at their disposal
mostly a single type of marking, namely notches, they were confined
to handling only one type of data at a time. One bone could keep track
of one item, but a second one was necessary to keep track of a second
set of data. Therefore, the simple method of tallies could only be
adequate in communities where only a few obvious items were being
recorded. This seems to be the case in the Upper Paleolithic period,
when food was not systematically hoarded, and in an egalitarian society
where all members of a band had equal access to common resources.

Mesolithic Symbols:
10,000-8,000 B.C.

There is no evidence for any major modification in the use of
symbols during the Mesolithic period in the Middle East. Artifacts

bearing linear markings continued to be part of archaeological assemblages from the Levant to Iraq. Incised bones were recovered, for example, at the two Natufian sites of Hayonim (Bar Yosef & Goren, 1973) and Ain Mallaha (Perrot, 1966), Palestine, about 10,000 B.C. A third Natufian settlement, Rosh Zin in the Negev (Henry, 1985), as well as Zawi-Chemi, a contemporaneous site in northern Iraq, produced pebbles and various bone implements engraved with parallel lines (Solecki, 1981).

Symbols of suspected magico-religious significance also persist in the form of funerary paraphernalia, amulets, and animal art similar to those of the Paleolithic tradition. For instance, the Natufians of the Levant are known for burying their dead with elaborate headdresses made of dentalium shells (Valla, 1975) and decorating their tools with animal motifs (Valla, 1975). A new feature worthy of mention, however, consists of schematic human figurines carved in stone (Valla, 1975) similar to earlier European examples (Leroi-Gourhan, 1971) and equally enigmatic.

Neolithic Symbols:
8000-6000 B.C.

The first agricultural communities of the Middle East carried on the age-old symbolic traditions. The early farmers placed antlers in house foundations (Cauvin, 1978) and painted their floors with pigments (Cauvin, 1972). They performed burial rituals that also sometimes involved red ochre (Braidwood, Howe, & Reed, 1961). Colorful stones like red carnelian, black obsidian, gray steatite, white alabaster, and mother of pearl continued to be worn (Contenson, 1972), and notched bones were still part of village assemblages (Redman, 1978). At that time, animal and human forms were translated into clay, which is the Neolithic material par excellence (Schmandt-Besserat, 1974, 1977). These figurines and other early Neolithic symbolic assemblages remain as enigmatic to us as the preceding Mesolithic and Paleolithic material, and are generally assumed to bear a magico-religious significance. However, the practice of agriculture which brought a new economy based on hoarding grains, a new way of life based on sedentariness, new settlement patterns in open-air villages, new technologies such as ground and polished stone, and the use of new raw materials such as clay also generated new symbols. These symbols were different in form and content from anything used previously. They were clay tokens modeled in distinctive stages, each representing one unit of a commodity (Schmandt-Besserat, 1980).

Tokens were clay artifacts modeled into multiple forms, either geometric or naturalistic. All of these forms were new, and none had antecedents in Paleolithic or Mesolithic times. As Cyril Smith (1983) has mentioned, the token system exploited for the first time all of the basic geometric shapes, such as the sphere, cone, cylinder, tetrahedron, triangle, quadrangle, and cubes (the latter surprisingly rarely). Some of these forms, such as the disks and cylinders—which stood for numbers of animals—were fully abstract, since they were not derived from the image of any animal or part of a animal. Others, such as the cones, may be argued to be iconic, depicting vessels of geometric shapes such as conical cups. All of these forms were arbitrary, exhibiting a deliberate choice of a particular set of features.

The token system was also novel in the kind of information it conveyed. Whereas Paleolithic iconic art probably evoked cosmological figures and Paleolithic or Mesolithic tallies may have recorded time, the tokens dealt with economic data, namely, each token stood for one precise amount of a commodity. For example, the cone and the sphere represented measures of grain probably equivalent respectively to our liter and bushel; the cylinder and lenticular disks showed numbers of animals; the tetrahedrons were units of work, and so forth. The new symbolic values originated, seemingly, as a direct consequence of agriculture. This is suggested by the following facts: First, tokens were never found in sites where hunting and gathering was the base of food procurement, but are part and parcel of the first agriculturalists' tool kits. Second, the timing of their appearance and their geographic extension in the eighth millennium B.C. precisely coincides with the time and region involved in experimenting with the domestication of plants and animals (Schmandt-Besserat, 1982). Third, the first tokens stood for products of the farm. Fourth, it appears logical that a lifestyle based on planning a harvest and hoarding food for survival would incite record-keeping. Fifth, and finally, it also makes sense that a socioeconomic system based on the redistribution of commodities would require a device for record-keeping in order to control goods. Situational and cultural indicators reveal, as is true with the study of written communication, that the development and use of such symbols is directly tied with social context; that is, symbolic meaning emerges as cultures evolve to a point that such forms of manifesting meaning are needed and valued.

THE PLACE OF TOKENS IN THE
EVOLUTION OF SYMBOLS

The tokens were the link between tallies and writing. On the one hand they perpetuated some basic features of the Stone Age and, on the other hand, the innovations they brought to communication presaged writing. The tokens shared with tallies the method of translating concrete information into abstract signs. Like the tallies, tokens removed the data from its context and separated the knowledge from its knower. Thus, like the Paleolithic notched bones, the token system promoted abstraction and objectivity. Tokens also shared with tallies the way of presenting information in one-to-one correspondence. Each token stood for one unit of a commodity, just as each notch on a bone stood for one item counted. Whereas tallies recorded only quantitative information, however, the tokens conveyed also qualitative information (Schmandt-Besserat, 1984). Each token indicated by its shape the type of item counted, while the number of units involved was shown by the corresponding number of tokens. For example, one bushel of grain was represented by one sphere; two bushels of grain by two spheres, and so on. The principle of one-to-one correspondence, inherited from the past technologies, made the system cumbersome because piles of tokens could not be handled easily. In particular, humans have difficulty identifying at a glance the number of artifacts in sets exceeding five to seven units.

The tokens differed from tallies, first in material; the counters were modeled of clay, a plastic material which can be shaped into multiple forms, easy to recognize and easy to duplicate. The primary singularity of the tokens was, therefore, that they were entirely manmade. Compared to tallies which communicated meaning by slightly altering a bone, the tokens were artifacts created from an amorphous mass into specific shapes, for the unique purpose of communication and record-keeping. The format of small tokens was an improvement over the notched bones. The tokens made it easy to manipulate data since the small artifacts could be arranged and rearranged in groups of any size and composition, while notches, once engraved on a bone, were fixed and irreversible. The token system brought more flexibility in the processing of information by making it possible to add, subtract, amend, and rectify data at will. The tokens were an entirely new medium for conveying information. Compared to the previous tallies, the conceptual leap was to endow each token shape with a unique meaning. Consequently, unlike markings of tallies (which had an infinite number of possible interpretations), each clay token was a distinct sign with a single, discrete, and unequivocal significance. While tallies were meaningless when out of context, the tokens could always be understood by anyone initiated into the system. The cone, for example, stood for a small measure of grain and could only have this one meaning. According to the late Ignacius J. Gelb's terminology (1974), the tokens were "word signs."

The greatest novelty of the tokens, however, was in that they formed a system. There was not only one type of token carrying a discrete meaning but an entire repertory of interrelated types of tokens, each with a corresponding discrete meaning. For example, besides the cone, which stood for a small measure of grain, the ovoid stood for a jar of oil, and so forth. The system made it feasible to manipulate simultaneously information concerning different categories of items, bringing a complexity of data processing never reached previously. It became possible to store with precision unlimited quantities of information concerning an unlimited number of goods without the risks of failure of human memory. Furthermore, the system was open; that is to say, new signs were added when necessary by creating new token shapes, and the ever-increasing repertory constantly pushed the device to new frontiers of complexity. The token system was, in fact, the first code—

the earliest system of signs used for transmitting information. The code included a number of token shapes, each bearing a discrete meaning. A sphere, for example, always signified a particular measure of grain and a cylinder always an animal. There were as many shapes of counters in the token repertory as was necessary to express.

The main features which ensured the success of the token system and explain its impact on communication can be summarized as follows:

1. The system was simple.
   a. The tokens were made of clay, a common material that required no special skills to be worked.
   b. The tokens' forms were plain and easy to duplicate.
   c. The system was based on one-to-one correspondence, which is an innate human capacity for dealing with quantities.
   d. The tokens were word signs. Therefore, they were independent of phonetics and could be meaningful in any dialect.
2. The tokens allowed new performances in data processing.
   a. It was the first mnemonic device able to store an unlimited quantity of data.
   b. It brought more flexibility in the manipulation of information by making it possible to add, subtract, and rectify data at will.
   c. It enhanced logic and rational decision making by allowing the scrutiny of complex data.
   d. It facilitated the communication of information.
3. The code was timely.
   a. It fulfilled new needs for counting and accounting brought about by agriculture.
   b. It was an intrinsic part of the "Neolithic Revolution," and therefore was adopted in the entire region which became involved in agriculture.

The tokens presaged Sumerian pictographic writing in form and contents. The use of clay as a writing material can no longer be explained by the fact that there is no other material available in the alluvial plain of Mesopotamia. Evidently, the use of clay to manufacture the Sumerian tablets can be traced to the tradition of communicating information by the means of clay tokens. Furthermore, particular tokens can be pointed out as being the prototypes of Sumerian pictographs. As discussed in earlier work (Schmandt-Besserat, 1980), this phenomenon can be explained by the use of clay envelopes to hold groups of tokens representing special accounts. The envelopes presented the disadvantage of hiding the tokens they contained. This problem was solved by the practice of pressing the tokens into the still-soft clay of the envelopes' surface in order to indicate the number and shape of the tokens enclosed. The impressed markings represent, therefore, the transition between the three-dimensional tokens and pictography. Not only did the custom of impressing some tokens on the surface of tablets continue, but the shapes of others were also drawn with a stylus, which could render more accurately the outline of the counters and their markings. It cannot be emphasized enough that such instances are few, numbering no more than a few scores. It is the case, however, for the signs representing grain measures, units of oil, sheep, textiles, and garments, which were among the most important items of the Sumerian economy of the third millennium B.C. and, obviously, were already significant in pre- or protohistory. However, the most important legacy of tokens to writing was the system of word signs they instituted. The tokens were semantic and, like the later Sumerian pictographs, each token stood for a discrete meaning. Furthermore, the economic content, which remained all along the hallmark of the system, also presages Sumerian writing. Namely, during the first two centuries of writing, the pictographic tablets dealt also exclusively with lists of goods including commodities such as grain, animals, oil, textiles, and garments (Nissen, 1986). Finally, it is presumable that the way the Sumerians organized signs on a tablet, in parallel lines and in placing them in decreasing order of magnitude from right to left, was probably inherited from tokens. It is likely that the counters were lined up in such a manner on the accountant's table (Schmandt-Besserat, 1981).

CONCLUSION

The use of visual symbols in the prehistoric Middle East became diversified in the course of 60 millennia, including more and more specific signs to deal increasingly with more concrete entities. The most ancient evidence of visual symbols, which date from the Mousterian period (c. 60,000-25,000 B.C.), such as the use of ochre and funerary deposits, seem to belong to the realm of magico-religious activities (Conkey, 1985). On the other hand, these symbols were part of a ritual communication system, expressing powerful but intangible realities such as, perhaps, life and death. During the last Upper Paleolithic period (c. 15,000-12,000 B.C.) graphic symbols in the form of tallies were used, seemingly, to note the passage of time. The calendrical information was more concrete because it translated perceptible physical phenomena, such as the successive phases of the moon. Finally, during the early Neolithic (c. 8000 B.C.) a system of clay tokens was invented to keep track of real goods. Symbolism was finally applied to daily, concrete commodities. The close affinity of the token system with agriculture shows clearly the relationship between economy and communication. It explains, in particular, how the Middle East became the cradle of civilization: It is in the Fertile Crescent that there developed an economy based on the domestication of plants, which in turn triggered the elaboration of a new symbolic system.

The tokens were a turning point in the use of symbols for communication. They inherited from tallies the methods of abstracting data and presenting it in one-to-one correspondence. The most significant and original contribution of the token system was to introduce the principle of word signs, whereby each token shape was bestowed with a discrete meaning. Furthermore, the repertory of tokens representing a set of interrelated commodities constituted the first code. In turn, the token system paved the way for the invention of writing. The Sumerian pictographic script borrowed major elements from tokens and, in particular, the principle of word signs, the morphology of certain pictographs, their economic function, the first rudiments of a syntax, and the selection of clay as a writing material. While written communication, particularly in the form of a phonetic script, would be a phenomenon occurring in the future, the generic traits of symbolization reveal much that is shared with later scripts. The use of stable as well as momentary symbols, the development of related symbolic meaning that would enable forms of discursive meaning to coexist with presentational meaning, the social and cultural contexts out of which new processes of symbolization developed are all occurrences that reveal traits compatible with the later developments of written communication. Consequently, and as this chapter has sought to make apparent, those studies which examine early efforts at symbolization can do much to reveal capacities and techniques that would later be used in written communication. A more refined knowledge of these developmental processes will not only enhance our understanding of the development of writing but the more generic capacity of symbolization of which it is a manifestation.

REFERENCES

Bar Yosef, O., & Goren, N. (1973). Natufian remains in Hayonim Cave. *Paléorient, 1*, 49-68.

Bordes, F. (1972). *A tale of two caves*. New York: Harper & Row.

Bostanci, E. Y. (1959). Researches on the Mediterranean coast of Anatolia, a new paleolithic site at Beldibi near Antalya. *Anatolia, 4*, 129-177.

Bostanci, E. Y. (1964). Important artistic objects from the Beldibi excavations. *Antropoloji, 1*(2), 25-31.

Bouyssonie, A., & Bardon, L. (1908). Découverte d'un squelette humain moustérien à la Bouffia de la Chapelle aux Saints (Corrèze). *L'Anthropologie, 19*, 513-520.

Braidwood, R. J., Howe, R., & Reed, C. (1961). The Iranian prehistoric project. *Science, 133*(3469), 2008-2010.

Bruner, J. S. (1966). On cognitive growth ii. J. S. Bruner, R. R. Oliver, P. M. Greenfield, et al. (Eds.), *Studies in cognitive growth*. New York: John Wiley.

Cauvin, J. (1978). *Les premiers villages de Syrie-Palestine du IXème au VIIe millénaire avant J. C.* Collection de la Maisons de L'Orient Meditérraneen ancien 4, Serie Archéologique 3. Lyon: Maison de l'Orient.

Cauvin, J. (1972). Nouvelles fouilles à Mureybet (Syrie) 1971-72, rapport préliminaire. *Annales Archéologiques Arabes Syriennes, 22*, 105-115.

Conkey, M. W. (1985). Ritual communications, social elaboration, and the variable trajectories of paleolithic material culture. In T. D. Price & J. A. Brown (Eds.), *Prehistoric hunters-gatherers*. Orlando, FL: Academic Press.

Contenson, H. de (1972). Tell Aswad Fouilles de 1971. *Annales Archéologiques Arabes-Syriennes, 22*, 75-84.

Copeland, L., & Hours, F. (1977). Engraved and plain bone tools from Jiita (Lebanon) and their early Kebaran context. *Proceedings of the Prehistoric Society, 43*, 295-301.

Gelb, I. J. (1974). *A study of writing* (rev. ed.). Chicago: University of Chicago Press.

Henry, D. D. (1985). Preagricultural sedentism: The natufian example. In T. D. Price & J. A. Brown (Eds.), *Prehistoric hunters-gatherers*. Orlando, FL: Academic Press.

Klein, R. G. (1966). *The Mousterian of Upper Russia*. Doctoral dissertation, University of Chicago.

Langer, S. K. (1960). *Philosophy in a new key*. Cambridge, MA: Harvard University Press.

Leroi-Gourhan, A. (1955). *Les hommes de la préhistoire*. Paris: Editions Bourrelier.

Leroi-Gourhan, A. (1961). *Les fouilles d'Arcy-sur-Cure. Gallia Prehistoire, 4*, 3-16.

Leroi-Gourhan, A. (1971). *Préhistoire de l'art Occidental*. Paris: Editions Lucien Mazenod.

Lumley, H. de. (1969). A paleolithic camp at Nice. *Scientific American, 220*(5), 42-50.

Marshack, A. (1972). *The roots of civilization*. New York: McGraw-Hill.

McLuhan, M. (1964). *Understanding media*. New York: American Library.

Movius, H. I. (1953). Teshik-Tash, a Mousterian cave site in Central Asia. *Mélanges en hommage au professeur Hamal Nandrin*, Société Royale Belge d'Anthropologie et de Préhistoire. Bruxelles: Imprimerie Administrative.

Nissen, H. J. (1986). The archaic texts from Uruk. *World Archaeology, 17*(3), 317-334.

Perrot, J. (1966). Le gisement natufian de Mallaha (Eynan), Israel. *L'Anthropologie, 70*(5-6), 437-484.

Peyrony, D. (1934). La Ferrassie. *Prehistoire, 33*, 1-92.

Redman, C. I. (1978). *The rise of civilization*. San Francisco, CA: Freeman.

Shackley, M. (1980). *Neanderthal man*. Hamden, CT: Archon.

Schmandt-Besserat, D. (1974). The use of clay before pottery in the Zagros. *Expedition 16*(2), 11-18.

Schmandt-Besserat, D. (1977). The earliest uses of clay in Syria. *Expedition 19*(3), 28-42.

Schmandt-Besserat, D. (1980). The envelopes that bear the first writing. *Technology and Culture 21*(3), 357-385.

Schmandt-Besserat, D. (1981). From tokens to tablets: A re-evaluation of the so-called numerical tablets. *Visible Language, 15*(4), 321-344.

Schmandt-Besserat, D. (1982). The emergence of recording. *American Anthropologist, 84*(4), 871-878.

Schmandt-Besserat, D. (1984). Before numerals. *Visible Language, 18*(1), 48-60.

Smith, C. S. (1985). A matter of form. *Isis, 76*(4), 584-587.

Smith, P. E. L. (1986). *Paleolithic archaeology in Iran*. Philadelphia: The University Museum, The University of Pennsylvania.

Solecki, R. S. (1972). *Shanidar*. London: Allen Lane.

Solecki, R. S. (1981). *An early village site at Zawi Chemi Shanidar*. Bibliotheca Mesopotanica 13. Malibu, CA: Undena Publications.

Tixier, J. (1974). Poinçon décoré du paleolithique supérieur à Ksar'Aqil (Liban). *Paleorient, 2*(1), 187-192.

Valla, F. R. (1975). *Le Natufien*. Cahiers de la Revue Biblique 15. Paris: J. Gabalda et Cie, Editeurs.

Vandermeersch, R. (1972). Ce que revèlent les sépultures moustériennes de Qafzeh en Israel. *Archeologia, 45*, 7-15.

2

An Historical View of the Relationship Between Reading and Writing

EDWARD P. J. CORBETT

In a talk on the connections between reading and writing that I prepared for the CCCC Winter Workshop in January of 1986, I remarked that like most teachers of English, I always presumed there were some connections between reading and writing. For many years, I proclaimed in my classrooms that reading and writing were interrelated, and I piously advised my students that if they wanted to become good writers, they would have to become good readers. I do not recall ever preaching that if they wanted to become good readers, they would have to become good writers; apparently, I did not recognize the connection between reading and writing as being a two-way street. In my playbook, reading benefited writing, but writing did not benefit reading.

I also recall telling my students that reading and writing were analogous to two other communications skills, listening and speaking: the listening that we did in the oral medium was comparable to reading in the graphic medium, and speaking was the counterpart of writing. I was so inclined to recognize the similarities between the pair of oral skills and the pair of graphic skills that I was not disposed to look for the differences between the two sets of skills.

It was not until I started to do some serious research for that paper that my presumptions about the relationships between reading and writing began to be shaken. Sheryl L. Finkle, a graduate student, called my attention to a collection of essays edited by Julie Jensen (1984) and titled *Composing and Comprehending*. The title itself suggested two alternative terms for *writing* and *reading* but also suggested that the relationships between writing and reading were much more complex than I had once imagined. One of the common themes of several of the essays in that collection was that although reading and writing were indeed complementary activities, researchers still do not have a very clear idea of the precise relations between the two. The conclusion that Robert J. Bracewell and two of his colleagues arrived at typifies the position that many researchers in the area of reading and writing have taken:

> Yet once one passes beyond decoding processes in reading and the mechanics of production in writing, to the essence of literary skill (namely, the appreciation and comprehension of literate texts and the ability to express oneself adequately in various text genres), it is not clear exactly what skills are developing. Furthermore, while we may feel intuitively that the more advanced skills of comprehension and self-expression are intimately related and that development of one should not only complement but reinforce the other, objective demonstrations that development of composition skills enhance comprehension and vice versa have yet to be achieved. Unfortunately, we lack an understanding of precisely what processes the activities have in common. (Bracewell, Frederiksen, & Frederiksen, 1982, p. 146)

I began to wonder whether the pedagogues in earlier ages had a more secure understanding of the relationships of reading and writing than we do, and whether in their classroom practices they were able to exploit those relationships so that the two skills were refined and reinforced. So I decided to review historically how the schools in earlier ages cultivated the literate skills.

A convenient starting point for such a review is the situation prevailing in the Greek schools of the fifth century B.C., because although the culture was still predominantly oral, the Athenian Greeks of that time had developed a sophisticated system of alphabetic writing. Literacy—the ability to read and write the native language—was then, as it continues to be, the key that opened the door to the privileged life. At the highest level of literacy, mastery of rhetoric—the art of oratory—

invested even the ordinary citizen with a tremendous power in public life. The regimen of instruction and practice that the pupils were subjected to, from the elementary schools where they learned their alpha/beta/gammas to the higher schools where they learned how to compose and deliver persuasive discourses, provides us with a good picture of how the ancient Greeks learned and perfected their skills in reading and writing. Fortunately, we have gained a great deal of information about the ancient schools from such classic works as Werner Jaeger's *Paideia: The Ideals of Greek Culture* (1943-1945), H.I. Marrou's *A History of Education in Antiquity* (1964), and Donald Lemen Clark's *Rhetoric in Greco-Roman Education* (1957).

Some of us were initiated into literacy by learning how to recognize and print whole words. But others of us gained entry into literacy by learning our ABCs first. Like the ancient Greeks and Romans, we started out by learning the letters of the alphabet, one by one and in the proper order. Like them, we recited the letters orally, sometimes in chorus with the whole class. The next step for us may not have been what it was for them: recognizing and printing syllables. We may have gone progressively from letters to words to phrases to sentences. If we persisted, we arrived at that satisfying stage which the plodding Greek and Roman pupils eventually achieved under the relentless tutelage and never-idle ferula of the *grammaticus*: the stage where we could read aloud a passage consisting of a succession of related sentences.

It may be disillusioning to us to find out that we learned the elementary stages of reading and writing in much the same way that the highly literate Greek and Roman pupils did. But we should be aware that those students had a much harder time of it in mastering those elementary stages than we did. Remember that they read from a manuscript rolled up on a spindle, and that they had to write with a stylus or a calamus on skins or wax tablets or papyrus; we read from a bound book and wrote on lined paper with a pencil or a pen. Furthermore, the texts that they read and copied not only lacked punctuation marks, but also lacked separations between the words. And the philosophy of "learning without tears" had not yet taken over in the schools: for them, any mistakes in reading or writing would be rewarded with the slash of a cane.

H.I. Marrou (1964) says of this pedagogy associated with the primary stages of literacy:

> This was the very essence of classicism—the antipodes of modern romanticism, with the systematic search for originality. The schoolboy of antiquity was not obliged to be original: all that was required of him was that he should learn to write and criticize according to certain rules. . . . This was verbal gymnastics all right, even if it was not highly intellectual. Here again, one feels the dead weight of these teaching methods, tolerable only because syllabuses were so limited and the cultural horizon more limited still, compared with teaching today. (pp. 241-242)

Once the Greek and Roman schoolboy had mastered his "letters," he graduated to the tutelage of the *grammaticus*, the Latin term for the teacher of literature and language. Quintilian (1920-1922) defined the province of the *grammaticus* very well:

> The profession may be most briefly considered under two heads, the art of speaking correctly (*recte loquendi scientia*) and the interpretation of poets (*poetarum enarratio*); but there is more beneath the surface than meets the eye. For the art of writing (*scribendi ratio*) is combined with that of speaking, and correct reading precedes interpretation (*enarratio*), while in each of these cases criticism (*iudicium*) has its work to do. (*Institutio oratoria* 1. 4. 2-3)

In relation to "speaking correctly" the *grammaticus* made sure that the student's pronunciation was proper and that his enunciation was distinct. In relation to writing correctly, the *grammaticus* made sure that the student's spelling, usage, and grammar were orthodox.

It was as the teacher of literature, however, that the *grammaticus* rendered the greatest service for the education of the student. According to Marrou (1964), consideration of a literary text involved four stages: (1) criticism of the text; (2) reading the text; (3) explaining the text; and (4) evaluating or judging the text. The first stage was a form of textual criticism, establishing the accuracy of the manuscript copy of the text and making sure that the student's copy was the same as the teacher's. The reading of the text was, of course, an oral reading, and—despite the run-together inscription of the words—the student was expected to read the text with the proper expression and understanding. The explanation or exposition of the text (what the Greeks called *exegesis* and the Romans called *enarratio*) was divided into the literal explanation (the lexical, grammatical, semantic, and stylistic dimensions of the text) and the literary explanation (the figurative and symbolic meanings, the structure, etc.). The evaluation (*krisis*) of the text was often based more on moral, rather than aesthetic, considerations. Odysseus' escape from the Sirens, for instance, was to be perceived as teaching us to flee from physical and spiritual temptations.

Often, however, this whole process was preceded by the teacher's *praelectio*, or pre-reading. This pre-reading was intended to be exemplary, but it is possible that very often the performance was calculated to impress the students with the teacher's virtuosity. The teacher read the text aloud, pausing frequently to call the student's attention to common or unusual features of the text, to conjugate a verb, to explain a particularly difficult passage, or to offer an evaluative comment. Since these explanatory readings were delivered orally in the privacy of the classroom, virtually none of them survive today, but when texts were explicated in writing these pre-readings became commentaries, which became a distinctive and major genre of literature in the Middle Ages. Ultimately, they became the *explication du texte*, which became a prominent feature of French schools in the nineteenth and early twentieth centuries.

The Greek and Roman pupils than passed on to the tutelage of the *rhetor*, the teacher of rhetoric, who was entrusted with the duty of teaching them to compose and, eventually, to deliver persuasive discourses. The teachers of rhetoric in the sophistic schools expected their students to learn the art of oratory not by being exposed to precepts, but by observing and imitating eloquent speakers. These were spoken models, of course, which did not involve the students in reading, but although the students sometimes moved directly from observing the models to delivering a speech, most of the time the students had to compose their oration in writing before memorizing it and delivering it before an audience. Today in English classes, one of the commonest ways in which we teach composition is to have our students read and analyze model essays in an anthology of such readings and then write a comparable essay on their own subject.

In those schools of rhetoric, however, where the art of persuasive discourse was learned by exposure to the precepts or principles of rhetoric dispensed by the teacher, the students went through a more systematic regimen of studies. In addition to learning the rules or principles for composing effective speeches, they learned their craft by memorizing and reciting eloquent discourses of all kinds (even poetry) by translating texts from one language to another, and by paraphrasing texts. These three practices will be discussed in the next section on the schools of the English Renaissance. Note that the acts of memorizing, translating, and paraphrasing all imply a written text that is to be memorized, translated, or paraphrased; and wherever there is a written text, the act of reading is involved.

The rhetor eventually engaged his pupils in the *progymnasmata*, a cumulative series of written exercises that moved progressively from the simple to the more complex modes of discourse that are frequently components of the full-fledged persuasive oration. These exercises, too, engaged the students in reading and writing. The students read and discussed a model text. Sometimes they were required to copy the whole text verbatim, just to get a feel for it. Then they were asked to compose a text of that genre—a fable or a description or a refutation or an encomium. The student author was often asked to give his written text to a classmate, who read the text aloud to the other members of the class, and then the teacher stepped in to invite oral critiquing of the composition. We have oral critiquing of student essays in many of our composition courses, but usually there is not the close conjunction of reading and writing that there was in the Greek and Roman schools of rhetoric.

That is what this chapter seeks to emphasize in reviewing the practices in the Greek and Roman schools: the inexorable union of reading and writing exercises. In a culture that had become literate only relatively recently, the literate people in that milieu were so awed by the miracle wrought by the creation of alphabetic writing that they read intensely and wrote studiously. For them, reading and writing were ancillary skills, both of which had to be consciously learned; unlike the skills of speaking and listening, which seemed to come naturally to people just from being part of a community that had a common language. Consequently, they seemed to be more aware of, more convinced of, the connections between reading and writing than we are.

When we move to the Middle Ages, literacy seems to be a more exclusive property than it was in antiquity. First of all, if medieval people were literate, they were more likely to be literate in Latin than in their vernacular language. Secondly, even that Latin literacy seemed to be the province primarily—if not exclusively—of clerics in their monasteries. A poor farm boy, the son of illiterate parents, could hope to achieve literacy in his lifetime only if he was willing to become a celibate monk. He had to pay a heavy price to gain that literacy: endless hours of enforced silence and prescribed prayers, tedious hours in the scriptorium laboriously copying manuscripts. One of the ironies of his apprenticeship was that he was often assigned to copy manuscripts before he had become a good enough reader to be able to understand what he had copied. Writing for him was more often manual labor than intellectual labor. But even when he was able to savor the delights of the knowledge he gained from the texts that he copied, the rule of silence in the cloister prevented him from discussing those delights with his confreres.

The basic education of the medieval universities and cathedral schools was grounded in the trivium, which consisted of the three language arts of grammar, logic, and rhetoric. Those arts were derived from the comparable arts in Greek and Roman culture, but the subject matter of the trivium tended to be confined to matters of philosophy, theology, ecclesiastical polity, and the Holy Scriptures. The great literature of the Greeks and the Romans was often available, and sometimes even copied in the monastic scriptoria, but was usually avoided as dangerous or scandalous pagan fare.

Even rhetoric was constricted in its province. For one thing, it took a decidedly subsidiary place in relation to logic and grammar. Moreover, it ceased to be the wide-ranging art that dealt with a variety of deliberative, judicial, and epideictic discourses and concentrated on two new kinds of rhetorical discourse: the art of preaching (*ars praedicandi*) and the art of letter-writing (*ars dictaminis*). But perhaps because of the solitary and isolated life of monastic students, scholars in general and rhetoricians in particular became superb readers. In the most influential rhetoric text of the Middle Ages, St. Augustine's *De doctrina christiana*, the first three books dealt with how to read the Scriptures, and the fourth book dealt with the most effective way in which to transmit the message of the Scriptures to the laity. One way to characterize this work is to say that the first three books are concerned with invention (with the discovery of something to say) and that the fourth book is concerned with elocution (with style). Another way to regard this work is to say that the first three books deal with hermeneutics or interpretation, and the fourth book deals with expression or communication. A third way is to say that *De doctrina christiana* is a work dealing with the art of reading and writing.

The genre, however, that most reveals the close connection between reading and writing in the Middle Ages is the commentary. In describing this distinctive genre, Jeffrey Huntsman (1983) said that in many cases, elaborate commentaries literally surround the text, "for the manuscripts often had the original in the center of the page with commentaries filling the margins on all sides" (p. 63). Ralph McInerny (1983) lists the points that, according to Boethius, a commentator should make: "to brood over a text, to explain its meaning, to paraphrase and unpack it, to reveal its order and arrangement—it is by doing these things that an adept [commentary] can aid a novice" (p. 262). Earlier, it was suggested that the oral *praelectio* that the Greek and Roman *grammatici* presented as a prelude to the detailed discussion of a text in the classroom was a prototype of the medieval written commentary.

In his *How to Read a Book*, Mortimer J. Adler (1940) confessed that he learned much of what he knew about reading from studying the medieval commentaries, which were written, he said, by "men who could read better than the best readers today . . . the rules I am going to prescribe are simply a formulation of the method I have observed in watching a medieval teacher read a book with his students" (pp. 96-97). The modern school practice that is most like the *praelectio* and the commentary is the French *explication du texte*, an exhaustive disquisition on virtually every facet of a written text. Perhaps the closest experience that American students have had of the elaborate French explication of a text is their exposure to the kind of close analysis of a poem practiced by the so-called New Critics. A significant difference is that the New Critics stayed within the text and did not, as the classical grammarians and the medieval commentators did, provide extensive historical, biographical, and cultural information as a background for the discussion of the work. But anyone who was exposed to the New Critical method, especially in those years right after World War II, can testify about how that kind of close reading of a text stimulated the writing that followed the reading.

A number of historians and literary scholars have spoken about how the invention of the printing press and the invention of relatively cheap paper in the late Middle Ages contributed to the growth of literacy. Another cultural phenomenon should be mentioned that gave a great impetus to the extension of literacy in the late Middle Ages and the early Renaissance: the invention of eyeglasses. Edward Rosen has written the definitive history of the invention of eyeglasses with convex or converging lenses, an invention that he established as having taken place in Pisa, Italy, in 1286. Vincent Ilardi has written about the five recently discovered documents revealing that eyeglasses with concave lenses were being manufactured in Florence, Italy, from at least the middle of the fifteenth century—almost a century before they were thought to exist. Anyone who has ever been fitted for eyeglasses knows how these instruments have opened up the world of script and print to those with impaired vision, and aging scholars know how eyeglasses have extended their productive lives. Petrarch (1304-1374), for instance, said in his autobiographical *Letter to Posterity* that "for a long time I had very keen sight, which, contrary to my hopes, left me when I was over sixty years of age, so that to my annoyance I had to seek the help of eyeglasses (*ocularium . . . auxilium*)" (Rosen, 204). Today we await the invention of some optical device that will enable dyslexic students to cope with the graphic medium.

Teachers in the Renaissance schools of Western Europe made use not only of the mechanical assistance of eyeglasses, but also of the pedagogical methods of classical and medieval mentors. In the Renaissance period in England, teachers such as John Brinsley in his *Ludus Literarius* (1612), Charles Hoole in his *A New Discovery of the Old Art of Teaching Schoole* (1660/1913), and Roger Ascham in his *The Scholemaster* (1570/1870) have given us a good idea of the methods that the grammar school teachers of this era appropriated from earlier teachers in order to teach students how to read and write. And in our own time, Donald Lemen Clark in his *John Milton at St. Paul's School: A Study of Ancient Rhetoric in English Renaissance Education* (1948) has given us detailed information about how pupils in this famous London school were trained in reading and writing. This chapter will focus now on those imitative exercises that Renaissance pedagogues, such as those at St. Paul's, inherited from the teachers of an earlier era and adapted for use in their classrooms.

The three main imitative exercises were memorizing, translating, and paraphrasing. These exercises presuppose a text that will be memorized or translated or paraphrased, and where there is a text to be memorized, translated, or paraphrased there will necessarily be reading. So all three of these exercises involved a combination of reading and writing. The texts that were memorized were usually recited orally, of course, but often the schoolmasters required the students to reproduce the memorized passage in writing before reciting it orally before the members of the class. Reproducing the passage both orally and scribally doubly reinforced the memorization.

The texts that were memorized were revered passages of prose or poetry from classical or vernacular literature or from the Holy Scriptures. Memorizing these passages served to etch into the students' subconscious awareness choice diction, elegant phrases, startling figures of speech, and stirring rhythms. There was a time, not more than fifty years ago, when the pupils in our grade schools and high schools had to memorize select passages and reproduce them on demand. Everyone knows some older person from that era who even today can still recite, with great pride and gusto, a poem or a rousing passage of prose once committed to memory as a school exercise. Students who have many such messages resonating in their heads will inevitably reproduce echoes of those passages in what they write.

Paraphrasing was an exercise that promoted *copia* of words and ideas, a much-admired accomplishment in the Renaissance. The quintessential example from the English Renaissance of *copia* of words and ideas is Robert Burton's *Anatomy of Melancholy* (1621). But the simplest form of paraphrase was for the student to take a thought as expressed in a particular sentence and express it in a variety of ways. A virtuoso performance on this exercise was exhibited by Erasmus in his *De Duplici Copia Verborum ac Rerum*, where he took the Latin sentence *Tuae literae me magnopere delectarunt* (Your letter pleases me very much) and produced 150 variations in Latin on that thought. Although an extreme performance of that sort is bound to produce many strained, awkward, quaint sentences, continual practice in varying the expression of a thought does promote verbal versatility.

Paraphrase, however, could also be exhibited in structures larger than the sentence. Students could be asked to render a poem in prose form or a piece of prose in verse. Or they could be given a passage of dialogue from a play and be asked to render that dialogue into indirect discourse. Or a stretch of dense philosophical discourse could be turned into a piece of expository prose that would be comprehensible to a subteenage child. For any of these exercises, the reader/writer would have to be in command of a large store of synonymous words, syntactic structures, and figurative expressions, not to mention a rich reservoir of facts and ideas.

The main difference between translation and paraphrase is that translation works from one language to another language, whereas paraphrase produces alternative expressions within the same language. The English schoolmasters in the Renaissance schools required their pupils to do a lot of translating—from Latin to English or from English to Latin, or both ways. And sometimes they required their pupils to engage in "double translations"—translating a text from Greek to Latin, and then to English. All these exercises in translation required intensive reading and precise writing. Nothing resembling these exercises prevails in our schools today. Whether these students were, by and large, better readers and writers than students today remains to be proven, if it could ever be proven. But it seems safe to say that because of all this intensive concentration on written words in more than one language, Renaissance pupils were more language-conscious than their counterparts today.

After the Renaissance, there are no notable innovations of pedagogical practices that conjoin reading and writing. In the eighteenth century, the rising middle class was anxious to be instructed in what to read and how to read, and turned for such instruction to such arbiters of taste and elegant expression as the Joseph Addison issues of the *Spectator Papers*. The novel was created in that century to satisfy the literary appetite of those aspiring middle-class readers. By the Victorian period of the nineteenth century, that middle class had achieved widespread, if not universal, literacy, and its appetite for printed material was insatiable. These eager readers did not have radio or movies or television to distract them from the printed material that either entertained them or instructed them. This was the era of the three-decker novel and the multivolumed collected works of authors. In short, this was the age, above all others, of legions of omnivorous readers and cadres of prolific authors.

Although the English and American citizens of the twentieth century have access to the elementary and secondary educations that can make them literate, the society in which they live has by no means achieved universal literacy. While 80% of those citizens can be classified as being at least functionally literate, it could be argued—and certainly has been claimed—that they are not, by and large, readers and writers as adept as those citizens of periods when the proportion of literate people was considerably lower than it is now. We have not yet reverted to the state of what Walter Ong (1982) has called "primary orality," but, as Ong and his former colleague Marshall McLuhan often reminded us, we have reached a state of "secondary orality," where the print medium has to compete with the audiovisual appeal of the electronic media. Our students in preparing to write a research paper no longer have to copy notes on 3 × 5 cards from the books and articles they have read; they simply photocopy the pertinent pages and highlight with a marking pen the relevant passages. So they have lost even the union that was effected between reading and writing when people had to copy by hand the words that other people had written. And it is difficult today to motivate students or teachers to do the kind of intensive reading that was once manifested in the classical *praelectio* or in the French *explication du texte*, or in the Brooks-and-Warren style of close reading of a poem. Nevertheless, I am not yet prepared to proclaim that we have "lost something valuable" in our drift away from the close relationship that once seemed to exist between reading and writing. I will not be prepared to make that kind of doomsday proclamation until scholars have determined—more firmly than they have so far—just what the mutual effects are of reading and writing upon one another. Meanwhile, I shall continue to lament that all the reading and writing I have done in my lifetime has not made me a better reader and writer than I am.

REFERENCES

Adler, M. J. (1940). *How to read a book: The art of getting a liberal education*. New York: Simon & Schuster.

Ascham, R. (1870). *The scholemaster*. London: Muir & Paterson. (Original work published 1570)

Augustine (St.). (1958). *On christian doctrine (De doctrina christiana.)* (D. W. Roberson, Jr., Trans.). Indianapolis, IN: Bobbs-Merrill.

Boswell, G. M. (1986). The rhetoric of pedagogy: Changing assumptions in seventeenth-century English rhetorical education. *Rhetoric Society Quarterly, 16*, 109-123.

Bracewell, R. J., Frederiksen, C. H., & Frederiksen, J. D. (1982). Cognitive processes in composing and comprehending discourse. *Education Psychologies, 17*, 146-164.

Brinsley, J. (1917). *Ludus literarius: Or the grammar schoole*. Liverpool: University of Liverpool Press.

Clark, D. L. (1948). *John Milton at St. Paul's school: A study of ancient rhetoric in English Renaissance education*. New York: Columbia University Press.

Clark, D. L. (1957). *Rhetoric in Greco-Roman education*. New York: Columbia University Press.

Erasmus, D. (1963). *On copia of words and ideas (De duplici copia verborum ac rerum.)* (D. B. King & H. D. Rix, Trans.). Milwaukee, WI: Marquette University Press.

Hoole, C. (1913). *A new discovery of the old art of teaching schoole, in four small treatises*. Liverpool: University of Liverpool Press. (Original work published 1660)

Huntsman, J. F. (1983). Grammar. In D. L. Wagner (Ed.), *The seven liberal arts in the Middle Ages* (pp. 58-95). Bloomington: Indiana University Press.

Ilardi, V. (1976). Eyeglasses and concave lenses in fifteenth-century Florence and Milan: New documents. *Renaissance Quarterly, 29*, 341-360.

Jaeger, W. (1943-1945). *Paideia: The ideals of Greek culture*. (G. Highet, Trans., 3 vols.). New York: Oxford University Press.

Jensen, J. M. (Ed.). (1984). *Composing and comprehending*. Urbana, IL: ERIC Clearinghouse on Reading and Communication Skill.

Lechner, J. M. (1962). *Renaissance concepts of the commonplaces: An historical investigation of the general and universal ideas used in all argumentation and persuasion with special emphasis on the educational and literacy tradition of the sixteenth and seventeenth centuries.* New York: Pageant.

Marrou, H. I. (1964). *A history of education in antiquity.* (G. Lamb, Trans.) New York: New American Library.

Mathews, M. M. (1966). *Teaching to read: Historically considered.* Chicago: University of Chicago Press.

McInerny, R. (1983). Beyond the liberal arts. In D. L. Wagner (Ed.), *The seven liberal arts in the middle ages* (pp. 248-272). Bloomington: Indiana University Press.

Minnis, A. J. (1984). *Medieval theory of authorship: Scholastic literary attitudes in the later middle ages.* London: Scholar.

Ong, W. J. (1982). *Orality and literacy: The technologizing of the word.* New York: Methuen.

Quintilian (Ed.). (1920-1922). *Institutio oratoria.* (H. E. Butler, Trans., 4 vols.). Cambridge, MA: Harvard University Press.

Rosen, E. (1956). The invention of eyeglasses. *Journal of the History of Medicine and Allied Sciences, 11,* 13-46, 183-218.

3

Sophistic Formulae and the Emergence of the Attic-Ionic Grapholect: A Study in Oral and Written Composition

RICHARD LEO ENOS

In its most creative period, that is when the great works of literature were produced, Greece was politically and linguistically fragmented. The "Greek language" was in fact a collection of local dialects which were used by separate city states in their public documents. (Palmer, 1980, p. 174)

For centuries Hellenic sophists were considered an intellectual embarrassment to the otherwise brilliant and lucid contributions that characterize Greece's Classical period, particularly with respect to Athens' preeminent literary contributions. Characterized as opportunistic, glib, and amoral, centuries of scholars took on presumption the opinion that sophists had little or nothing to do with Greece's "literate revolution" but to exploit writing for their own pragmatic, selfish purposes. Research in the last few decades, however, has largely amended this perception to the point that sophists are now recognized as having made significant cultural and artistic contributions. Not the least of these achievements—as this chapter argues—is their contributions to the written form of the Attic-Ionic dialect and indirectly its emergence as the substance of what we now consider to be Classical Greek. How, what, and in what fashion sophists contributed to the transformation of the Attic-Ionic dialect to a grapholect—the inscribed literary mode of preference—is the chief concern of this chapter.

The dispelling of centuries-old presumptions about the merits of sophistic rhetoric has undermined formerly unchallenged starting points for inquiry into Hellenic expression. Recent efforts, for example, now give us assurance that Plato's characterization of the sophists, and sophistic rhetoric in particular, was colored by his intolerance for their views and imprecise in his portrayal of their glib attitude toward discourse (Enos, 1976a, 1987). Acknowledging Plato's characterization of sophistic rhetoric as unrepresentative has implicitly induced scholars of rhetoric to waive past presuppositions and inquire into the nature of the sophistic rhetoric with the objective of reconstructing its composing processes and, for the focus of this chapter, its contributions to literacy.

Initial efforts to re-evaluate sophistic contributions make it all too apparent that as our understanding of the sophists deepens an error of category becomes apparent, for to consider the "sophists" as a group is to underscore similarities and downplay differences. While the diversity and complexity of sophistic discourse may make for convoluted accounting, it does provide a starting point that offers a more sensitive understanding of their diverse impact than thinking of sophists in a uniformity monolithic manner would permit. Sophists, speaking in dialects from all parts of the Greek world, came to Athens frequently adapting their discourse to the local Athenian tongue, but bringing their own techniques of composing. That is, and as will be discussed in more detail later in the chapter, while sophists often changed over to the Attic dialect they kept the modalities of expression indigenous to their primary tongue.

Cultural and political forces help explain the funneling of this uniformity of literary expression. Athens, the oratorical and literary center of the Greek-speaking world, attracted and valued intellectuals. Coming from a tradition of oral composition and speaking from one of a number of Greek dialects, many of these sophists adapted their expression and wrote and spoke in the Attic dialect. The Attic dialect, a form of Greek in the local Athenian tongue, itself assimilated features of dialects, particularly the Ionic (Buck, 1955), which had evolved as the oldest and most dominant form of expression for oral, epic poetry. So thoroughly did these two cultures mix (Herodotus 1.56; Thucydides 6.82; 7.57) that their dialects become known as one: the Attic-Ionic dialect. Such a concentration of talent continuously empowered that dialect with the best thoughts and forms of expression from throughout the Hellenic world to the extent that it became the dialect of preference for writing (i.e., the grapholect). In the process of conforming to the Attic-Ionic dialect, sophists contributed not only their wisdom but also transferred their modes of expression. Further, in the process of traveling throughout Greece, sophists helped greatly to establish the Attic-Ionic grapholect as the literary expression of choice.

To examine only the testimony and fragments of sophistic discourse would prompt the belief that the Attic-Ionic dialect was the sole mode of expression and synonymous with what we now consider Classical Greek. There is little doubt that what we term "Classical Greek" is predominantly the inscribed artifacts of the Attic-Ionic dialect. Yet, how the spoken Attic-Ionic dialect emerged as the dominant form of written composition and the role that the sophists played in facilitating a virtual monopoly of literary expression with the Attic dialect is largely unrealized. The Attic-Ionic prose style that has come to stand as synonymous for the literary efforts of classical Greece was in intellectual competition with other Greek dialects and benefited by many sophists who were themselves non-Athenian speakers. Understanding how the orality of distinct Greek dialects influenced and even contributed to a uniform, literary language is realized in large part by the sophists who helped contribute to this intellectual transition that prompted the emergence of literacy. Various Greek dialects emphasized different genres and modes of expression, each carrying with it formulae that facilitated ways of shaping thought and expression. The incorporation of these modes of discourse into the Attic-Ionic dialect not only enhanced its nature but facilitated its literate evolution. Thus, in subject, form, and transmission, sophists helped to solidify the literary form of Classical Greek. The best example of a sophist illustrating this phenomenon, Gorgias of Leontini, will be discussed later in the chapter.

PREVIOUS AND ANALOGICAL EFFORTS

The importance for understanding Hellenic literacy by realizing both the influence of orality and the constituent practices and traits of the composers is well grounded in pioneering research efforts. By tradition and preference, Plato and Aristotle were seen as the pinnacle of classical thought. Unfortunately, classical scholars inferred that Plato and Aristotle were also the best representatives of an intellectual tradition and that their contemporaneous intellectuals, the sophists, were inferior in thought. This inference is understandable particularly because it mirrors the sentiments of Plato and Aristotle, both of whom had harsh comments about their predecessors (Enos, 1987). Yet, it is clear that Plato and Aristotle did not give accurate renderings of either the oral tradition which preceded them nor the merits of the sophists who were their contemporary rivals. Rather, Plato and Aristotle were two of the early examples of literate minds, and therefore unrepresentative of their own contemporary or historical intellectual climate. That is, their ability to utilize the advantages of literacy to foster abstract thinking free from stylistic devices used to facilitate memory was a turning point in the epistemology of discourse. The advantages of literacy provided much easier access to prosaic and hypotactic patterns of thought than grew out of the oral tradition which dominated pre-Socratic and sophistic thought. In short, Plato and Aristotle were critics of the sophistic tradition, a phenomenon which they only dimly understood in its context but unhesitatingly disparaged.

Several contemporary classical scholars began to re-examine the sophists and question the opinions of Plato and Aristotle. Untersteiner (1954), Segal (1962), Bowersock (1969), Guthrie (1971) and Kerferd (1981) established the continuity of sophistic thought with pre-Socratic philosophy, the sophistication of notions warranting serious philosophical inquiry, and the sustained tradition of the sophistic movement which flourished through antiquity. Eric Havelock's *Preface to Plato* (1963) argued convincingly that conceptual processes growing out of the Homeric tradition, and grounded in oral discourse, were sophisticated in their own terms but (again) not by the restrictive standards of Plato. The contributions of these and other scholars compelled contemporary historians of rhetoric to recognize the oral nature of early Greek discourse and its complexity while recognizing that the sophists, as beneficiaries of this tradition, were refining their own composing processes in a manner different in nature and kind from both Plato and Aristotle.[1]

These contemporary scholars paved the way for a re-examination of the sophists so that a more sensitive rendering of their composing process and the written artifacts of the period can be reconstructed. Such a task is clearly important for, despite the acknowledgment of the place of the sophists in philosophy and social history, some prominent scholars of rhetoric remain unconvinced that sophistic composition will provide any new or significant insights for the history of rhetoric. Jacqueline De Romilly (1975) and George Kennedy (1963, 1980) are two of the most prominent skeptics who hold such a view, choosing to accept literally the views of Plato and Aristotle on sophists such as Gorgias and their "minimal" contributions to rhetoric. The focus of the debate centers on the notions of epistemology: Did the sophists have an epistemology driving their discourse? Was such an epistemology identifiable and unified enough to be labeled "sophistic" and, if so, is such a process deserving of attention? Efforts at resolving this debate and, in the process, opposing the views of Kennedy and later De Romilly, were made in the previously cited studies on the epistemology of Gorgias' rhetoric (Enos, 1976a, 1987). Gorgias was a paradigm of the sophistic movement, and observations advanced in those works assert that Gorgias was both a challenging thinker and the possessor of an epistemology that was compatible with his heritage of orality but amenable (and adaptable) to writing. More important to the purpose of this chapter, Gorgias and his fellow sophists influenced the literary tradition of ancient Greece and ultimately had a role in shaping the Greek literary style. In more pervasive terms, sophists not only refined techniques of oral composition, they facilitated the emergence of Hellenic grapholect; that is, the melding and transformation of the Attic and Ionic dialects to the literary medium of Hellenic expression that would come to represent nothing less than Classical Greek itself. One such aspect of what Havelock (1982) terms this "literate revolution" is the contribution of sophists to the literate style of classical Greece.

THE NATURE OF THE GREEK
LANGUAGE AND ITS DIALECTS

The impact of sophistic contributions to the Attic-Ionic grapholect is best assessed by understanding the Greek language and its dialects. It is particularly important to recognize that Greek dialects are not the result of diffusion and splintering of tongues from one, univocal source of language but rather a semi-autonomous but shared group of *oral* dialects. The "unification" of these Hellenic languages is not—as it is still today—the solidification of the spoken tongue. Rather, Classical Greek is a literate phenomenon, a confluence of dialects dominated by the Attic-Ionic forms resulting from efforts to create a *literate* language. The evolution from natural, oral dialects to the artificial written dialect is the result of a number of factors, only one of which is linguistic-philological in nature. Social, cultural, and political preferences and sources of power controlled the evolution of the grapholect. The sophists, as expert theoreticians and practitioners, were instrumental in not only its development but its dissemination throughout the Greek-speaking world.

The nature of the Greek language masks a diversity and a phenomenon in orality that has implications for literary composition. The earliest evidence of a "Greek Language", the Linear B fragments of the Bronze Age (c. 1200 B. C.), reveal a remarkable conformity and pervasiveness irrespective of the archaeological cite in Greece from which they were excavated. Yet the clay tablets of Linear B texts also reveal that the script was little more than what Palmer (1980) terms a "chancellary language" (p. 53) or a "fossilized administrative language" (p. 54), used for record-keeping but no more representative of the diversity of the actual language than grocery lists would be for our everyday speech. Excluding the uniformity that characterizes the craft literacy of Linear B, there is no evidence of a singular "Greek" language but rather a number of decentralized dialects which persisted throughout ancient

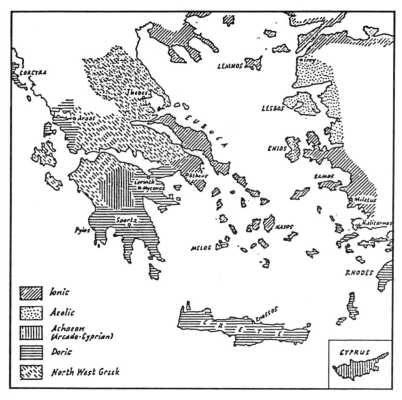

Figure 3.1. The Distribution of the Greek Dialects in the Alphabetic Period
SOURCE: Reproduced from L. R. Palmer, *The Greek Language*, by permission of Faber & Faber

Greece. Although it is quite probable that numerous oral dialects ceased to be spoken, were never preserved beyond the memory devices of oral composition, and thus were forgotten, five major dialects evolved from oral discourse to written texts and thus preserved their features: Attic-Ionic, Arcado-Cyprian (Archaean), Aeolic, North West Greek, and Doric. These dialects, illustrated in Figure 3.1, reveal their regional and cultural territoriality.

There are two distinguishing features that arise from the diverse origin of the Greek language. First, and obviously, each dialect is rooted in oral discourse. Second, and less obvious, each came with identifiable traits indigenous to its mode of discourse. The Ionic and Attic dialects

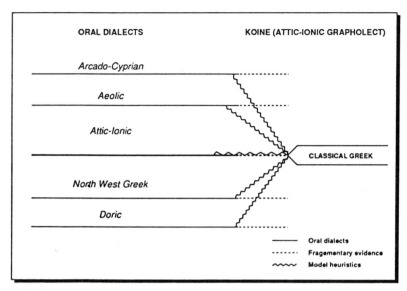

Figure 3.2

each have their own respective characteristics but, for reasons to be discussed later, coexisted in their chief forms in a manner that greatly influenced writing. Despite the dialect elisions, apparent also in the Arcado-Cypriate group, this diversity persisted actively throughout the Classical Period, particularly when orality dominated composition and the emphasis in literacy was emerging throughout Greece but widely evident only in Athens. Figure 3.2, extensively modified from a simpler diagram offered by Allen (1974), illustrates this diversity at the point of origin.

Figure 3.2 illustrates that the principle dialects existed independent of a uniformly generic tongue. What is important to stress is that *during* the classical period, "Greek" meant a diversity of dialects, each of which took shape by its features or oral discourse. Classical Greek did not evolve from a single, indigenous, and centralized tongue uttered initially at a single locale, transformed into script, and then "frozen" as the classical language as was Latin (Allen, 1974). Isolated by virtue of some of the most hilly terrain of the Mediterranean, multiple local dialects evolved throughout the Greek world. Some of these dialects came to be written and preserved. The eventual creation of a single "Classical Greek" is not the consequence of a uniform assimilation but rather various linguistic, cultural, and what is termed here *extra-rhetorical* features. As writing emerged and literacy became widespread, select features of dialects became incorporated into the dominant writing dialect or the grapholect; that is, features of oral dialects that were considered effective and elegant were assimilated into the written style, which became the *Koine* (Allen, 1974) or common mode of literary expression. What was assimilated was not only unique words and phrases, which capture the surface features of dialects, but modal heuristics of thought and expression. That is, ways of structuring and composing ideas were transferred from the dialect into the grapholect. In our postclassical history Classical Greek came to be dominated by (if not synonymous with) the Attic-Ionic dialect, the dialect that constituted literary prose. Creation of this Classical Greek script, however, was the result of the confluence of these factors, and one of the forces shaping this phenomenon was the sophists of the classical period. Their contribution, however, cannot be fully understood without understanding the nature of these dialects and the processes they helped to transfer to the Attic-Ionic dialect that became the classical Greek script or *Koine*.

THE GREEK DIALECTS AND
SOPHISTIC POLLINATION

The constituent features of Hellenic dialects provide a basis for understanding the evolution of the literate mode of classical Greek. Hellenic dialects emerged, as do all dialects of natural language, as orality. The five major dialects of ancient Greece each had their own unique linguistic properties but each came into existence long before scripts and, despite the natural interaction of people that results in "borrowing" and transference, continued to persist in their chief features throughout the classical period. These features were distinguished primarily by their phonetic characteristics, for while it is doubtless that local terms and phrases existed, basic features of grammar, syntax, and vocabulary were generally shared. The salient and distinguishing oral features of the dialects were the differences in sound patterns. The phonetic features of each dialect greatly contributed to its uniqueness and flavor, and the formulaic expressions that emerged were distinguished not only by nuance in their linguistic properties but their tonal qualities.

The orality of Hellenic dialects offers insight that cannot be understood fully if we consider literary artifacts alone; that is, if we see evidence of composition solely from the literary texts that have survived. Hellenic dialects were distinguished in large part by their tonal features and, as Aristotle indicates in *Rhetorica* (1403b), such stress was based on pitch; in fact, as Allen (1974) indicates, "tonal accent was one of the most characteristic phonetic features of ancient Greek" (p. 118). An illustration will reveal the significance of this oral dimension: Greek dramatic literature was composed to be recited aloud. Pitch, one of the chief features in shaping meaning, is realized through oral renderings. Hearing Aristophanes' *Birds*, as Stanford (1967) indicates, will enable listeners to capture a dimension of the play's meaning, for in saying their lines of the play in pitch actors "chirp" their parts. No silent rendering of the play, or even one whispered for that matter, would capture the oral orthography of its tonal features; in short, the tonal features of discourse, as with a Gregorian chant, provide a meaning as well as the words themselves. Alexandrian grammarians of the second century B. C. recognized this phenomenon and provided accent marks to help preserve the tonal pattern of ancient Greek; by the fourth century A. D. however, accent was altered in meaning when stress replaced tone, and the oral quality of pitch was lost (Allen, 1974).

While euphonic features of Greek dialects were lost even to ancient scholars, their impact on shaping Classical Greek was enormous, for tonal patterns shaped the formulae of the dialects. These formulae or modes of expression, in turn, helped to facilitate expression not only as aids to memory but as ways of helping to compose thought. Dialogues such as the "Gorgias" and the "Phaedrus" reveal the sophistic concern with oral style, poetic patterns, and tonal qualities. Endemic to these dialect features, sophists brought with them the heuristics of their own dialect. The earliest forms of literature are oral and the composing processes are shaped by the tonal patterns of the dialect. These patterns, in turn, facilitate configuration of thought in ways best revealed by how mnemonic devices of rhythm and cadence shape memory and even creativity. Dialects, transmitted in part by sophists who traveled throughout the Greek-speaking world, helped to shape not only oral literature but the conceptual modes that facilitated their expression and eventually the scripts that ensured their preservation.

One of the best examples of this pollination—one which even pre-dates sophistic influence—is the transmission of Homeric literature by rhapsodes (Enos, 1978; Palmer, 1980). Homerica is primarily eastern Ionic, and the pan-Hellenic sweep of the *Iliad* and the *Odyssey* estab-lished a dominance in expression that came to associate epic oral com-position with the Ionic expression. The further contributions of Hesiod, Pindar, and Simonides only ingrained the Ionic dialect as the medium for poetic expression, and centuries of *aoidoi* and rhapsodes further created and preserved the dialect as the mode for expressing great literature. It is important to stress that what became established as the medium of expression was not only the tonal features of the Ionic dialect but the formulaic patterns and modes of expression; in short, the heuristics of the dialect. Similarly, Ionic became the first fully developed prose style, and the range of expression—from the scientific/ medical tracts of Hippocrates (*Corpus Hippocratium*) to the histori-ography of Herodotus (Enos, 1976b)—associated the Ionic dialect with literate expression. Again, however, more was disseminated in Ionic literature than the tonal quality of the dialect. The formular techniques of composition and the methods of analysis and inference in the sci-entific and historical writings also were heuristics that were assimi-lated along with the oral orthography of the Ionic tongue.

As an intellectual center the fruits of Ionic wisdom were naturally attractive to Athenians, and social and cultural forces fostered an assimilation of the two dialects. In 494 B. C. Ionia fell to Persia and the once strong Greek leaders of the city-states of Ionia, who so avidly sponsored and nurtured the arts of expression, fell or succumbed to "barbarian" tyranny. Lacking an atmosphere of patronage, and sensing a climate of oppression, many artists and intellectuals welcomed the benification of Athens, who not only opposed Persian tyranny but offered the city as a school for Greek intellectuals (Thucydides 2.41.1).

The pollination of Ionic forms and thought, so apparent in rhapsodic composition, and its harmonious compatibility with the Attic dialect is evident also in the sophists of the classical period. Protagoras, an ardent traveler of the Greek world, was attracted to Athens but—unlike other sophists who followed—persisted in writing in the Ionic dialect (Palmer, 1980). His impact on Athenian thought is best known for probability and advantage, and his popularization of arguing from inference is well recognized in Plato's "Protagoras." Yet, unlike Protagoras, many other thinkers who came from Ionia and throughout Greece "Atticized" their dialect for Athenians. Despite these modifications to Athenian discourse sophists still transferred the modality of the expressions acquired in their native tongue, referred to in Figure 3.2 as the modal heuristic of the dialect. Gorgias of Leontini (Sicily) and Thrysamachus of Chalcedon (Asia Minor), for example, both wrote excellent Attic while transferring the poetic and periodic features of their respective grand and middle styles that had earned them fame in their "foreign" dialects (Palmer, 1980). Thus, while sophists immigrated to Athens from throughout the Greek world and modified their discourse to Attic, they nonetheless transferred the modal heuristics endemic to their dialect onto the written Attic style, thus enriching the Attic-Ionic dialect with the most lucid modes of expression each dialect had to offer.

As indicated above, one of the best examples of a sophist influencing the Attic-Ionic style was Gorgias of Leontini. Regarded as one of the oldest, if not the "father," of the sophistic movement, Gorgias's impact on Athenian expression is well testified by a number of ancient sources and most likely the motivating force driving Plato's "Gorgias." Several ancient sources call particular and repeated attention not only to the substance of his addresses and public performances but to the style of his expression. An acknowledged master of stylistic devices (*Schemata Gorgieia*), Gorgias was acclaimed for both this performance and teaching (Athenaeus 504E; Xenophon 2.26; Norden, 1909-1918/1974). Diodorus Siculus (12.53.1-4) notes the many rhetorical techniques he popularized with Athenians, who quickly regarded him as a man of letters and paid handsomely to attend his school. Philostratus (*Epistle* 73; *Vitae Sophistarum* 1.9.3) provides convincing proof of Gorgias' impact on Athenian expression, citing how his style ("Gorgianize" [γοργιάζει]) influenced the expression of such prominent orators and writers as Pericles, Critias, and Thucydides. In fact, as Philostratus writes, "the detached phrases and approaches of Gorgias' discourse influenced many circles, particularly epic poets" (*Epistula* 73). Chided by Plato ("Gorgias"), Aristophanes (*Aves* 1694; *Vespae* 420), and Aristotle (*Rhetoric* 1404a, 1406b), the impact that Gorgias made on the oral and literate style of the Attic-Ionic dialogue through his modes of expression and popularization of rhetorical techniques is nonetheless acknowledged through the time of Cicero (*Orator* 39, 165) and into the Second Sophistic. Coupling Gorgias's popularization of modes of expression with the models revealed by extant fragments reveals the nature and source of his influence on the Attic-Ionic grapholect. Yet, as will be discussed later, the contribution of sophists such as Gorgias to the grapholect extended beyond the adaptation of their dialects to the Attic-Ionic. As persistent, itinerant travelers, sophists helped to spread the literate mode of expression throughout Greece and thereby disseminate not only literacy but its Athenian-oriented mode of expression throughout the Greek world.

Athenians were not without gifted stylists of their own dialect, each of whom further added to the sophistication of literate Attic expression. Thucydides, earlier mentioned as having been influenced by Gorgias's style, and one of the great historians of antiquity, is considered a master of Attic prose and his accounts of the Peloponnesian War became a model of literary expression as well as historiography. Similar examples from other forms of expression also contributed to the Attic literary style. The dramatic literature of playwrights such as Euripides, the masterpieces of Attic oratory by Antiphon and Demosthenes helped to enshrine the Attic prose style as the medium of expression. Many literary scholars believe that Isocrates and his school of logography perfected Attic diction (Enos, 1974; Palmer, 1980). In short, the assimilation and association of the Ionic dialect, the attraction which drew intellectuals from throughout Greece, and the local excellence of Athenian intellectuals all contributed toward the preeminence of the Attic-Ionic dialect. This distinction was enshrined not only by artful prose features but by the modal heuristics that facilitated the creation and conception of discourse. Most significant of all, and concomitant with the forces mentioned above, Athens became the first literate society of Greece. The richness and sophistication of oral composition which gave preeminence to the Attic-Ionic dialect provided the heuristics for literary composition. Thus as writing was popularized and reading became widespread, the techniques of oral composition assimilated from masters of other dialects complemented the contributions of Attic stylists to provide unparalleled literature which became written down for posterity. Eventually, techniques derived from oral composition began to be directed to literary composition, a phenomenon which George Kennedy (1980) popularized as *letteraturizzazione*. Through this process, principles of effective oral expression are adopted to become principles for effective literary expression. The strong relationship between oral and literate expression is clear. Significantly, and as illustrated in Figure 3.3, this phenomenon, which provided the emergence and refinement of the Attic-Ionic literary style, was facilitated by sophistic rhetoric.[2]

Social forces, in addition to literary phenomena, further helped result in the creation of an Attic-Ionic grapholect. The Ionic alphabet was made the official script (μεταγραμματισμός) in Athens in the archonship of Eucleides in 403-402 B. C. (Palmer, 1980). The Panathenenaic festivals and the great Dionysia provided both regular occasions for performances of literature and a spectacle for proficiency in the Attic dialect. Further, the distribution of Athenian policy in the form of epigraphical inscriptions presumably aided in both the spread and assimilation of the dialect throughout the empire. Eventually, Philip's conquest of the Hellenic world made his adoption of the Athenian dialect as the official language of Macedonia an imperially recognized form of literary expression (Buck, 1955; Palmer, 1980; Welles, 1974). Thus social, political, and intellectual forces contributed to the concentration of the Attic-Ionic dialect as the preferred literary mode of expression. Yet, even in their departure from native dialects, writers transferred the modal heuristics of style and argument that earned them

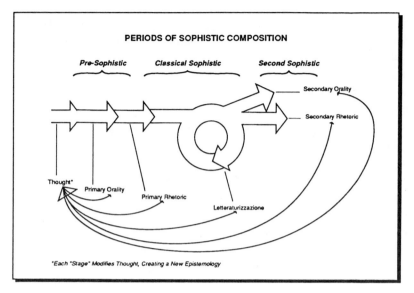

Figure 3.3

initial recognition. Thus, the best features of other dialects became absorbed by the Attic-Ionic grapholect, which only further strengthened its position as the dominant mode of literary expression and, through the constant travel of sophists, was doubtlessly disseminated throughout Greece.

CONCLUSION

The significance of these events provides a context for understanding why Classical Greek was largely a confluence of the Attic and Ionic dialects and the role sophists played in its creation and transmission. First, Athenians readily assimilated the Ionic dialect with their own Atticism and thus conjoined the best and oldest of the oral literature of Greece with their own tongue. Second, Athens aggressively attracted the most eloquent thinkers from throughout Greece and many of the most prominent stylists adapted to the Attic dialect while contributing some of the best heuristic features of their own dialects. The impact of Gorgias of Leontini, perhaps the most influential of all sophists, reveals the nature and extent of such influence on the creation of a literate mode of expression. Third, as the first literate society of Greece, Athens transferred features of oral composition to the Attic script. This process of *letteraturizzazione* contributed directly to the emergence of Athens' literary process, which became the standard of written expression. Most importantly, when the Attic dialect was deemed official by Philip and later by Roman conquerors, it established the Attic-Ionic dialect as the gracholect (in Ong's [1982] terms) that made the written script (Buck, 1955) the *Koine* or recognized language of expression. It is clear, however, that this transition of oral and written composition was aided by several social and political forces that on the surface appear to be only tangential, but in actuality were nothing less than a pan-Hellenic phenomenon. There is little doubt that sophists were an enormous aid in establishing the *Koine* by enriching the Attic-Ionic dialect with their own techniques of composition and then transmitting that mode of expression throughout the Greek-speaking world in their travels. As an educational and cultural force, sophists were not only the medium for transmitting Hellenic literature, but eventually in disseminating the Attic-Ionic dialect as the preferred tongue of artful expression. Thus, as writing shifted from an aid to memory to an art form it is understandable why the Attic-Ionic dialect would dominate as the gracholect. The forces operating on the sophistic transmission of the Attic-Ionic dialect help to reveal features in the creation of a gracholect not readily apparent in an examination that concentrates solely on the literary artifacts.

At first, the contributions of sophists to the literary tradition of Greece appear minimal, and would also appear to have little to do with the choice and selection of the Attic-Ionic dialect as the literary mode for Classical Greek. Yet, when we consider that Hellenic discourse moved from a developed oral tradition to a literary medium in a relatively brief time, the importance of the sophists becomes apparent. The factors of travel, the custom of mentor-apprentice education, the reliance on memory, the dissemination of oral literature to public audiences, and the physiological characteristics necessary for such a lifestyle reveal that sophists were an important link in the transformation of oral to literate discourse. Growing out of an established oral tradition, sophists nonetheless assimilated and even refined principles of rhetoric for pragmatic prose composition as well as high art, frequently using writing to facilitate their work. The pervasiveness of sophists throughout Greece and their transmission of a vast amount of discourse in the Attic-Ionic dialect helped to direct that dialect as the preferred script. From this perspective, it is apparent that the phenomenon of *letteraturizzazione* was brought about in no small way not only because great literary works emerged, but because sophists helped to share in the creation and transmission literature (including written oratory) throughout the Greek world. Thus, when Philip eventually decreed that the Attic dialect would be the literary medium of expression for the Greek-speaking world, he was formalizing a phenomenon of *letteraturizzazione* which sophists informally and indirectly had been nurturing for decades.

NOTES

1. The monumental contributions of Milman Parry (1971) and Albert B. Lord (1976) in demonstrating the complexities of Homeric oral composition must be noted, even by analogy to this topic, as providing the paradigm for studying the relationship of oral and literate expression. A detailed account of their specific contributions, restating what is so aptly detailed in the works cited in this note, would require a synopsis disproportionate to the thesis of this chapter.
2. This model is adapted from an earlier version (Enos & Ackerman, 1987).

REFERENCES

Allen, W. S. (1973). *Vox graeca: The pronunciation of classical Greek* (2nd ed.). Cambridge: Cambridge University Press.

Allen, W. S. (1974). *Accent and rhythm: Prosodic features of Latin and Greek: A study in theory and reconstruction.* Cambridge: Cambridge University Press.

Aristophanes. *Aves.*

Aristophanes. *Vespae.*

Aristotle. *Rhetoric.*

Athenaeus. *Deipnosophistae.*

Avotins, I. (1975). The holders of the chairs of rhetoric at Athens. *Harvard Studies in Classical Philology, 79*, 313-324.

Bowersock, G. W. (1969). *Greek sophists in the roman empire.* Oxford: Clarendon Press.

Buck, C. D. (1955). *The Greek dialects.* Chicago: University of Chicago Press.

Cicero, Marcus Tulins. *Orator.*

Davison, J. A. (1963). The Homeric question. In A. J. B. Wace & F. H. Stubbings (Eds.), *A companion to Homer.* New York: Macmillan.

De Romilly, J. (1975). *Magic and rhetoric in ancient Greece.* Cambridge, MA: Harvard University Press.

Diodorus Siculus.

Enos, R. L. (1974). The persuasive and social force of logography in ancient Greece. *Central States Speech Journal, 25*(1), 4-10.

Enos, R. L. (1976a). The epistemology of Gorgias' rhetoric: A re-examination. *Southern Speech Communication Journal, 42* (Fall), 35-51.

Enos, R. L. (1976b). Rhetorical intent in ancient historiography: Herodotus and the battle of Marathon. *Communication Quarterly, 24*(1), 24-31.

Enos, R. L. (1978). The Hellenic rhapsode. *Western Journal of Speech Communication, 42*(2), 134-143.

Enos, R. L. (1986). The art of rhetoric at the Amphiareion of Oropos: A study of epigraphical evidence as written communication. *Written Communication, 3*(1), 3-14.

Enos, R. L. (1987). Aristotle, Empedocles and the notion of rhetoric. In R. J. Jensen & J. C. Hammerback (Eds.), *In search of justice: The Indiana tradition in speech communication.* Amsterdam: Rodopi.

Enos, R. L. & J. Ackerman (1987). *Letteraturizzazione* and Hellenic rhetoric: An analysis for research with extensions. In C. W. Kneupper (Ed.), *Visions of rhetoric: History, theory and criticism.* Arlington, TX: Rhetoric Society of America.

Guthrie, W. K. C. (1971). *The sophists.* Cambridge: Cambridge University Press.

Havelock, E. (1982). *The literate revolution in Greece and its cultural consequences.* Princeton, NJ: Princeton University Press.

Havelock, E. A. (1963). *Preface to Plato.* Cambridge, MA: Belknap Press.

Herodotus. *The Persian wars.*

Kennedy, G. A. (1963). *The art of persuasion in Greece.* Princeton, NJ: Princeton University Press.

Kennedy, G. A. (1980). *Classical rhetoric and its Christian and secular tradition from ancient to modern times.* Chapel Hill: University of North Carolina Press.

Kerferd, G. B. (1981). *The sophistic movement.* Cambridge: Cambridge University Press.

Lord, A. B. (1976). *The singer of tales.* New York: Atheneum.

Norden, E. (1974). *Die antike kunstprosa* (2 vols.). Stuttgart: B. G. Teubner. (Original works published 1909, 1918)

Ong, W. J. (1983). *Orality and literacy: The technologizing of the word.* New York: Methuen.

Palmer, L. R. (1980). *The Greek language.* Atlantic Highlands, NJ: Humanities Press.

Parry, A. (Ed.). (1971). *The making of Homeric verse: The collected papers of Milman Parry.* Oxford: Clarendon Press.

Philostratus. *Vitae sophistarum.*

Philostratus. *Epistula.*

Plato. "Gorgias."

Plato. "Phaedrus."

Plato. "Protagoras."

Segal, C. P. (1962). Gorgias and the psychology of the *logos*. *Harvard Studies in Classical Philology*, *66*, 99-155.

Stanford, W. B. (1967). *The sound of Greek: Studies in the Greek theory and practice of euphony*. Berkeley: University of California Press.

Thucydides. *The Peloponnesian war*.

Untersteiner, M. (1954). *The sophists*. (K. Freeman, Trans.) New York: Philosophical Library.

Welles, C. B. (1974). *Royal correspondence in the Hellenistic period: A study in Greek epigraphy*. Chicago: Ares.

Xenophon. *Symposium*.

4

The Auditors' Role in Aristotelian Rhetoric

WILLIAM M. A. GRIMALDI, S. J.

For the most part in the history of Greek and Roman writing on rhetoric the auditors' contribution to discourse has not been seen as something significant. From the evidence at our disposal, the auditor is usually viewed as a passive presence. He was, of course, recognized by those who wrote on rhetoric as the object of any practical or theoretical suggestions made to the speaker but solely as one whose attention was to be caught, his reason convinced, his emotions and feelings aroused; all to gain his support for and acceptance of what the speaker proposed. In fact, one might say that attention was devoted exclusively to the speaker and to the ways whereby he might achieve his goal successfully. Thus we hear much of invention, style, argumentation, and parts of speech. This emphasis on the speaker is quite visible in the one rhetorical handbook which has come down to us from among the many of ancient Greece. This is Anaximenes' *Ars Rhetorica*, commonly known as the *Rhetoric to Alexander*. The same limited perspective is reflected in comments on teachers of rhetoric by two men who entertained a larger understanding of rhetorical discourse, for example, that of Plato in the "Phaedrus" (266d-268a), or Isocrates' dismissive remarks about "those who promise to teach political discourse" or those "who dared to compose the so-called arts of rhetoric" ("Against the Sophists," 9,

AUTHOR'S NOTE: The author wishes to acknowledge the support provided in part by an NEH Senior fellowship for a commentary on Aristotle's *Rhetoric II* from which this chapter is a development.

16). It is seen, too, in works like the *Rhetorica ad Herennium* and Cicero's *De Inventione* that are derivatives of the Greek handbooks of rhetoric. This understanding of the auditor is also taken to be that of Aristotle in his *Rhetoric*. However, this treatise on rhetoric, which either by reason of its virtuosity and excellence or a chance accident of history has survived into the present as the only example from ancient Greece of a serious study of the art of discourse, deserves a further look. For the *Rhetoric* is unique in a number of ways: It is a treatise on discourse given to us by one of the most distinguished minds in Western thought. It is not a handbook on the techniques of good speaking, but an analysis of the nature of language when it is used by men to communicate effectively with others by the spoken (or written) word. Furthermore, it is an analysis that assumes and rests upon the author's philosophical commitments in ethics, psychology, political science, dialectic, and logic. To the best of our knowledge it is a work of his maturity, and possibly the fruition of a continuing interest in the discipline as indicated by the references in later literature to rhetorical works of his such as *Gryllus, Theodectea*, and *A Compilation of Rhetorical Handbooks*. Furthermore, it stands alone among Greek, Latin, and later rhetorical works as a well-articulated and comprehensive grasp of the essentials of the art (Grimaldi, 1972). The *Rhetoric* (as all else that Aristotle took up) is an effort to come to an understanding of the kind of thing discourse is when it is used in the attempt to communicate effectively with others. It is not a handbook of 10 easy lessons on how to be a successfully popular speaker. If one should insist that it is, then it can be said with the same assurance that the *Poetics* is an exercise book on how to write poems like the real poets.

Among notable contributions to be found in the *Rhetoric* is a study of the emotions in the second book. This study, as far as can be known, is unique for its own time and indeed for centuries later, and still commands attention. It is described in a recent book on emotion thus: "This picture of emotions . . . is by and large the correct one" (Lyons, 1980, p. 34).

Apart from its excellence as a critique of the nature of the various emotions (i.e., the state of the person experiencing the emotion, the things which cause the emotion, the persons toward whom it is experienced), this detailed analysis has the practical purpose of alerting the speaker to the auditor and the changes which can occur in him and thus affect what he hears.[1] Indeed, from what Aristotle says such an awareness is clearly intended to help the speaker dispose the auditors to cooperate with him, for as he says, "matters appear in a different guise to those who love and to those who hate and to those who are angry and to those free from anger" (1377b31-1378a3). Clearly, in Aristotle's view this study of emotion is not meant to enable the speaker to manipulate the auditor and twist him about by arousing an unjustified and irrational emotional response, and so corrupting his judgment, since such a use of emotions is strongly condemned in the opening chapter (e.g., 1354a16-26).[2]

In Aristotle's *Rhetoric* the sense of the primary importance of the auditors as cooperating partners in discourse is present from the beginning and is clearly stated. We are told early on that the function of rhetoric as a technique is not to persuade the auditors, but to discover those aspects in the subject under discussion which are suasive (1355b10-11); we learn, too, that rhetoric is the ability to discover that which is possibly suasive in any subject (1555b25-34), but "the suasive is that which is suasive to someone" (1356b28). In the *Rhetoric*, the someone is the auditor who is thereby enabled to arrive at a judgment. In fact, the auditors (ἀκροαταί) as judges (κριταί) are the final telos of the whole rhetorical praxis. Aristotle makes this clear when, in the third of the three opening programmatic chapters of the first book, he examines the proximate and the ultimate telos of each kind of rhetoric (1358a36-b29). There we learn that the auditors are the final goal of all rhetorical discourse, for they are the ones who must reach a judgment on their own when that which is possibly suasive on the subject has been placed before them (1355b10-11, 26-27, 32-34). In this kind of role, in which they must make a judgment on their own, the auditors cannot be totally passive partners completely subject to the technical skills of the speaker. They are viewed rather as nonspeaking partners actively engaged in the exchange taking place between speaker and auditor. Aristotle understood rhetorical discourse to be an eminently reasonable activity; purely passive auditors make it an exercise in the irrational.

Thus it is that when we turn to a pivotal part of his rhetorical theory, the *entechnic pisteis*, as he names them, we are confronted with a problem. These pisteis—logos (reason), pathos (emotion), and ēthos (character)—direct the entire process of invention apart from (at least formally) the atechnic proofs (laws, witnesses, etc.). They are called entechnic because they submit to the reasoned activity of the speaker and form an organic, logical whole for the development of argument. Aristotle describes them in this way: "entechnic pisteis are those that can be provided by ourselves and the methodology of rhetoric" (1355b37-38). Rooted in rational and psychological sources, they provide evidentiary material of a probative quality (thus the term πίστεις [pistis]) that enables the auditors by means of the speaker to move on their own toward a decision. As pisteis they are presented as coequal[3] and, depending upon how one interprets the meaning of ἦθος, they receive relatively equal treatment.

It is the meaning of ἦθος (ēthos) as entechnic pistis that is the problem. Does it mean simply and exclusively the ἦθος of the speaker? Or does is signify as well the ἦθος of the auditors, an ἦθος which the speaker must know and whose probative force he must utilize in his argument? If this last is so, it would present us with further evidence of Aristotle's acceptance of the active presence of the auditors in discourse. It is this point that this chapter would like to argue.

The common interpretation of ἦθος as entechnic pistis is that it signifies the speaker's ἦθος alone as Aristotle identifies it (1356a2). There are contra-indications in the text, both extrinsic and intrinsic, that such an interpretation is not correct. Let us look at the extrinsic first, not because they prove the incorrectness, but because they locate the problem more clearly and reveal the difficulties attached to such an interpretation.

First of all, there are structural difficulties. After naming the three entechnic pisteis, Aristotle devotes I.4-14 to the explanation of logos and II.2-11 to pathos. The only explanation of the speaker's ἦθος is at 1378a7-20, with a reference to I.9 as support. But, as this reference (1378a16-19) also indicates, I.9 presents the ways to show the ἦθος of others as well. A sketchy 14 lines versus 11 and 10 chapters is certainly a skewed structure for key concepts, but not impossible. Some,

Dufour (1960) for one, would consider II.1 as a chapter also given to the speaker's ἦθος; this is incorrect. A study of the chapter reveals that it is a transitional chapter focusing on two things: (a) a summary (1377b16-20) of I.4-14 on logical pistis (logos); (b) a general introduction to II.2-17, psychological pistis, by means of (1) a general observation on ἦθος, πάθος, (1377b21-1378a6); followed by (2) a brief comment on the speaker's ἦθος (1378a7-20); and (3) on how the πάθη can affect judgment (1378a20-28). Even were we willing to accept this oddity in the explanation of the three entechnic pisteis—with the one called the most effective of the three receiving a scant 14 lines of exposition—we next face the problem of how we are to understand II.12-17. Where do these chapters on the ἦθος of the auditors fit into the analysis? What purpose do they serve? Süss (1910) and others assumed them to be a part of the entechnic pistis, pathos. But ἦθος is not pathos as Aristotle says at *EN* 1105b19-1106a12,[4] and it could not be from his explanation of each. The one merit in such an interpretation is that is recognizes that the ἦθος of II.12-17 is as much an entechnic pistis as pathos. This, of course, is denied by those who restrict this pistis to the speaker's ἦθος. Cope (1867) seemingly escapes the problem by finding three meanings for ἦθος in the *Rhetoric*: (a) the ἦθος of the speaker which is the entechnic pistis, (b) that of the forms of government in I.8 and that of II.12-17, and (c) that of style. But this is really not valid, since ἦθος for Aristotle belongs properly to the person. Consequently, Cope's other meanings are contained in his first meaning. For example the meaning of ἦθος at II.12-17 would be the same as that of the speaker; similarly, in I.8 in using ἤθη of governments, Aristotle understands politeia as a moral person. The use of ἦθος for style is by analogy. Furthermore to interpret II.12-17 to mean that the speaker must adapt his ἦθος to that of the auditors (Cope, 1867, 1877) is to admit actually that the speaker's ἦθος by itself is inadequate as entechnic pistis and to suggest in fact that the auditors' ἦθος was for Aristotle a necessary part of ἦθος[5] as entechnic pistis.

Such are some of the extrinsic indications which run counter to an interpretation which confines ἦθος as entechnic pistis exclusively to the speaker. They become more significant when we consider the meaning of the word and the way Aristotle uses it in the text of the

Rhetoric. Aristotle does not explain the meaning of ἦθος as he uses it in the *Rhetoric*. To say, however, that it carries the ordinary meaning found in the ethical works (i.e., moral character) would be a secure statement.[6] We can arrive at an understanding of its meaning in the *Rhetoric* from what Aristotle calls its root idea, ἔθος (1369b6-7).[7] This is the name given to an action repeatedly done by a person. Thus, at 1370a6 τὰ ἔθη refer to specifically different actions repeatedly performed by an individual. As we are told there (1370a6-9) this manner of acting is like, but not the same as, that which flows from our nature. In fact, ἔθος is said to be like a second nature (*EN* 1152a20-32). Ἔθος as an action done over and over is the ground for what Aristotle calls ἕξις (habit, acquired habit) which is important for determining the meaning of ἦθος. A ἕξις is a disposition present in the individual that receives the effect of a repeated action and so becomes further disposed for doing that action (*EN* 1103b7-25 and see b21; 1114a9-10).[8] Such ἕξεις (stable dispositions) together with δυνάμεις (capacities), and πάθη (transitory motions proceeding from the capacities), are present in what Aristotle calls the orectic (appetitive) part of the psyche (*EN* 1105b19-28; *EE*1220b7-20). The dynameis appear to have no specific determination from nature (*EE* 1220a38-b6) and may be influenced one way or another. This influence comes from the hexeis which shape the dynameis to function in a certain way (*EE* 1105b23-28; *EE* 1220b16-20). If a dynamis is shaped partly under the direction of reason by an elective hexis (ἕξις προαιρετική) to a habitual way of acting in the area of moral activity, the result is a firm direction of the person toward or away from the good proper to man. Such a tendency toward or away from the standard of goodness proper to man Aristotle calls virtue or vice. He also calls it ἦθος (*EE* 1221b32-34; *Poetics* 1448a2-4), or what we call moral character. This is a meaning found frequently in the *Rhetoric*;[9] certainly it is the meaning presumed to be present by those who talk of the speaker's ἦθος as entechnic pistis. For their supporting evidence, 1378a7-20 and I.9 have in mind the moral character of the speaker. Moral character is also the meaning found in II.12-17. These chapters in reality are a presentation of patterned ways of acting which are both typical and indicative of a good or bad moral character.[10] In fact when Aristotle speaks of ἦθος, either as he specifies it for the speaker (1378a7-20) or describes it for the auditor (II.12-17), he is speaking of "moral character." This may well be the way one should think of ἦθος as entechnic pistis.[11]

If one were to make specific the meaning of ἦθος as found in the *Rhetoric*, it could be described in this way: ἦθος is a firm dispositon in a person formed partly under the direction of reason (*EE* 1220b5-7) with respect to that part of the appetitive soul represented by the emotions; this firm disposition reflects the quality of the individual's dominant habits in the sphere of moral activity.[12] In brief, it denotes a stable and established attitude in a person with respect to good or bad moral actions, an attitude which is the result of some kind of reasoned and repetitive activity.

This is the meaning of ἦθος (singular, plural) in all of its 58 appearances in the *Rhetoric*,[13] omitting 1413b31 which is not certain. What is evident, however, from the instances is that any *exclusive* reference in them to the speaker's ἦθος as entechnic pistis is minimal. For example:

- 4 clear instances pertain to the speaker's ἦθος as entechnic pistis (1356a2, 5, 13; 1366a26) while 3 others probably do the same (1359a23, 26-27; 1418b23).
- 4 instances can only be the ἦθος *of others as entechnic* pistis: 1366a13, 14-15; 1390a26-27; 1391b20-21.
- in 1 use the ἦθος of both the speaker and another is denoted *indirectly* as entechnic pistis: 1376a28.
- in 43 instances ἦθος signifies or can signify the ἦθος of the speaker, or auditors, or others, and it is an ἦθος which is a probative force (i.e., entechnic pistis). Some instances are 1356a23; 1376a25; 1384b11, 12-13; 1395b14; and 1417a17-24.
- there are 3 uses where "moral character" is a possible meaning. But equally possible is: "a trait, quality of character," "characteristic" (e.g., 1390b29, 1391a20-21, 1391b2).

This extensive use of ἦθος as moral character and signifying either directly or indirectly the ἦθος of the auditors or others[14] as entechnic pistis causes one to question an interpretation which confines it to the first category. Furthermore, when we look at the passages that seemingly refer clearly to the speaker's ἦθος as entechnic pistis, it is somewhat difficult to understand what can be meant by the text. For without a knowledge and a use of the auditors' ἦθος by the speaker (i.e., employing the auditors' ἦθος as entechnic pistis) the text statements are unclear. For example, at 1356a4-13 the speaker's ἦθος as entechnic pistis cannot be totally divorced from his knowledge and use of the auditors' ἦθος. The crucial words are at 1356a5-6; ἀξιόπιστον, ἐπιείκεσι. How can the speaker present himself as "worthy of belief," "a good man" without an understanding and use of the ἦθος of his audience? Both are qualities to which different audiences respond in different ways, for example, the old, the young, the uneducated, and the cultivated to name a few. In fact, in the other passage (1366a8-16) where Aristotle also has the speaker's ἦθος in mind, he notes that the speaker must know the ἦθος of different kinds of government (the subject of I.8) and must do so "since its own ἦθος is necessarily (ἀνάγκη εἶναι) most suasive with respect to each."[15] Indeed Aristotle himself points explicitly to this role of the ἦθος of others, particularly the auditors, as entechnic proof when he says at the end of II.13 (1390a25-28): "Such, then, are the ἤθη of the young and old. Consequently, since men give a favorable hearing to discourse which is addressed to and in accord with their own ἦθος, it is quite clear how the speakers by the language they employ will reflect such character both in themselves and in their discourse." This observation sets forth unambiguously what he thinks to be the purpose of his presentation of ἦθος in II.12-17. In fact, cc. 12-17 (owing to the method Aristotle uses to develop these varied "characters") are related to his brief treatment of the speaker's ἦθος at II.1 (1378a7-20). In this passage at II.1, he mentions three components which he considers essential for a speaker's ἦθος if it is to influence the auditors and win their favor: sound judgment (φρόνησις), moral integrity (ἀρετή), and good will (εὔνοια.) In his examination of the ἦθος of others (cc. 12-17) as it is affected by age and fortune (1388b31-32: κατὰ τὰς ἡλικίας καὶ τάς τύχας) these are the qualities which appear (unnamed as such) continually in the analyses. A brief example from the first character studied, that of the young, will illustrate this: sound judgment in the young is limited (1389a17-26, b5-7); moral integrity is changeable (1389a3-16, 35-37); and good will is present (1389a37-b2, b8-11).

The intrinsic indications are such that those who insist that Aristotle meant that ἦθos as entechnic pistis was exclusively that of the speaker must offer a more satisfactory explanation than the statements at 1356a1-13 and 1378a7-20 along with I.9. This is particularly true when we reflect upon Aristotle's statements about the auditors and the role he assigns them in discourse. Aristotle has made the auditor the telos of rhetorical discourse (1358a36-b8) and judgment (κρίσις) on his part essential to the whole process (1358b2-8, 1377b21, 1391b8ff.). By themselves, these two facts offer an argument to include the auditors' ἦθos under the term ἦθos as entechnic pistis. For in such a perception of rhetoric the speaker, to be effective, must always recognize and utilize the fact that he is speaking to a certain kind of audience with a particular set of established attitudes, interests, intellectual and emotional convictions, desires, and needs, all of which flow into the judgments and decisions they make. In brief it is this ἦθos, as Aristotle tells us at 1369a7-31, that affects a person's decisions and judgments: "And in general all the circumstances which cause men's characters to differ (must be considered), for example if a man views himself as rich or poor . . . this will make a difference in him." He ends this comment (1369a28-31) by stating that he will discuss these matters later. This is commonly understood to mean the discussion at II.12-17, even by those who maintain that the speaker's ἦθos is the only entechnic pistis.

From the tenor of the remarks in cc. 12-17, it is clear that the only purpose they serve is to call attention to the ἦθos of different kinds of auditors. The ostensible purpose for doing this is unavoidable, namely, to alert the speaker to the fact that he must attend to and adjust himself to the type of auditors addressed if he is to address them successfully. But to say this is to say that the auditors' ἦθos is an entechnic pistis. This would also be the conclusion one would draw from the comment at 1369a7-31, that at 1390a25-28, from the indications given by the transitional statements made in II.1, and from the general use of ἦθos in the *Rhetoric*. The success or failure of what the speaker wishes to convey is contingent upon the kind of cooperative listening response he evokes from his knowledge of the auditors. As Demosthenes, an experienced speaker, said: "While other artistic or technical attainments are fairly autonomous, the art of the speaker is ruined should the auditors prove recalcitrant" ("On the Embassy" 340).

This is the kind of close affinity between speaker and auditor that Aristotle recognizes and presents in the *Rhetoric*. Should the speaker overlook the salient features of the ἦθος of his auditors, or dismiss them as insignificant or irrelevant to his purpose, he effectively negates or weakens the force of his own ἦθος as entechnic pistis. In such a relationship the auditors' ἦθος cannot be anything but an entechnic pistis, for it must be understood and addressed by the speaker to ensure the credibility of his own ἦθος with the auditors. From the evidence of the text statements the impression is received that the speaker's ἦθος cannot function autonomously and exclusively as a force for establishing conviction in an audience. In fact, it may well be that the more realistic assessment of the speaker-auditor relationship in Aristotle is that the auditors' ἦθος not only exerts an influence on the speaker's ἦθος, but also on the emotional resonance (πάθος) he lends to his argument as well as its intellectual temper (λόγος). If any distinction were to be drawn between the speaker's and the auditors' ἦθος as entechnic pistis in the *Rhetoric*, one could say that Aristotle gave the speaker's ἦθος primacy of importance: it is the ἦθος which is mentioned first, the only one formally identified as entechnic pistis, and while it is tempered by the auditors' ἦθος it is the one which comes into play openly in rhetorical discourse.

By way of conclusion we might ask whether or not Aristotle's concept of the ἦθος of the speaker and of the auditors as an entechnic source of establishing conviction and assisting proof continued in the subsequent tradition. Our one substantial store of evidence for that would be in the Latin tradition which is a derivative of, and so a witness to, the later Greek tradition. From the *Rhetoric to Herennius*, the rhetorical works of Cicero, the *Dialogus* of Tacitus, and Quintilian's *Institutio oratoria* the answer would be negative. There may be suggestions of an understanding, but there are no signs of a clear apprehension of a role for the speaker's and less so the auditor's ἦθος as a probative force. What is notable is a superb confidence in the ability of the speaker to achieve what he wishes by himself, his style, and his command of rhetorical techniques, the *bene dicendi scientia*. This impression is actually reflected and borne out in the titles of the various works: *Orator, De Oratore, Brutus de Claris Oratoribus, Institutio Oratoria,* (*Education of the Orator*), *Dialogus de Oratoribus.* The speaker's ἦθos finds expression in Cato's *vir bonus* who would be for Cicero and Quintilian a well-educated and cultivated man. Apart from that, neither speaks in a formal way of ἦθos, or the comparable Latin term *mores,* to express the character of the speaker—or the audience—as a formal probative method for winning conviction. Cicero does not even use the word ἦθos where he might be expected to do so. It does appear once in his writings in the opening lines of *De Fato* and is explained as the word the Greeks use for *mores* (moral character). Ἦθos is not to be found in the Latin tradition in the meaning we find in the *Rhetoric.* We do learn that the speaker must make himself attractive to the audience, and that he does this by the image of himself which he presents "by proclaiming his own merits, etc. . . . by attributing the opposite qualities to the opponents . . . by indicating some hope for agreement with the judges."[16]

It is not difficult to accept the fact that the Latin tradition (as seen in our four sources) recognized the importance of the speaker as a person, and to a degree, of the auditors, and the contribution each makes toward establishing acceptance of the subject proposed by the speaker. But this recognition is not formalized either as the ἦθos, or the *mores* of each, and developed as a form of winning conviction in the same way that reason and emotion are. In the *Rhetoric to Herennius* 1.4.7-8 we meet the typical acknowledgment of the need for a receptive audience. At 3.6.11 we find an awareness of the role of speaker and audience: "Principium sumitur aut ab nostra . . . aut ab eorum qui audient persona."[17] At Cicero's *Orator* 8.24 we read of the auditors: "Semper oratorum eloquentiae moderatrix fuit auditorum prudentia"[18] (*Brutus* 51.191-192 and cp. 184; *De Inventione* 1.16.22; *De Oratore* 2.79.321.)

Yet when we turn to the remarks of Cicero and Quintilian on what Cicero says the Greeks called ἠθικόν and Quintilian that they called ἦθos, we do not find the remarks relevant to Aristotle's entechnic pistis ἦθos;[19] Cicero's comment is at *Orator* 37.128. At first eye-catching, it shortly dissipates whatever it seemed to promise: "Duae res sunt enim quae . . . admirabilem eloquentiam faciant. Quorum alterum est quod Graeci ἠθικόν vocant, ad naturas, et ad mores et ad omnem vitae consuetudinem accommodatum; alterum quod idem παθητικόν nominant."[20] In the very next sentence, this ἠθικόν is described as something that is "courteous, pleasant, capable of winning good will" and is contrasted with παθητικόν, which is described as "violent, inflamed, highly aroused." This is an intriguing explanation for ἠθικόν. But before considering it and its contrast with παθητικόν, a contrast found elsewhere in Cicero, let us look at Quintilian.

In the *Institutio oratoria* there is a reference (5.10.17) to *Rhetoric II* which is commonly taken to be cc. 12-17. Unfortunately, the passage cannot be reconciled with Aristotle's text as we have it. Furthermore, when Quintilian takes up ἦθος itself at 6.2.8-9 he tells us that it has long been accepted (*antiquitus traditum*) that ἦθος is an emotion, one of the two kinds of emotion, the other being πάθος. He continues on to tell us that ἦθος is a word for which Latin has no equivalent and that while *mores* (moral, character) is used he does not quite agree with the interpretation. He remarks further that actually those who are more careful (*cautiores*) do not translate the word, but give its sense. Thus it is that they explain πάθος as a violent emotion while ἦθος is a mild calm, continuing emotion. As can be seen, he actually uses at 6.2.9 in speaking of ἦθος the Latin word *adfectus*, "properly used" as he says at 6.2.20 for Greek πάθος. For Quintilian this meaning of ἦθος and πάθος, as already noted, is "traditional." Certainly Aristotle is not part of that tradition from the manner in which he explains ἦθος.

At this point we can return to Cicero, his explanation of ἠθικόν, and its contrast with παθητικόν. The brief explanation of each given in the earlier citation (*Orat.* 37.128) is quite acceptable for Aristotelian ἦθος and πάθος. It is the further statement in the very next sentence (cited in part) which brings to mind what Quintilian calls the "traditional interpretation" of ἦθος as emotion. Cicero sets up a contrast between ἦθος as mildness or agreeableness and πάθος as vehemence or strong agitation. This does sound as though Cicero may be thinking of ἦθος as emotion. In fact, when we turn to the *De Oratore* (2.53.212-213) the language with its contrast between mildness and vehemence in the speaker or in his style recalls that of the *Orator* 37.128. This is also true at 2.43.182-184. In these instances, if Cicero is not actually speaking of the speaker's ἦθος as an emotion, he is speaking inescapably about an emotional response aroused in the audience by the speaker as a person, by his *lenitas, humanitas*, and his "style of speaking which is adapted to his *vita* and *mores*" (2.53.212-213). For Aristotle, however, an emotional response is won by the entechnic pistis πάθος.

Quintilian, in his discussion of ἦθος (6.2.2-20), is not much clearer than Cicero. After stating that ἦθος is an emotion and the kind of emotion it is, Quintilian on occasion draws confusingly close to Aristotle's view of ἦθος but the observations never sharpen or stay in focus. At 6.2.13 the word denotes goodness, integrity, or genuineness in the speaker, and then drifts off in another direction. At 17 it is moral character (*mores*) that should be found in a speech when the talk is of moral character. At 18 it means that the speaker be a *vir bonus*, but by 20 we are back with the idea of emotion.

Fundamentally Quintilian and Cicero, when speaking of the effect of the speaker as a person (his ἦθος) on the auditors, are speaking of an emotional effect upon the audience. This is not the response to the speaker's ἦθος in Aristotle. There the response of the auditors is to the credential quality of the speaker (1356a5-8, 1377b25-28); it is a response which is more intellectual than it is emotional. Roth (1866, p. 856) puts it well: "The speaker's ἦθος is the prominent disposition in his personality and his style which responds to the understanding of his hearers."[21]

What emerges from this brief survey of the later rhetorical tradition as seen in treatises on rhetoric by Quintilian, Cicero, Tacitus, and the *Ad Herennium* is that the Aristotelian concept of ἦθος as entechnic pistis, whether it be that of the speaker or of the speaker and auditor, is not present. It has been lost somewhere along the way, and perhaps early on. What we find is the presence of the orator as the dominant and controlling factor in discourse. The auditors are effectively in his hands to dispose of as he will. In fact, comments throughout the works on the emotions and the way they have been or may be used reinforce this view. Those cited at n.3 are not untypical.[22]

What has also accompanied the disappearance of Aristotelian ἦθος as entechnic pistis is Aristotle's sense of the importance of the auditors. His clear understanding of the auditors as cooperative, and in some ways codeterminative, participants in discourse is not really the perception of the auditors we now find. Aristotle's emphasis at the outset (I.3) on the auditors as the ultimate objective of rhetorical discourse in their role as judges and his study of the emotions to which they are subject, as well as their varied types are not met as part of the formal theory of later rhetoricians.

NOTES

1. Another facet of this concern of Aristotle for the auditors' participation in discourse is seen in the matter of logical pistis (*logos*). The speaker's argumentation should be such that it is not so brief as to confuse, nor so detailed in stating the obvious as to bore, but should challenge the audience in its very first enunciation. This is first suggested at 1357a16-21. At 1400b27-34 Aristotle is more explicit, saying in part: "All such refutative and demonstrative syllogisms which the auditors foresee as soon as they are stated—and not because they are superficial—are particularly applauded, for at one and the same time (i.e., as they hear the argument) the auditors are delighted with themselves as they anticipate its conclusion; further, all those enthymemes are applauded which the auditors are slightly behind in apprehending only to the extent that they apprehend them when they have been completed." At 1410b21-27 Aristotle first notes that the auditors do not care for reasonings that are obvious and which call for no effort. He then remarks: "All those enthymemes are highly esteemed which either are understood as soon as they are stated particularly if the knowledge is new (not on hand before), or those which the mind is a step behind in grasping." The kind of attention Aristotle apparently wants from his auditors in the matter of argumentation is that of which he speaks (1412a20-21) in describing the auditor's response to a good metaphor: "How true! And I failed to see it!" In Grimaldi (pp. 87-91) there is a brief word on Aristotle's insistence that the audience obtain a quick and understanding grasp of the speaker's reasoning.

2. See also 1355a21-24 and Aristotle's argument for the art of rhetoric on the grounds that it serves truth and justice. In Cicero one can be disconcerted at times by the strong references to the emotions. At *Brutus* 279 we read that an orator's "highest praise" is to "inflame the emotions of the auditors and bend them to follow along whatever way the subject demands." At 89 we come upon this: "the speaker who inflames the auditor (*iudicem*) accomplishes far more than the one who instructs him."

3. See, however, 1356a13 on the preeminence of the speaker's ἦθος as pistis (κυριωτάτην), with which compare Isocrates ("Antidosis," 278-280); on the other hand see 1366a13-14 on the ἦθος of the politeia as a *moral person* and as something that is definitely not the speaker, but which he calls the most suasive πιθανώτατον.

4. From the passage cited Aristotle is speaking of moral virtues, which at 1106a11-12 he identifies with the *hexeis* and specifically at 1106b36f with the *hexeis prohairetikai*, the elective habits or habits of purposeful choosing. Such habits are equated with the presence of ἦθος (1366a14-16, 1395b14-17, 1417a16-19). Thus moral virtue is in our passage equated with ἦθος. In fact at the end of the discussion we read (1138b35f.): "In our analysis of the virtues of the soul we noted that some are virtues of character (ἤθους),

some of the intellect. We have, then, completed the virtues of character (ἠθικῶν)." So, we cannot confuse ethos with pathos.

5. Here attention might be called to 1369a18-31 where Aristotle speaks of the influence of ἦθος in the actions of men and so the need to know the ἦθος in order to know how and why men might act. Once again we see that by itself the speaker's ἦθος as an entechnic pistis will be relatively ineffective unless it is able to utilize the resources of the auditors' ἦθος.

6. Aristotle (1356a20-27) explicitly remarks that to use the three entechnic pisteis correctly, we must among other things make a study of types of human character, a study found in the discipline of Ethics, ἡ περὶ τὰ ἤθη πραγματεία, which is primarily a study of moral virtue and the moral life.

7. See, also, EN 1103a17-18, EE 1220a39-b1.

8. Aristotle expresses this notion at the outset of the Rhetoric, 1354a7: "because of the habitude derived from a stable disposition."

9. 1366a14-16, 1369a15-19, 28-29; 1389a35-37; 1390a16, 17-18; 1395b14-18; 1414a21-22; 1417a17, 18, 19-20, 22, 23-24; 1418a16-17, b23.

10. In the analysis of the different kinds of character in II.12-17 there are constant references to moral character, that is, the virtues and vices as they are found in EN 1107a28-1108b10, EE 1220b38-1221a12. In describing the characters he speaks of courage, temperance, liberality (and so on) and self-indulgence, irascibility, meanness, cowardice (and so on).

11. Thinking of ἦθος as entechnic pistis to signify the moral character of both speaker and auditor and the mutual influence of each upon the other makes much sense. It explains, for instance, a number of statements in the text on the ἦθος of each and also explains in a simple way the development between I.4 and II.17. With the introduction of the three entechnic pisteis at I.2 Aristotle develops the idea by illustrating each pistis between I.2 and II.17; reason (logos) at I.4-14; emotion (pathos) at II.2-11; moral character (ethos) at II.12-17.

12. As Burnett (p. 66) remarks, it was the formation of this kind of ἦθος that was the object of the first education in the Republic and Laws of Plato.

13. See Wartelle for the uses. The word ἠθικός appears 12 times (in the singular 7 times, in the plural 5) and ἠθικῶς once. In a number of instances there is obvious reference to ἦθος as entechnic pistis.

14. Anaximenes' meaning for the word ἦθος is similar to Aristotle's, that is, the way a person habitually acts (1428b11) in the area of moral activity (see, for example, the actions he mentions). He employs the word 10 times in the following manner: referring to the speaker twice (1430a28-29; 1446a14; possibly 1445b17); in one instance to the auditors (1434b28-31); in three instances it refers to others and their habitual ways of acting (1429a11; 1430a35; 1441b19-20) and in two instances akin to this it could be taken in the same way, or as "moral character" (1445b3, 12); in one case (1441b22) the meaning is unclear.

15. If we think of the ἦθος of the speaker as the sole entechnic pistis we are forced at passages such as II.1 (1377b22-28) to ask how a speaker can develop the auditor's character without an intelligent knowledge of what probably makes it tick. Or again at 1377b28-1378a6 one wonders how he can make the auditors well-disposed, in fact dispose them at all without such knowledge. Such an effort sounds unpleasantly like the remarks of Gorgias in Plato ("Gorgias," 458e-460e).

16. *De Partitione Oratoria* 8.28. This idea reappears often in the formulaic expression "that we win over the auditors to ourselves" (*De Oratore*, 2.27.115). But as is seen from the citation this is done in other ways than by what the speaker himself is as a person. Enos and McClaran, however, in their study of the speakers and audience in Cicero's works (including the nonrhetorical) present a different reading of their place in Latin tradition. So, too, does Fantham in her study of the Ciceronian idea of what Aristotle calls the speaker's ἦθος. In the course of it she indicates that Cicero may also have in mind the ἦθος of others. There is a problem, however, as will be seen in the meaning of ἦθος in the Latin tradition. This cannot be resolved by interpreting *Rhetoric* 11.12-17, as Fantham does (p. 270), as a continuation of "the analysis of the emotions in the audience." In this view she is not alone (e.g., Süss, p. 163). However, it overlooks two facts: Aristotle denies that ἦθος is πάθος; in Aristotle's concept of ἦθος the emotions enter in as a part. As was said earlier an ἦθος for Aristotle is a firm disposition in a person formed partly under the direction of reason with respect to that part of the appetitive soul represented by the emotions and reflecting the quality of the person's dominant habits in the sphere of moral activity.

17. "The introduction is drawn from the person of the speaker . . . or from that of the prospective auditors"; see also Cicero (*Orator*, 25, 123): "The speaker should make the greatest use of this kind of discretion—that he be a controlling influence with respect to occasions and persons."

18. The practical good sense of the auditors has always been a guide for the eloquence of speakers."

19. In fact this pistis is understood to be a form of πάθος; see, for example, Martin (pp. 97, 158-160), Kroll (p. 69) and Roth (pp. 855, 858).

20. "There are, to be sure, two factors which make one's eloquence worthy of wonder. One of them is what the Greeks call 'expressive of moral character' and is conformed to the natures of men, their moral conduct, and all the customary ways of life; the other is what they term 'emotive.' "

21. "Es ist die in seiner Persönlichkeit und seiner ausdrucksweise hervortretende Gesinnung, welche dem Sinne seiner Zuhörer correspondiert."

22. At times even passing comments (objectively quite correct) emphasize the importance of the speaker and convey the idea that if he uses his wits he can have his way, for example, speaking on "propriety" at *Orator* 72, Cicero says: "Although a word (*verbum*) without reference to the thing it denotes possesses no power at all, still time and again that same thing is accepted or rejected if it is expressed in one way or another (*alio atque alio verbo*)."

REFERENCES

Burnet, J. (1900). *The ethics of Aristotle*. London: Methuen.
Cope, E. M. (1867). *An introduction to Aristotle's* Rhetoric. London: Macmillan.
Cope, E. M. (1877). *The Rhetoric of Aristotle with a commentary i-iii* (Rev. and ed. by J. E. Sandys). Cambridge: Cambridge University Press.
Dufour, M. (1960). *Aristote: Rhétorique i-ii*. Paris: Association Guillame Budé.

Enos, R. L., & McClaran, J. (1978). Audience and image in Ciceronian Rome: Creation and constraints of the *vir bonus* personality. *Central States Speech Journal, 29,* 98-106.

Fantham, M. (1973). Ciceronian *conciliare* and Aristotelian ethos. *Phoenix, 27,* 262-275.

Grimaldi, W. M. A. (1972). Studies in the philosophy of Aristotle's *Rhetoric. Hermes, 25.*

Kroll, W. (1918). "ἐν ἤθει." *Philologus, 75,* 68-76.

Lyons, W. (1980). *Emotion.* Cambridge: Cambridge University Press.

Martin, R. (1974). *Antike Rhetorik ii.3.* I. Muller, W. Otto, & H. Bengston (Eds.). Munich: Handbuch der Altertumswissenschaft.

Roth, C. L. (1866). Was ist das ἦθος in der alten rhetorik? *Neue Jahrbücher für Philologie und Paedagogik (36),* 855-860.

Süss, W. (1910). *Ethos.* Leipzig: Scientia Verlag.

Wartelle, A. (1982). *Lexique de la "rhétorique" d'Aristote.* Paris: Les Belles Lettres.

5

A Sophistic Strain in the Medieval Ars Praedicandi and the Scholastic Method

JAMES L. KINNEAVY

THE HYPOTHESIS: THERE REALLY WAS A MEDIEVAL SOPHISTIC

Studies of rhetoric during the Second Sophistic emphasize its historical importance as a period of transition between antiquity and the Middle Ages. The perspective for measuring its impact, however, is often done in relationship to and in comparison with rhetoric of the classical period. A more complete understanding of sophistic rhetoric requires an understanding of its subsequent impact on later periods. The hypothesis of this chapter is that, in the Middle Ages, there was a third sophistic movement in rhetoric, paralleling the first and second Greek sophistic periods in rhetorical history. A comprehensive recurrence of even a majority of the traits of the first in the second would not be proposed; even less could one argue for a double mapping of both of the movements in antiquity onto the medieval sophistic. There are, however, a few significant features which are repeated. The first sophistic occurred mainly in the fifth century B. C., and was dominated by such figures as Protagoras, Gorgias, Hippias of Elis, and Thrysamachus. For the purposes of this chapter, it is helpful to point out that epistemologically all of these thinkers tended to avoid absolutism and to court some kind of relativism, sometimes even skepticism. They all also emphasized rhetoric in their teachings, and three of them left distinct stylistic influences on subsequent rhetorical thought. In the opinion of Plato and Aristotle and the tradition these two engendered, sophists tended to emphasize style over matter, persuasion over truth, and rhetoric over dialectic. One of the favorite genres (especially of the later sophists) was the epideictic oration—a speech often intended neither for a political nor a legal audience, but rather for an audience that was often more interested in the brilliant display of the rhetorical techniques of the author than in any immediate issue at hand. Not all of the epideictic speeches which we have from antiquity betray this major aim; for example, Pericles' famous funeral oration in Thucydides epideictic lauded and displayed the aspirations of the Athenians, not the rhetorical virtuosity of Pericles. However, many of the epideictic speeches were exercises in virtuosity, serving the practical purpose of enticing students to the orator's school. In any case, much epideictic rhetoric was more interested in craft and artistry than in matters of the polis.

Although the roots of the Second Sophistic have been traced to the fourth century B. C., it is generally considered to have flourished in the second to fourth centuries A.D. More even than in the first sophistic, the writers of the Second Sophistic regarded declamation and the display of rhetorical powers as their most important activity, as Kennedy (1972) has said. They also were hopeful of "attracting high-paying pupils" (Kennedy, 1972, p. 560), though sometimes some of the second sophists, such as Dio of Prusa, Lucian, and Apuleius, became important philosophically or literarily. Dio of Prusa, however, is famous for his "Encomium of Hair" and for his "Trojan Discourse," in which he attempts to prove that the Trojans won the war. Even his most famous work, his Olympic speech, is conceded by Kennedy (1972) to be more sophistic than philosophical. Other important names in the Second Sophistic were Philostratus and Eunapius (these were also the historians of the movement), Herodes Atticus, and Libanius (the teacher of St. Basil, St. Gregory of Nazienzen, and St. John Chrysostom).

One of the reasons for the dominance of the epideictic in rhetoric in the Second Sophistic was the absence of any motivation to real political speech in the period of the emperors. Rhetoric declines in periods of tyranny, as Tacitus (1967) explains at length in his "Dialogue on

Orators," and for this reason Tacitus turned from rhetoric to history in his later years. The "Dialogue" was written in the early period of the Second Sophistic, probably in A. D. 101.

Religion did allow a serious alternative to politics in this period, but the Sophistic spirit also invaded the pulpit. Speaking on this issue, St. John Chrysostom (Armeringer, 1921) wrote:

> This has turned the Churches upside down, because you do not desire to hear a discourse calculated to lead you to compunction, but one that may delight you from the sound and composition of the words, as though you were listening to singers and minstrels. . . . Just such is our case, when we vainly busy ourselves about beautiful expressions, and the composition and harmony of our sentences, in order that we may please, not profit; [when] we make it our aim to be admired, not to instruct. (p. 26)

Chrysostom opposed applause for sermons, even when he received it, and blamed the audience as well as the competitive preachers: "For the public are accustomed to listen not for profit, but for pleasure, sitting like critics of tragedies, and of musical entertainments" (Armeringer, 1921, p. 26). It is this aspect of the Second Sophistic that recurs in certain aspects of the *ars praedicandi*, the scholastic method in theology. In addition, and related to the epideictic nature of the *ars praedicandi*, the scholastic method and the *disputatio* also clearly display another aspect of the sophistic movement in antiquity, one to which Aristotle devoted the last book of his *Organon*. In *Sophistici Elenchi*, Aristotle considered at some length the use of sophistic or contentious refutations. In fact, in common parlance, this is the most usual means of "sophistry." Let us then look at these facets of sophistic rhetoric recurring in two major genres of the Middle Ages, for it is clear that preaching and argument dominate the study of rhetoric, and from this perspective we may be better able to judge its nature and impact.

THE SOPHISTIC STRAIN
IN THE *ARS PRAEDICANDI*

Two of the three medieval rhetorical arts, the *ars praedicandi* and the *ars poetica*, came almost unheralded onto the medieval scene at approximately the same time, reached their maturity almost immediately, and were passed on to succeeding centuries virtually unchanged. The *artes poeticae* started in 1175 with Matthew of Vendome and finished in 1280 with Laborintus. The *artes praedicandi* started with Alain de Lille in 1199 and were definitely established almost as a finished genre by 1220, although there were hundreds of imitations in the remainder of the century and the next two centuries. The diffusion of this genre roughly follows the intensity of the university life and the use of the Scholastic *disputatio* in France in the thirteenth century, in England in the fourteenth, and in Germany in the fifteenth, says Charland (1936).

Authorities agree that one of the most typical and comprehensive of these arts was that of Robert of Basevorn, written in A. D. 1322 (Charland, 1936). Murphy (1974) says that Basevorn "almost perfectly embodies the entire movement" (p. 276); his work will guide the examples used in this chapter. The sermons preached following this genre were usually given in Latin by the master of theology to the young clerics (Charland, 1936). In contrast to the previous homiletic sermons, which followed the text of the Scripture and interpreted it seriatim, these sermons were thematic and used Scripture and other authorities to develop the theme. Basevorn illustrates several themes throughout his treatise, but he returns again and again to one theme in particular, "The intelligent minister is acceptable to the king" (Proverbs 14:35), recommended for use on the feast of St. Peter the apostle. The following illustration represents graphically the development of this theme in the sermon as it is given throughout Basevorn's treatise:

> So far only the first part (R) has been developed. The development of S (Minister) parallels that of R. The transition from R to S is accomplished through a paraphrase from St. Jerome: since virginity was known to the angles, Peter's mind (R,a) through his virtue (S,b) is angelic. Through three passages from Proverbs, R, S, and T are reviewed (and the theme repeated). Then because Peter's mind is angelic, the hierarchy of acts of the angelic mind, according to Dionysius, can be applied to Peter: purgation, illumination, and consummation. These become the development of S (d, e, and f).
>
> S is developed paralleling R, but now both the generic R, S, and T and the specific a, b, and c can be reechoed. Within d, we see that Peter is purged

by b (his actions); and a quotation from Proverbs echoes R, a, and b. Similarly, e is developed by echoing S; then two quotations from Proverbs echo R, a, and b and R and a, respectively. Within f, consummation is developed by echoing R, T, a, c, and d. Thus because S can build on both the original theme (R, S, T) and its first subdivision (a, b, c), its development can become more complex.

The third principal member, T, follows a similar development by building upon three new subdivisions (memory, intelligence, and prudence). These are led up to by a quotation from St. Bernard which echo R, a, S, b, and T; this is followed by a quotation from Proverbs which bring back R, S, and T. So St. Peter's intellect (R, a), because of its virtuous life and death (S, b), is to be awarded a jewel (T) because it had the three parts of the human intellect spoken of by Cicero: memory, intelligence, and prudence (g, h, and i). These are developed by relating them respectively to the past, the present, and the future. Then g is developed by relating it to T; h is developed by relating it to T, R, and a, and by a quotation from 1 Corinthians which echoes R, and a; similarly, i is developed by a quotation from Psalms which echoes R, a, T, and f. (Murphy, 1971, pp. 160-164, 192-195)

In the conclusion, the major statements of the theme are brought together in a single statement. Thus the previous development can be unified by this statement: "O that they would be wise and would understand, and would provide for their end." This is the end of the sections which Basevorn presents in *Forma Praedicandi* (Murphy, 1971). It is true that the convolution development, probably the second most complicated development which he mentions, is chosen here. Basevorn mentions the correspondence method, the congruence of correspondence, the circuitous development, the convolution development (illustrated here), the simple method to be used with "ordinary people in any vulgar idiom," and finally the elegant method of virtual authorities and virtual divisions—the latter to be used "in Latin to the very intelligent."

What did these echoings or recurrences of the thematic motive consist in? Throughout the entire treatise Basevorn is quite explicit on this matter: they are either verbal or real concordances. A *verbal concordance* is the repetition of some of the same words or roots used above; for instance, for the theme for the First Sunday of Advent (*Dies appropinquavit*) the antetheme could well be a verse from Ecclesiastes, 4:7 *Approprinqua ut audias*. But in moving from the theme to the

TABLE 5.1: A Sermon on St. Peter Illustrating the Convolution Development

ANTETHEME & PRAYER	Not given.		
THEME:	THE INTELLIGENT	MINISTER	IS ACCEPTABLE TO THE KING
DIVISION & DEC. OF PARTS	R	S	T (Prov 14:35)
	Wise man, truth	Service, virtue	God's reward
DEVELOPMENT			
*Intelligent-*R	a	b	c
	Peter preached truth Isaias-R,S,T	Peter elevated by resisting (repugnans) R attacking (impugnans) S conquering (expugnans) T R,S,T Aug-R, Jer-S, Ecclus-T	Peter is made sublime Isaias Holy Spirit-R Son-S Father-T

(continued)

Table 5.1 Continued

Minister-S. Transition: Jerome; therefore Peter's mind (R,a) is angelic. Prov: the wisdom of a discreet man is to know his way, a wise man declines from evil (R,a,S,b). Prov: A wise servant is acceptable to the king (S,b,T,c). So Peter shows the hierarchic act of the angelic mind:

d	e	f
Purgation	Illumination	Consummation
By [b] he is purged	by virginity-S	R,T,a,c,d
Prov: R,a,b	Prov: R,a,b	
	Prov: R,a	

Made Acceptable to the King-T. Trans.—St. Bernard, R,a,S,b, T. Prov: R,S,T. So Peter's intellect (R,a) because of his virtuous life and death (S,b) is to be awarded a jewel (T) because it had:

g	h	i
Memory	Intelligence	Prudence
past	present	future
T	T,R,a	Psalms: Ra, T, f
	1 Cor: R,a	

CONCLUSION (Unification): O that they would be wise and would understand, and would provide for their end.

SOURCE: From Robert Basevorn, *Forma Praedicandi* (tr. Leopold Krul, O.S.B.), in James J. Murphy (Ed.), *Three Medieval Rhetorical Arts* (Berkeley: University of California Press, 1971), pp. 160-164, 192-195.

declaration of parts, Basevorn specifically cautions against using the same roots: synonyms or words related in meaning are to be used; not even words of the same root are allowed (see Chapter XXXIII). This is *real concordance*, but the motive recurrence must be either verbal or real. That is, there must be a verbal rhyme or a semantic rhyme for each echoing.

Such a requirement makes for a very tight structure. Given an antetheme, a theme, a declaration of parts, and a triple sub-subdivision of each part, plus unification conclusion (21 sections), there must be either a verbal or a real concordance repeated 21 times. In addition, in the development of each part there may be verbal or real concordances; attention has been called to several of these (*repugnans, impugnans, expugnans; rapitis, rapiat, rapit, eripiat*). The result is a 21-cell prose poem with major divisional verbal rhymings and semantic rhymings, and with other root rhymings and puns interspersed. It is not difficult to document these concordances for every part of the structure (antetheme, theme, declaration of parts, digression, amplification, correspondence, agreement of correspondence, circuitous development, convolution development, and unification).

The exegesis of this rhetorical text illustrates the intricate relationship of oral and written composition. The presumptions of seeking aesthetic excellence through phonetic and textual features is itself a statement of the disposition such authors had toward discourse. Hours can be spent figuring out how the text is put together, working in one's native language with the Latin on the side. It is a wondrous puzzle, and it is possible to see how most of the parts go together. If someone were to read the sermon aloud, one would be able to hear most of these recurrent motives, in English and even more in Latin, and be amazed at the verbal craft of the entire piece. The response would be primarily that of response to the artistry—the typical response to the epideictic piece in sophistic rhetoric.

Basevorn was aware of this danger. Early in the treatise, he refers to both the English and the French methods, saying that they have their origins in the famous Church fathers, and adds:

> They use in part the method of one of the other and in part their own and also add many devices which, as it seems to me, appertain more to

curiosity and vanity than to edification: that concordances be vowels—
e.g., if the theme is *Veni, Domine Jesu* (Come, Lord Jesus), the gerundive,
veniendi, or the noun *adventus*, or the verb *dominari* or the noun *salvator*
(which is equivalent to Jesus) could not function at all. . . . What excuse
they have before God I cannot well see. . . . Indeed, so great is men's
vanity, especially that of the English, that they only consider the curious
and do not commend anything else. (Murphy, 1971, Ch. 7)

This warning and reaction is repeated quite a few times. Thus, the
circuitous development is compared to a labyrinth, and is "more decorative then useful" (Ch. 44); the convolution method is "useless, and in
the whole, as I think, impossible," although Basevorn admits it pleases
him (Ch. 45); the unification in a convolution development is formed
("if it must be formed," Ch. 46); and finally, after the development he
turns to seven additional ornaments, which Basevorn admits, "are more
extrinsic, but they serve for beauty" (Ch. 50). Other remarks can be
added to these (Ch. 45). St. John Chrysostom would have railed at the
audience and preachers alike for these performances. Yet, these cautions are also an index of both the tendencies and techniques of composition; that is, a concern with creating discourse that has aesthetic
effects which can be captured in both oral and written performance.

THE SOPHISTIC STRAIN
IN THE SCHOLASTIC METHOD

From this perspective we should now turn to the scholastic method,
the dialectical method exemplified in the *summa*. The *summa* incorporated the methods of the other three major medieval instructional
techniques, the *lectio*, the *disputatio*, and the *sententia*. The development of the scholastic method has been brilliantly chronicled by
Grabmann (1909/1957) early in this century, and his analysis has not
been seriously challenged since. He contends that this history of the
method was the continuous conflict between authority and reason and
that the method finally harmonized both of these methods of argumentation, mainly under the influence of Abelard, Lanfranc, Peter Damian,

and especially Anselm of Canterbury, whom Grabmann regards as the real founder of the method.

Regardless of the historical process, however, the product should be analyzed. Aquinas certainly epitomizes the confluence of these various influences of authority and reason. Let us look at a typical question from the *Summa Theologica*, "Whether Man's Happiness Consists in Fame or Glory?" (Aquinas, 1952). The article consists in the three usual parts of the scholastic method: the objections and contrary instances; the solution of the question given in the corpus; and the replies to the objection. The contrasting texts of the first part come from Abelard and the dialecticians, and the synthesis comes from Ivo of Chartres, Bernold, Anselm, and Aquinas, among others (see Grabmann, 1909/ 1957). It is easy to see why some have called these three parts the thesis, the antithesis, and the synthesis, but the analogy is perhaps not quite accurate.

In the first part, Aquinas had to search the authorities, whether Biblical, partristic, classical, Islamic, or Jewish, for arguments which would assert that man's happiness actually did consist in fame or glory. These arguments were clearly fallacious, for they were to be disproved by the subsequent section and specifically by the answers to the objections. They were *sophistici elenchi* (sophistic arguments), to use Aristotle's terms for the section of his *Organon* devoted to fallacies. And, of course, as Anselm of Canterbury claimed, Aristotle's *Organon*—especially the *Analytics*, *Topics*, and *Sophistici Elenchi*—was one of the major sources of the scholastic method (Grabmann 1909/1957). In a real sense this was sophistry, because particularly for a topic such as this there was no real issue: no serious student of Christian theology could entertain the thought that happiness could consist in human fame and glory. Aquinas had to be clever even to set up intelligent arguments for this position in the section on objections, and in so doing reveals a conceptual framework that is not only classical in heritage but sophistic in orientation.

Of course, not all of the questions and articles in the *Summa* are as one-sided as this one. In many there are really debatable issues within the context of the Christian theology, and the sophistic content of these questions disappears in favor of a real dialectic. But there are enough questions where the received dogmas or tradition in the Church did not permit of much tolerance and where, therefore, the objections had to be heavily sophistic. While no claim is advanced for a completely sophistic scholastic method, any more than one has been argued for a completely sophistic art of preaching, there is clearly a sizable dose of sophistic in both. The sophistic is clear in the first section: the objections are fallacies, and the argumentation is of necessity sophistic. One does not have to examine the quite intelligent case that Aquinas made for human fame and glory in the three objections. Students of theology must concede the sophistic craft in slipping from human fame and glory to heavenly glory in the first objection, buttressed with a quotation from St. Paul; they will also recognize the equivalence of good with happiness and the serious authorities, Dionysius, Ambrose, and Augustine, used in the second; and finally they will concede that the employment of an appeal to an element of the eternal ("after a fashion"), with Boethius as a backup, in the third argument is a clever ploy. The corpus does not generally participate in the sophistic nearly so much as the objections and the answers to them, for a fairly obvious reason. Here the truth, as it is conceived, is being argued—not fallacies.

The return of a healthy dose of sophistic recurs also in the third part of the method, the reply to the objections. But the measure of the sophistic in the replies is almost inversely related to the measure in the objections. In other words, if the objections were really trivial (and therefore sophistic), then the replies can be solid and not just a matter of display of dialectic prowess. If the objections were strong, then the incorporation of the authorities quoted in the objections becomes more problematic.

They must, however, be incorporated. This is the effort of harmony which had to be brought about and which is the second and more serious problem of sophistic in the *Summa* methodology. The authorities belong to the tradition; that is why they were quoted in the first place. Therefore, they cannot be peremptorily dismissed as wrong. The replies to the objections must somehow interpret their earlier sayings in a way that allows the authority to remain in the tradition. This hermeneutic can sometimes be sophistic: even though the objections in this case were fairly trivial, there is a touch of the sophistic in the treatment given the first objection, which had been dignified by slipping from the notion of human fame and glory to the glory of heaven in the passage from St. Paul. The reply is easy: St. Paul was not speaking of human glory, so that heavenly glory is indeed happiness. But the reader has to ask why St. Paul had been quoted in the first place. In any case, St. Paul's authority is not impugned.

The second objection is somewhat different. The argument of the objection develops by equating goodness with happiness, and by quoting Dionysius in saying that goodness diffuses itself. But a person's goodness is diffused by glory "being well known and praised," according to Ambrose. The reply points out that if the knowledge of glory is false, it does not come from goodness. Aquinas does not say what part of the objection is fallacious; Dionysus is not harmed. Ambrose's definition of glory is not false, although Aquinas has shown that not all diffusion by glory is of goodness. What the reply seems to show is that the objection was not really valid, since glory is an ambiguous term. In any case, the stature of none of the authorities is hurt. The fallacy consists in applying Ambrose's statements about glory to eternal glory and happiness; Aquinas points out the fallacy. It is exactly that, a *sophisticus elenchus*, a sophistic argument.

The third reply is the easiest because the third objection is the weakest. The objection had argued for some kind of eternity in fame; it is easy to dislodge that assertion, and Boethius had only said, "You seem to beget unto yourself eternity, when you think of your fame in future times." The misinterpretation of Boethius hardly disturbs his stature either. This, however, is a typical treatment of many of the routine questions in the *Summa*, particularly those in which the issue is practically decided ahead of time. The dialectical method has been traversed, objections to the main thesis have been raised with suitable authorities, the thesis itself has been established, and the seemingly conflicting authorities have been assured of their place in the theological tradition. It has been a good show. And sophistic has been an essential part of the performance.

The point of this chapter is to reveal the sophistic strain in the rhetoric of the subsequent period, and not merely to assess its nature from classical origins. This chapter simply suggests that the Middle Ages, like most ages, have a place in their language arts for the operation of a sophistic. In the case of preaching, it operates somewhere between rhetoric and poetic, the usual place for much epideictic oratory. And in many cases there is possibly more of the aesthetic than of the persuasive on the part of the audience—more pleasure than profit, St. John Chrysostom would have said. In the case of the scholastic method, it operates as the sophistic fallacy opposing the true thesis, and later as the disclosing of the fallacy in the reply to the objections. In both cases, the use of authorities—Biblical, partristic, and classical—is an integral part of the methodology.

In the case of the sophistic involved in posing objections, the sophistic is ranked normally even lower than rhetoric or poetic on the usual epistemological planes. In the Middle Ages, McKeon (1942) recognizes three kinds of proof in Aristotelian logic, "scientific or demonstrative, dialectical, and sophistical" (p. 8), which are expounded in Aristotle's *Posterior Analytics*, the *Topics*, and the *Sophistici Elenchi*. Such distinctions can be seen in Remigius of Auxerre, Gerbert, Hugh of St. Victor, John of Salisbury, and especially St. Thomas Aquinas (McKeon, 1942). Aquinas makes the most elaborate distinctions, ranking according to level of certainty: understanding, intellect, science, dialectic, rhetoric, poetic, and finally sophistic (Aquinas, 1970). One of the implications of this chapter is to reveal that subsequent efforts to study the relationship of oral and written discourse from the sophistic tradition will not only provide a more complete understanding of rhetoric's history but, in many instances, a more sensitive understanding of the discourse under examination. Actually, there is even in the sophistic elements of the scholastic method more than a touch of the aesthetic as well. But that topic is one that is the subject of another inquiry and another hypothesis.

REFERENCES

Aquinas, Thomas (1952). *Summa theologica*. Tr. Fathers of the English Province, Rev. Daniel J. Sullivan. In *Thomas Aquinas, I*. Great books of the Western World. Ed. Robert Maynard Hutchins. Chicago, IL: Encyclopedia Britannica, Inc.

Aquinas, Thomas (1970). *Commentary on the posterior analytics of Aristotle.* (F. R. Larcher, Trans.). New York: Magi.

Armeringer, T. E. (1921). *The stylistic influence of the Second Sophistic on the panegyrical sermons of St. John Chrysostom: A study in Greek rhetoric.* Washington, DC: Catholic University of America.

Charland, Th. -M. (1936). *Artes praedicandi: Contribution a l'histoire de la rhetorique au moyen age.* Paris: Libr. Philosophique, J. Vrin.

Grabmann, M. (1957). *Die Geschichte der scholastichen Methode* (2 vols.). Darmstadt: Wissenschaftliche Buchgesellschaft. (Original work published 1909)

Kennedy, G. A. (1972). *The art of rhetoric in the roman world, 300 B. C.-A. D. 300.* Princeton, NJ: Princeton University Press.

McKeon, R. (1942). Rhetoric in the Middle Ages. *Speculum, 17,* 1-32.

Murphy, J. J. (1974). *Rhetoric in the Middle Ages: A history of rhetorical theory from Saint Augustine to the Renaissance.* Berkeley: University of California Press.

Murphy, J. J. (Ed.), (1971). *Three medieval rhetorical arts.* Berkeley: University of California Press.

Tacitus (1967). *Dialogue on orators.* (H. W. Bernario, Trans.). Indianapolis, IN: Library of Liberal Arts.

6

The Illiterate Mode of Written Communication: The Work of the Medieval Scribe

DENISE A. TROLL

If we are to understand the relationship between technology[1] and the diffusion of culture and knowledge, we must understand how human cognition since the invention of print differs from human cognition prior to the invention of print. We must understand what print technology acted upon to produce the modern mind, which is to say that we must reconstruct medieval consciousness. Possessing such knowledge, we may begin to speculate reasonably about the long-term effects of present and future technologies on human consciousness, culture, and knowledge.

H. J. Chaytor argues that the significant areas of study should be "the mental attitude of the scholar and literary man in the ages before print" and the mental attitude of the scholar and literary man after print (1950, p. 138), but to narrow the focus to the *scholar*'s mentality biases the study along the unfounded assumption that the only habits of importance in the diffusion of culture and knowledge are those of an academic class. This assumption is dubious, and a study driven by it can only produce dubious results. Rather than focusing on the locus from which culture and knowledge are presumably diffused (the scholars), the intention here is to focus on the locus that enabled the diffusion: the technology. This chapter will illustrate how preprint technology constrained medieval culture and knowledge, and how the consciousness of those who wielded the technology was gradually (re)structured by it. The discussion will overturn some of our assumptions about the medieval scribes.

Medieval culture and knowledge were no doubt diffused by medieval manuscript technology and those who manipulated and developed it, specifically, medieval monks and scribes,[2] personalities who may or may not have been "scholars" depending on how the term is defined.[3] The goal of this chapter is to probe manuscript technology, in the context of medieval monasticism, for clues to the techniques it demanded and therefore the constraints it placed on human culture and knowledge. These clues can then be used to reconstruct medieval consciousness and contribute to our understanding of how the modern (postprint) mind differs from its ancestor.

CLEARING OUR MINDS

The millennium in which manuscript technology reigned spans the evolution of human consciousness from, in Eric A. Havelock's terms (1982), the second period of *craft literacy* through the period of *scriptorial literacy*—roughly from the fall of the Roman Empire to the invention of print; we will come back to these terms later in the chapter. Havelock (1982) warns us not to read backwards through history and project our modern biases onto earlier stages of consciousness; for example, we must not assume that the medieval mind operated out of the same cognitive organization of reality as we do. The danger is apparent in the following scenario.

Many of us have an image of medieval scribes as silent, dedicated monks producing illuminated manuscripts at tilted desks. We value their work because it preserved the treasures of antiquity. We feel certain that, as the monks worked, they absorbed the meaning of what they copied and themselves became storehouses—veritable libraries—of the genius that preceded them. We envy their freedom to concentrate on every word, to commit each one to parchment or vellum so painstakingly that they must have memorized certain passages and been able to recall them at will. We believe that the monks were religiously devoted to preserving and translating the best intellectual and literary efforts of the past, and that they valued the technology of writing, knowing that they were paving the way for social literacy by providing the basic necessity: texts.

This "reading" of the medieval scribes is based on four assumptions that operate covertly in the modern literate mind, itself the product of print. First, we assume that the scribes could read and were intelligent enough to remember what they read. Second, we assume that they worked on their own volition in order to learn, and that they questioned and memorized what they read. Third, we assume that they were devoted to preserving and translating written discourse because of the intellectual content it perpetuated. And fourth, we assume that they valued writing because they understood its social, epistemological, and psychological ramifications. In short, we assume that they were literate in the modern sense of the word.

Behind these four assumptions lurks the pervasive notion that reading and writing were always experienced and appreciated as they are in the twentieth century. The modern noetic habits of connecting reading and writing and equating the two with literacy produce a misreading of the medieval scribes if our goal is to know medieval consciousness on its own terms—the way medieval minds and events organized it, rather than the way we would. The depiction of medieval scribes presented above says more about our minds and values than it does about medieval consciousness. We must replace this misleading, modern literate view of the scribes with a more responsible view that takes into account their historical, religious, intellectual, and psychological situation. Only by putting the scribes and their work into *their* context can we approach the medieval experience and their understanding of manuscripts and literacy; only then can we see how manuscript technology constrained medieval culture and knowledge. We must clear our minds of tacit assumptions.

Chaytor's (1950) designation of a gap between print or paper literacy and what preceded it may be restated as a gap between our view of who the medieval scribes were and what they did, and the medieval scribes' self-concept and perception of what they did. A methodical and self-conscious look at medieval history can expose our modern biases and help us conceptualize the cognitive structure of our ancestors. Let us begin with what manuscript technology demanded.

THE DEMANDS OF MANUSCRIPT TECHNOLOGY

While modern writers are free to choose from among a variety of tools, materials, and working conditions (and even choose these to suit different phases of the writing process), medieval scribes did not have this liberty. The demands of manuscript technology interacted with the demands of medieval politics and monasticism to severely constrain the scribes' choices.

Materials and Tools

In comparison with modern writing materials and tools, those wielded by medieval scribes were rare, expensive, cumbersome, and primitive. The historical situation dictated the materials available for writing: wax tablets for temporary notes; papyrus, parchment, and vellum for important text. The stylus, pens, and inks were likewise constrained by history. There were tools for preparing the parchment, for ruling lines, for marking the beginnings of lines, and for doing the writing itself.[4] The materials and tools were so problematic that they affected the process of book production and the appearance of the books produced—which in turn affected the cost, availability, and quality of books, and the medieval experience of reading and writing.

For centuries, each scribe did every step in book production—from tediously preparing the materials to copying, illuminating, and binding the manuscript. Marc Drogin estimates that, writing large manuscript pages, the scribe averaged about two to four pages a day; an average manuscript took three to four months to copy. A manuscript with colored initials and miniature art work produced by a single scribe could take several years (Drogin, 1983). During this period, each scribe was a veritable publishing house, a master craftsman able to wield a variety of difficult tools and hence a member of an elite guild.

For pragmatic reasons, the paradigm of the copyist/writer as master craftsman slowly changed. The scribes gradually specialized in a particular step in book production, for example, in illuminating or rubricating. Ironically, though specialization enabled them to produce manuscripts more efficiently, it devalued their labor: the scribes became factory workers, members of an assembly line. As books became more readily available and the ability to read and write became less of an oddity, the scribes' talent no longer branded them as elite, and when the printing press was invented and the scribes failed to unionize, they lost their jobs.

Besides affecting the process of book production, the tools and materials of manuscript technology affected the appearance of the finished books by constraining the shapes of the letters. For example, the material surfaces and inks often interacted poorly; ink trailed along hairlines on the parchment, directly affecting the physical appearance of the letters—which subsequently made reading and copying difficult. Furthermore, the slow speed of manuscript production and the limited availability of parchment, evidenced by the continued practice of using palimpsests,[5] led to the conscious and subconscious evolution of new scripts. According to John B. Morrall (1967), the eighth-century invention of the Caroline minuscule[6] at St. Martin's in Tour, France, under the direction of the English monk Alcuin, was an attempt to produce a smaller script so that more text could be placed on a page, and to standardize a medium of communication so that systematic education would be possible.[7] Cursive script apparently evolved from the minuscule in the twelfth century for the purpose of producing manuscripts more quickly. T. A. M. Bishop argues, "The cursive script is the result of license, not discipline; it is evidence not of a common training but of something simpler and historically more interesting: a common pressure of urgent business" (1961 p. 13).[8]

The difficulty of mastering all of the tools of manuscript technology slowly shaped book production and the lives of those engaged in it. During the early Middle Ages, writing was a craft and the writer (copyist) a member of an elite guild—those who could wield all of the tools. During the late Middle Ages, writing was industry and the writer an assembly-line worker who could wield only a limited subset of tools.

The paradigmatic shift from guild to factory heralds the shift from what Havelock (1982) calls *craft* to *scriptorial* literacy. To fully appreciate the shift, we must examine the working conditions of the scribe.

Working Conditions

The medieval scribes' working conditions were constrained by manuscript technology and monastic life, both of which were harnessed for political ends. Charlemagne's mandate of 795, *De Litteris Colendis*, which encouraged verbal education by requiring churches and monasteries to teach grammar and rhetoric so that people could read Scripture, in effect required every monastery to have a scriptorium. The mandate slowly ushered in the period of scriptorial literacy, still visually oriented as a craft, but bureaucratically sanctioned and multiplied. Understanding the slowly changing context in which the scribes encountered manuscript technology will help us reconstruct their experience and organization of reality. For ease of discussion, the scribes' working conditions may be viewed on four critical levels—but keep in mind that the separation is somewhat artificial; the levels interacted with one another. The four levels pertinent to a critical examination of the scribes' working conditions are religious, intellectual, physical and psychological.

Religious conditions. Manuscript technology and monastic life interacted with one another in ways that constrained both. In most monasteries, regulations regarding reading and writing were an intrinsic part of the operating rules. As early as the sixth century, Benedict of Nursia (Monte Cassino) and Cassiodorus (Vivarium) emphasized reading and the accurate copying of Christian and secular texts. As late as the thirteenth and fourteenth Centuries, the Statutes of the Benedictines read: "By this constitution we order that every monk not otherwise reasonably prevented at the time and place [appointed] be occupied in the study of reading, or in writing, correcting, illuminating, and likewise binding books" (quoted in Drogin, 1983, p. 5). Abbots assigned the books to be copied and the monks copied them in silence, in keeping with monastic rule. If they spoke, they spoke in hand signals.

The monks copied manuscripts because it was their religious duty to fight the devil by multiplying God's words. Copying was promoted as manual labor that would lead to salvation (Drogin, 1983). No manual labor was considered more becoming to monks than writing ecclesiastical books. On the one hand, according to the Abbot of St. Evroul (c. 1050), a scribe could be saved by industry in the scriptorium because one sin was pardoned for each letter he copied (Boorstin, 1985). On the other hand, "To make an error was to commit a sin" (Drogin, 1983, p. 12), and the scribes could be physically punished and forced to recopy a manuscript if the abbot or elders found an error while proofreading. A quotation from Alcuin (Boorstin, 1985) summarizes many of the constraints on the scribes:

> Here let the scribes sit who copy out the words of the Divine Law, and likewise the hallowed sayings of the holy Fathers. Let them beware of interspersing their own frivolities in the words they copy, nor let a trifler's hand make mistakes through haste. Let them earnestly seek out for themselves correctly written books to transcribe, that the flying pen may speed along the right path. Let them distinguish the proper sense by colons and commas, and let them set the points each one in its due place, and let not him who reads the words to them either read falsely or pause suddenly. It is a noble work to write out holy books, nor shall the scribe fail of his due reward. Writing books is better than planting vines, for he who plants a vine serves his belly, but he who writes a book serves his soul. (p. 495)

Copying, then, was important in context, not so much in and of itself, which according to Ong (1982) is evidence of the orality of the medieval mind: "Orality relegates meaning largely to context whereas writing concentrates meaning in language itself" (p. 106).

Intellectual conditions. The medieval monks preserved and amplified knowledge—the knowledge that the religious and political authorities chose. If they could read the text they copied, they were held responsible for learning its contents (Drogin, 1983). But "learning" here should not be misconstrued with our modern sense of being able to draw inferences or generate new knowledge. For the monks, living in a world where everything was believed to have been revealed in Scripture, learning was reiterating what was known, not questioning or rearranging it. Learning was memorizing and reciting what was given, that is, participating in traditional knowledge. The very act and popularity of copying indicates the medieval frame of mind wherein reading was not an intellectual exercise, but "the symbolic expression" of assimilating and retracing facts—the facts of a predominantly oral culture and religious tradition (Curtius, 1953, p. 326).

Physical conditions. Manuscript technology was physically debilitating. The scribes worked outside for centuries, protected from the elements only by their clothing and the ceiling, until respect for their work moved them indoors. When they worked outside, they worked in an enclosed place called the *claustrum*, a rectangular area formed by the surrounding walls of the monastic buildings. Whether outdoors or indoors, they sat on backless stools and wrote on severely tilted work surfaces. Adequate heat and light were exigencies for the medieval monks in ways that they are not for modern writers privy to electricity and fossil fuels. Artificial heat and light could not be used, because they endangered the precious manuscripts. This made writing a seasonal activity. Oderic Vitalis writes, "winter cold prevented me from writing," although evidently he meant writing with pen on parchment, not taking notes with a stylus on wax (*Oderic Vitalis*, Bk. IV, Vol. II, 360-361, and Bk. VI, Ch. 3, Vol. III, 218; in Clanchy, 1979). Many monks went blind from long hours of tedious work with insufficient light. Heat was occasionally provided, but primarily for drying the ink on damp days, not for keeping the scribes warm.[9]

Psychological conditions. The scribes could not refuse to copy the assigned text; to do so was to be denied food and wine, and to be chained to the desk until its completion (Drogin, 1983). Daniel J. Boorstin quotes from a medieval manuscript: "Jacob wrote a certain portion of this book not of his own free will but under compulsion, bound by fetters, just as a runaway and fugitive has to be bound" (1985, p. 494).

The monks were strongly urged to keep the same spacing and pagination as the original, and were reluctant to take credit or risk blame for innovation (they could be punished and forced to recopy a manuscript if they made a mistake). In a world of copying, forgeries, and formula, the notions of originality and intellectual property were unknown.[10] Plagiarism did not become a crime until the end of the Middle Ages (Drogin, 1983).[11]

The *claustrum* provoked feelings of being surrounded and trapped (from which we get our word "claustrophobia"), which depressed the monks. They often became violent, hurting themselves and each other (Drogin, 1983). The situation worsened when "overstrained chastity degenerated into erotics" (Workman, 1913, p. 63). The scribes' proclivity for violence surfaces in their insertion of explicit curses at the ends of manuscripts. Though they were ordered not to alter the text they copied, they often appended personal appeals to protect the manuscripts they produced. These snippets of self-expression reveal both relief and anxiety upon finishing—what Drogin compares to post-partum blues (1983). The scribes lament external and internal disorders as the result of sitting too long uncomfortably and being forced to concentrate on material they neither understood nor appreciated. Fear of error and ominous deadlines for completion added to the tension. They plead with their readers not to touch or tear the pages, to touch only the covers. Their anxiety regularly exploded in curses on careless handlers of their manuscripts. For example:

> The finished book before you lies;
> This humble scribe don't criticize.
> Whoever takes away this book
> May he never on Christ look.
> Whoever to steal this volume durst
> May he be killed as one accursed.
> Whoever to steal this volume tries
> Out with his eyes, out with his eyes!
>
> *Explicit iste liber*
> *sit scriptor crimine liber.*
> *Non videat Christum*
> *qui librum subtrahet istum.*
> *Hunc qui furetur*
> *anathematis esse necetur*
> *Ut me furetur*
> *qui nitatur exoculetur.*
>
> —13th C. (?) Rome, Vatican Library
> Ms. Palat. Lat. 978, folio 25r, col. 2.
> (From Marc Drogin, ANATHEMA!
> [Allanheld & Schram, 1983];
> permission granted by Abner Schram,
> Ltd., Montclair, New Jersey)

The curses often invoked pestilence on careless book handlers and their children and their children's children. The medieval curse of *anathema* or excommunication was a decision of the medieval scribes, not a Council of the Church. Its development indicates the difficulty of book production, the value of books, and the forces that threatened them (Drogin, 1983).

THE IMPLICATIONS OF MANUSCRIPT TECHNOLOGY

Due to the length of time it took to produce a manuscript and the cost of material and labor,[12] books were extremely rare and expensive. Few people owned or had access to books, which increased their value and made book safety and production a priority. Books quickly became so integral to monastic life that they affected monastic architecture: cloisters were arranged with niches or stalls for reading and writing, and much of the space in the monastery was devoted to the production of writing materials.[13] Furthermore, the scribes invented devices to protect the books and Church officials checked to see that the devices were maintained.[14] Drogin (1983) speculates that manuscript technology even affected monastic dress, that is, that the monks' wide sleeves were used to hold and protect books from dirty hands and moisture.

Book safety was such a priority that eventually books were chained to the library shelves or to a horizontal bar above the desk where they were to be consulted (Boorstin, 1985). In some communities, the sentence for stealing or burning a book was death (Drogin, 1983). As late as the fourteenth and fifteenth centuries, books were still scarce and expensive, and access to libraries was limited to a privileged few (Chaytor, 1950). Book purchasing involved as much legal complexity as purchasing a house or land. Ownership was even passed on in wills[15]; the long-standing practice of inserting curses in manuscripts, which continued into the first printed books, made proof of ownership an important issue (Drogin, 1983).

The cost and limited availability of books in turn affected book production, since copying depended on an available exemplar. Monks often spent weeks or months negotiating to have a book on loan; they had to pledge large sums of money or goods of comparable value as security, wait an equally long time for the arrival of the book, and then spend months—often with several monks working on one text—to copy, proofread, decorate, and bind the new book. Sometimes monasteries had to return the original and a copy in return for the loan. Most monastic libraries would only loan to neighboring churches or people of conspicuous worth; some refused to loan books at all (Drogin, 1983).

The proliferation of languages and scripts, the rarity and expense of books, and the notion of learning prevalent in the Middle Ages made books mysteries, magical entities to be preserved rather than created. In the early Middle Ages, books were stored with religious relics and valuable jewelry; "the difference between writings and other precious objects was not as obvious [to the medieval mind] as it is to a modern literate" (Clanchy, 1979, p. 126). Illuminated copies of the Bible were treated as shrines, believed to be hallowed by age and associations. The medieval book edified by its presence; it was an object of contemplation: "For monks in the old Benedictine tradition, books, with their precious and brightly illuminated words, were images which produced a state of mystical contemplation and understanding" (Clanchy, 1979, p. 130). The monks were in awe of their books, in awe of making the spoken word visible, storable, able to be respoken at any time; the technology was a magic gift from God, and a way to salvation (Drogin, 1983).

Only gradually did books begin to be collected into libraries, and only in the late Middle Ages were they seen as reference materials: "At the time of the Norman Conquest documents were special objects which were treasured as shrines; whereas by 1300 Edward I, like the friars, expected them all to be available for scrutiny and comparison whenever he wanted" (Clanchy, 1979, p. 131). Here again we see the paradigmatic shift from craft to industry: from books considered as religious objects (valued for their visual aesthetic) to books considered as a product line (valued for their reusable content).

MEDIEVAL ORALITY AND LITERACY

Medieval manuscript technology made reading and writing extremely difficult. Few people had access to books, and even if they did, few had the education to read the variety of languages and scripts that proliferated at the time. Chaytor (1950) argues: "In the medieval world, those who could read or write were the few, and it is likely that most of them did not read or write with our methods or with our facility" (p. 5); "Of the few who could read, few were habitual readers; in any case, the ordinary man of our own times probably sees more printed and written matter in a week than the medieval scholar saw in a year" (p. 10).

Reading was constrained by both the availability of manuscripts and the lack of uniformity in scripts and spelling. The tedious process and expense of manuscript production account for the limited supply of manuscripts; the writing materials, state of education, and difficulty of travel account for the lack of uniformity in scripts and spelling. The state of education, in turn, was affected by the limited supply of manuscripts, the lack of standardization therein, and the constant political upheaval of the Middle Ages. The situation was further irritated by the fact that written language differed from ordinary spoken language, deriving not from ordinary speech but from tradition, political authority, and social status (Clanchy, 1979).

The difficulty of reading affected medieval culture: "Medieval writing was mediated to the non-literate by the persistence of the habit of reading aloud and by the preference, even among the educated, for listening to a statement rather than scrutinizing it in script" (Clanchy, 1979, p. 150); and "Writing was converted into the spoken word by the habitual practice of reading aloud and of listening to or making an 'audit' of a statement, rather than scrutinizing its text on parchment" (Clanchy, 1979, p. 263). Consequently, reading was conceptualized primarily as an oral phenomenon in the Middle Ages; the medieval mind cycled even the written word back into the oral realm. Reading was linked not with writing but with composing through dictation and with public performance. The role of the composer (*dictator*) was kept distinct from that of the scribe (*scriptor*) (Clanchy, 1979).[16] Though reading and writing had been around for centuries, the medieval mind was still dominated by residually oral cognitive connections promulgated by an oral religious tradition. The practice of public readings emphasized orality and downplayed literacy by devaluing learning to read.

This oral emphasis made silent reading practically impossible in the Middle Ages. Silent reading was so unusual that it provoked comment.[17] The common manner of reading to oneself in the Middle Ages involved whispering or muttering, as evidenced by an eighth-century copyist's description of the process: "Three fingers hold the pen, the eyes see the words, the tongue pronounces them as they are written and the body is cramped with leaning over the desk" (*qui scribere nescit nullum putat esse laborem. Tres digiti scribunt, duo oculi vident. Una lingua loquitur, totum corpus laborat, et omnis labor finem habet, et praemium ejus non habet finem* [in Wattenbach, *Schriftwesen in Mittelalter*, Leipzig, 1896, p. 495]; quoted in Chaytor, 1950, p. 14). The scribe is obviously unable to avoid pronouncing each word as he deciphers it, regardless of the monastic rule of silence.[18] Chaytor (1950) argues that the only explanation for the private niches or stalls for reading and writing, in a community where members spent most of their time together in (supposed) silence, is that the noise of reading aloud while copying distracted the other monks, themselves engaged in the arduous tasks of reading and writing.[19]

According to Havelock (1982), oral and literate modes of experience and communication coexist in tension, a tension medieval scribes experienced firsthand but could neither understand nor articulate. Ong (1967) concurs that the Middle Ages were "impossibly oral despite [its] possession of and fixation on writing" (p. 268),[20] adding that the shift from oral to literate consciousness was a movement in which the ear was seduced into collaboration with the eye. Throughout the Middle Ages, the scribe emphasized the eye: writing was to be visually pleasing, hence the artistic scripts we call *calligraphy* (Greek for "beautiful writing"); though Charlemagne and Alcuin attempted to standardize script, the monks added flourishes and hooks, eventually transforming

minuscule into Gothic script. Ong (1967) argues that the scribe "heightened the visualist, quantified quotients of awareness, but he did so with
minimal reflectiveness" (p. 221). Perceiving writing as a visual craft,
the medieval scribes did not grasp the opportunity that having words
"out there" on the page presented for purposeful and careful rearranging—which is to say, learning. Purposeful and careful rearranging was
not allowed.

Chaytor, too, argues that the shift from script to print involved the
"gradual substitution of visual for auditory methods of communicating
and receiving ideas" (1950, p. 4); the copyist's "instinctive question,
when deciphering a text, was not whether he had seen, but whether he
had heard this or that word before; he brought not a visual but an
auditory memory to his task" (p. 14). Chaytor explains that during
medieval reading

> The acoustic image may be translated into the visual image of a book, and
> if the hearer is illiterate [in modern parlance], this is probably the end of
> the process. If the hearer can read, he will substitute for the visual image
> of a book the printed word "book," and in either case there may be a
> half-felt tendency to articulate the word. . . . If the thinker is illiterate, the
> images that arise in his mind will be auditory; if he is literate, they will
> be visual; in either case, immediate vocal expression can be given to them,
> if necessary. (pp. 5, 9)

The medieval copyist was an "oral performer" (Ong, 1982, p. 63).
Sight and sound were disconnected in medieval consciousness, which
meant that the scribe had to work hard to connect the visual with the
auditory. Regardless of the rule of silence, medieval monks read aloud
because words were sounds, that is, they concentrated on first recognizing the letters visually, then sounding them out in order to recognize
if they had heard the words before. The task was further complicated
because spelling and scripts were not yet standardized. This separation
of sight and sound and the lack of standardization probably account for
some of the errors the scribes made. "If a scribe was copying a text
composed in a dialect not native to himself, he was likely to substitute
his own auditory memory of the text for his visual impression of it, and
to write *er* instead of *ar*, *el* for *a* and the like" (Chaytor, 1950, p. 19).

This practice made reading very slow and tedious: "Such a man would have read but little and that little very slowly" (Chaytor, 1950, p. 139). Archbishop Lanfranc explains in the constitution for Christ Church Canterbury that each monk was issued one book a year to read, indicating that "a monk who read with attention and understanding every word of St. Augustine's *City of God* . . . had achieved a great deal in a year" (Clanchy, 1979, p. 130).

Medieval consciousness both enacted and resisted the transition from oral to literate consciousness. According to Clanchy (1979), "Literate modes could not be imposed by royal decree" (p. 12), despite efforts such as the *Domesday Book*, which attempted to govern conquered people by the threat of written records, and Edward I's *quo warranto* proceedings, which attempted to reduce government and property holding to writing. As late as the twelfth century, oral testimony was considered the legally valid "record," not written documents; by the thirteenth century, written records had gained status, but they still required oral ceremonies and/or a personal seal, the symbol of oral confirmation, to be considered legally binding.[21] The written record was considered a "mummified semblance" of living eloquence and trust in an oral tradition (Clanchy, 1979, p. 233). Thirteenth century politics reveal that "where literate modes were relatively novel, written records were of limited value to government" (p. 146). "Literate habits and assumptions, comprising a literate mentality, had to take root in diverse social groups and areas of activity before literacy could grow or spread beyond the small class of writers" (p. 149). Problems and prejudices had to be overcome to make literate modes acceptable to rulers and knights "upon whose lead further change depended" (p. 149).

> Because literacy had been identified with Latin for a thousand years, it had first to be learned by the laity in this clerical and alien form. Those old rivals, the *clerici-litterati* and the *laici-illiterati* had to come to terms and absorb each other's thought processes before literacy could become a common vernacular habit. The extension of literacy was therefore a complex social problem in the Middle Ages and not a simple matter of providing more educational facilities. Bridges had to be built across the divide of speech and script. (p. 201)

The growth of social literacy demanded the restructuring of consciousness, the substitution of visual/spatial representations for the oral/aural phenomenon of language. The development of medieval punctuation provides evidence of the interiorization of visual/spacial categories, that is, for the development of literacy as we know it. Though the scribes were told not to change anything, they did. Besides adding book curses to the manuscripts they copied, the scribes changed the physical appearance of the text by adding punctuation marks and explicit spaces between words and paragraphs. Before Charlemagne, there were no spaces between words, no periods, commas, semicolons, or explicit paragraphing; these developed after copying was institutionalized by *De Litteris Colendis*. According to James J. Murphy (1978), the scribes devised important characteristics of medieval punctuation: they "punctuated . . . where they thought that confusion was likely to arise in the minds of the readers for whom the text was prepared" (p. 137), but in the process meaning often perished. Boorstin (1985) argues that scribes began to put spaces between words to help "prevent ambiguities in meaning and so preserve the pure text. . . . Scribes in Ireland, England, and Germany felt more secure when they saw the words separated" (p. 497). These blank spaces restructured consciousness: the concept of discreet, visual objects called *words* was born—a clear movement away from the oral world with its invisible stream of sound. The creation of punctuation and blank spaces indicates the visual placement of silence or pauses in reading (vocalizing) a text. Since punctuating and spacing for semantic purposes, even if erroneous, presupposes some "reading" of the text, punctuation and spacing were obviously the contributions of scribes who could read.

Manuscript technology and medieval monasticism constrained the scribes' experience and conception of writing. Writing was not a matter of self-expression or intellection, but a manual labor that produced a pleasing visual product. The monk was obliged to perform this labor by religious duty. Writing was a way to have sin forgiven, to partake manually in mystery and missionary effort. Evidence suggests that the scribes had no respect for learning, regardless of monastic rule or the mandate that they teach.[22]

Writing was difficult and time consuming because of the manuscript technology. Reading was difficult because it required swift recognition of the sounds and a fluent vocabulary—neither of which were common because of the low level of education and the variety of languages and scripts that circulated in manuscript form.[23] Because of the difficulty of reading and writing, the two processes were not connected in the Middle Ages (Chaytor, 1950; Clanchy, 1979). As late as 1533, Sir Thomas More wrote in his *Apologye* that reading and writing were "Not acquired concurrently in the local schools, where writing was regarded as a superior skill" (quoted in Chaytor, 1950, p. 111).[24]

THE ILLITERATE MODE
OF WRITTEN COMMUNICATION

In modern society, people are considered literate if they can read and write with minimal skill. In medieval society, however, the *litterati* were erudite scholars, people who knew Latin—which, given the educational method of recitation, was possible without the ability to read and write.[25] Reading and writing were not prerequisites for medieval literacy (Clanchy, 1979). The tacit cognitive connections of the medieval mind powerfully diverge from those of the modern mind: the modern mind cannot easily conceive of literacy in terms other than the ability to read and write; the medieval mind did not connect literacy with reading and writing, but with esoteric scholarship. Modern literacy is measured by minimum and utilitarian standards; medieval literacy was measured by maximum and seemingly impractical standards, since Latin served no purpose in daily life. The modern mind has difficulty conceiving of literacy without practical value because illiteracy has such powerful social and economic implications today. Regardless of the difficulty, this bizarre position is where we must begin: medieval literacy was not a social medium in the marketplace.

Redefining literacy from an esoteric exercise to a practical affair took centuries. Clanchy (1979) argues that the "shift from sacred script to practical literacy" (p. 183) began in the twelfth and thirteenth centuries, but that even at the end of the twelfth century minimal reading and writing skills still did not constitute literacy. According to Chaytor (1950), by the twelfth century at least one person in a household could read and write, yet "He was often regarded with some amazement and an explanation of the phenomenon was thought to be necessary" (p. 111). By the fifteenth century, a *litteratus* was reduced from a person of erudition to a person with a minimal ability to read Latin. "What had changed, however, was not necessarily the proportion of persons in the population who had mastered reading and writing, but the meanings of words" (Clanchy, 1979, p. 185).

In medieval terms, then, literate men often dictated books, letters, and Church and government documents to scribes because they could not write themselves. For example, evidence suggests that Charlemagne did not know how to read or write, yet he "wrote"—in modern parlance—a book with Alcuin. Meanwhile the scribes, who obviously could write because they copied or took dictation, were considered illiterate if they did not know Latin. The separation of writing ability from literacy is evident in Walter Map's description (Clanchy, 1979) of a boy "educated among us and by us [and yet] he was not *litteratus*, which I regret, although he knew how to transcribe any series of letters whatever" (p. 181). Obviously good handwriting was no substitute for good scholarship; handwriting was a craft, not an intellectual exercise.

Medieval manuscript technology made writing a craft whereby difficult manual labor produced a pleasing visual product. Writing was a special and valued skill that ideally, theoretically, presupposed the ability to read, but the variety of languages and scripts that flourished after the fall of Rome,[26] in combination with the low level of education,[27] make it highly unlikely that all medieval scribes could fluently read and understand every manuscript they copied. According to Clanchy (1979), "The variety of languages in which spoken and written thoughts were formulated . . . made any capacity to read or write an intellectual achievement. This variety also obstructed the spread of literacy, in the modern sense of a majority of people acquiring a minimal ability to read or write the language they spoke" (p. 184).

The obvious conclusion is that the Middle Ages were populated by copyists who often could not read what they copied: the text could be in a foreign language or script that the scribe could not understand. Even if the language and script were familiar, the handwriting could be illegible.[28] Neither script nor spelling were standardized. Furthermore, the abbreviations and ligatures that proliferated sometimes made the manuscripts unintelligible. The early Middle Ages was a period in which grapholects were actually dialects reflecting the idiosyncracies of particular locations and scribes.[29] Consequently, medieval scribes often copied only marks on a page, marks they misunderstood and mismanaged.[30]

Instead of assuming that the scribes worked on their own volition to learn, we now know that they worked because of a religious obligation reinforced and compounded by government sanction. They could not question, memorize, and contemplate everything they copied because they could not always read what they copied. Moreover, what they did read or have read to them was selected and restricted by their abbots, who censored so-called problematic texts, thereby positioning the monks in a unilateral world. Medieval education was limited, in a sense "closed," because all that could be known was already known: education was a matter of committing the recorded fund of knowledge to memory or to additional manuscripts for future recall. The monks did not observe and discover, but remembered and participated in an oral tradition bound by religious law. Questioning and contemplating were beyond the intellectual capacity or personal desire of many scribes; furthermore, such activities were certainly not encouraged, and the notoriety and innovation they represented ran counter to the humility and obedience of monastic rule.

Instead of assuming that the scribes were religiously devoted to preserving and translating written discourse, we now know that they were religiously devoted to salvation and to avoiding punishment. Their identities are more accurately defined by their roles in the medieval Church and "factory" than by their roles as promoters of literacy per se. The goal of personal salvation led them into monastic life and, subsequently, into the manual/spiritual labor of copying. Warriors engaged in battle with the devil, they multiplied God's words that evil might be banished. Literacy, the social literacy we know today, was the furthest thing from their minds.

Instead of assuming that the scribes valued writing because it expanded both their knowledge and their intellect, we now know that they valued writing as a craft and a manual/spiritual exercise, perhaps a penance, but not as an instrument of knowledge or self-analysis. If they read, what they read only reiterated what they heard; if they composed, they primarily wrote what they heard. Writing was a visual product and a commodity to be sold, not an intellectual process. The new technology had not yet restructured consciousness to the extent that the scribes were capable of sustained inquiry or interior processing of texts—probably because they were not interested in or assigned to such activity.

In our modern conception, if the scribes could not read what they copied, they were illiterate and copied only marks—which may account for some of the (supposedly) bad handwriting. Even if they could read the language of the texts they were assigned to copy, there is no guarantee that they could read the scripts in which they were written. Again, if they could not read the texts, we would call them illiterate—like the immigrants who arrive in America only to be forced into manual labor, regardless of their intelligence. Furthermore, even if the script was familiar to the scribe, the handwriting could be illegible. Here we would not call the scribe illiterate, but we would not call his copying a lofty, learning, literate exchange either. In a manuscript culture, if the exemplar text was illegible or unintelligible, the copy could only be worse. If the scribe was illiterate, we can only speculate about his consciousness when copying marks verbatim—a comparable experience might be if we were to copy Egyptian hieroglyphics or Sanskrit.

We now know that the scribes were manual laborers; craftsmen-turned-factory workers in a politically and religiously sanctioned guild, not intellectuals. The medieval monks and scribes lived a life of contradiction and contrast—a vow of poverty turned to wealth, a quest for privacy and individuality turned to community and conformity, an oral tradition compelling and binding them to turn the culture to a written tradition. The reconciliation of interior poverty and exterior wealth was a challenge the medieval monks were ill-equipped to meet. Fortunately for them, they saw nothing to reconcile. Their fragmented consciousness and culture did not encourage abstract thinking, and real-life situations made it such that abstract reasoning would have been detrimental to their survival: to question or create new texts was to be accused of heresy, not to make any money, not to do their duty within the community, and not to save their souls. Drogin's (1983) terminology of "the medieval secretarial pool" captures the bureaucracy of scriptorial literacy; add to that the assembly-line procedure of manuscript production in the late Middle Ages, and the result is a rudimentary factory staffed by literate and illiterate scribes whose consciousness was slowly being transformed by manuscript technology.

The scribes' cognitive categories were oral and, for the most part, illiterate in comparison to our literate cognitive categories. Further, the scribes did not perceive writing as an intellectual feat of composition, but rather as a debilitating craft, a kind of manual labor, that resulted in a visually pleasing product. The scribes engaged in their craft as a spiritual and penitential exercise under monastic rule, in collaboration with government and Church support; reading and writing were duties imposed from outside, not learning experiences motivated from inside. Texts were copied, not necessarily because the scribes valued the meaning they stirred, but because the medieval bureaucracy compelled them to write. Nevertheless, they contributed to the shift from an oral to a literate culture.

CONCLUSIONS AND IMPLICATIONS

According to Ong (1982), there is a marked contrast "between deeply interiorized literacy and the more or less residually oral states of consciousness" (p. 29). Havelock (1982) argues that there is a distinction between "modern paper [socialized] literacy and the literacy of our ancestors" (p. 335); "A literate mastery of any alphabet requires that visual shape and acoustic value or set of values be matched with lightning speed and certitude" (p. 198); and "the effective use of the alphabet depend[s] upon the requirement that the oral vocabulary of the reader first be fluent and educated" (p. 318). Given the limited education of the scribes, the psychological effects of their working conditions, and the variety of languages, scripts, and handwriting that they copied, there is no reason to believe that they rapidly recognized (read) everything that they encountered, or that their vocabulary was commensurate to the task.

If "true literacy is a social condition" (Havelock, 1982, p. 203), that social condition was not present to the medieval scribes: restrained by oral cognitive categories and bullied by bureaucrats, the concept of the private reader and student was paradoxically beyond their ken. Working out of a mental framework dedicated to producing pleasing visual products—focusing on actions, situations and attributes that forever remained disconnected—the medieval scribes were not literate in the sense that we mean today. Ironically, regardless of the scribes' magical understanding of texts and writing, their oral roots made them devalue the capacity of a text to be a vehicle for thought and expression. Language was a vehicle of preservation and transmission, not a heuristic for exploration and discovery. Their focus on the visual written product, rather than the intellectual composing process, actually deterred interior processing of texts, retarding the development of social literacy: "Calligraphic virtuosity of any kind fosters craft literacy and is fostered by it, but is the enemy of social literacy" (Havelock, 1982, p. 328).

"Monks would not have understood the modern demand for mass literacy. There was no point in teaching writing to people who would never have anything worth committing to the permanence of script. What was written down was carefully selected" (Clanchy, 1979, p. 118). "So far from advocating the mass production of literates or documents, the monastic writer aimed to use records to convey to posterity a deliberately created and rigorously selected version of events" by distinguishing between memorable events (*memorabilia*) and those worth remembering (*memoranda*) (Gervase I, 89 [in Clanchy, 1979, p. 118]).

To the modern mind, reading and writing are directly—supposedly "naturally"—linked. The current trend is to even equate these two, because reading involves interpreting, which is a kind of composing, which is to say writing. In contrast, to the medieval mind, reading and writing were not intimately linked. For the modern person, writing is a portable skill; we can do it any time, anywhere, and select among a wide variety of implements and materials. For the medieval scribe, writing was a seasonal activity often constrained to certain structures or rooms. For the modern person, writing is composing; a creative intellectual enterprise, original and interior. For the medieval scribe, writing was a craft; a redundant, exterior activity. Writing as manual labor, as a seasonal activity like football, is an entirely different experience from the modern experience of writing, which is ironically closer to the medieval notion of literacy as scholarship.

The implications of these findings should make us rethink some of our scholarly claims. For example, we can no longer claim with absolute certainty that the scribes were "careless" copiers whose "concentration failed" (Reynolds & Wilson, 1974, p. 150); if they could not read what they wrote, the most careful and concentrated scrutiny could not guarantee an accurate, readable copy. Surely some scribes were too motivated to be careless, since accurate copying could secure their place in heaven and their freedom from punishment on earth. We can no longer casually claim that the book curse "was so familiar to scribes that it probably was inserted without thought, as seems to be the case where it occurs near the end, as though it were remembered almost at the last moment" (Drogin, 1983, p. 24). Given that scribes also included complaints, prayers, jokes, amusements, puns, even salad and face cream recipes at the end of their texts (Drogin, 1983), we must wonder if they knew what they were doing or just copying pretty texts that they could not read. There is a very real possibility that literate monks composed the book curses, which were later copied from manuscript to manuscript by illiterate monks who either did not know what they said and thought they were part of the main text, or who had been told what they said and copied them because they appreciated the sentiment.

These findings should also make us rethink the serious distinction between writing and composing: composition is a more complex and intellectual process than the mere act of handwriting. Composition seems particularly difficult for a personality that conceives of writing as a (visual or oral) product rather than an instrumental process—an observation that coincides with twentieth-century classroom experience.[31] Viewing writing as a product seems to inhibit interior processing of texts.

Finally, we must look at the implications of the technology itself. Manuscript technology restructured consciousness and epistemology. After centuries of exposure to it, human consciousness had interiorized the alphabet; learned to read silently; developed the notions of authorship and intellectual property; and become familiar enough with writing to accept it as a legally binding record, and familiar enough with books to organize them in libraries and archives for reference. Reasoning analogously, computer technology is no doubt being interiorized; reading online is creating problems; our notions of intellectual property and copyright laws are being challenged by similar computer programs being implemented in different programming languages; and we are already familiar enough with electronic texts and record-keeping to rely heavily on the technology. What is in store for us has yet to be seen; however, we have a moral responsibility as educators to understand and acknowledge the implications of the technology we use. When we introduce our students to computers, we are inviting the restructuring of their consciousness in ways we cannot yet delineate clearly. Perhaps the modern-day "hackers" parallel the craft-literate scribes of the early Middle Ages: learning as they go, shaping and being shaped by the technology that is their obsession. If so, the consciousness and problem-solving strategies of these "hackers" should be a rich resource for understanding the relationship between computer technology and the diffusion of culture and knowledge.

In summary, the second period of craft literacy was populated by what we would consider illiterate or semiliterate scribes who connected writing with art and religion. The period of scriptorial literacy was populated by artistic serfs who manufactured textual notation from raw materials; like a factory assembly-line, their work was subject to many kinds of corporate and government regulations. The medieval scribes were valuable, diligent, oppressed, and often mediocre talents unaware of their contribution to the transition from an oral to a literate culture. They were writers—what a child would call "copycats"—not composers; more slaves than scholars. Still, their efforts created a manuscript culture that lasted a thousand years. Medieval literacy was an institution to preserve what was known, an institution erected on the bent backs of silent, anxious men. More often than not the scribes did not understand or appreciate the intellectual genius they preserved and transmitted, and they did not comprehend or respect the psychological and epistemological ramifications of the technology with which they worked.

According to Ong (1967), "Specializing in auditory syntheses and specializing in visual syntheses foster different personality structures and different characteristic anxieties" (pp. 130-131). The scribe lived in an oral, invisible, spiritual world but labored in a written, visual, physical one. The experience created high anxiety and a personality structure perhaps lost with the onslaught of print or paper literacy. Focusing on the visual enabled the scribes to exponentially multiply the number of available texts, and to design and promulgate an extremely efficient script, equipped with punctuation marks and spaces between words. The medieval scribe's historical situation, living an oral tradition while unconsciously establishing a written tradition, enabled his centuries of work to slowly reorient human cognition from oral/aural to visual/spatial categories—categories so necessary to learning (in our modern sense of the term).

Ironically, perhaps it is because the medieval scribes were not constantly slowed down by reading, questioning, and contemplating that they were able to accomplish so much. Had they questioned and argued with their abbots, perhaps even more restrictions and superstitions about texts would have been the result. Yet copying would go faster, presumably, if you could read what you copied! Scriptorial literacy remains a paradox: the saviors of literacy were coerced and often unable to read what they wrote; they reluctantly left their oral world to preserve a literacy they dimly understood and little appreciated. They paved the way for social literacy, regardless of their own lack of interest in it. Their contribution had little to do with what they thought they were doing, and nothing to do with their self-concept.

NOTES

1. *Technology* in this paper is used in Marshall McLuhan's (1967) sense of a human construction that artificially "extends" one sense while "amputating" another. It will be

shown that medieval manuscript technology extended the visual/spatial sense while amputating the oral/aural sense.

2. In this paper, the word *scribe* is used in M. T. Clanchy's sense (1979) of an author who writes a book that is being copied, specifically the monks who copied religious and pagan texts; "Before the Norman Conquest, and for a century after it, the majority of writers (in every sense of that word) were monks" (p. 117). According to L. D. Reynolds and N. G. Wilson (1974), Arethus (860-935), a churchman with an interest in learning, commissioned books from professional scribes "in the main monks of monasteries which accepted regular orders on a commercial basis" (p. 56).

3. Herbert B. Workman cites a veritable *potpourri* of the medieval monks' contributions, including

> The schools they founded, the libraries they gathered together, the writers on every branch of knowledge and culture then known to the world that they furnished, the manuscripts they copied, thus preserving to the world priceless treasures that would otherwise have been assuredly lost, [and] the chronicles of contemporary history they compiled. (1913, pp. 160-161)

4. "The knife or razor for scraping [the parchment], the pumice for cleaning and smoothing it, and the boar or goat's tooth for polishing the surface to stop the ink running. Then there are the tools for ruling the lines—the stylus, the pencil, and straight ruler, the plumb line, and the awl for pricking holes to mark the beginnings of the lines. Finally there is the writing equipment itself—the quill pens and penknife, the inkhorn, and the various coloured inks" (Clanchy, 1979, p. 89).

5. Though the monks copied and preserved, they also obliterated and destroyed. The blatant and bizarre contradiction here, in terms of our misreading of the scribes' appreciation for their work, is that often they valued the parchment more than the text that was on it, despite the fact that it took so long to produce a manuscript.

> Many texts which had escaped destruction in the crumbling empire of the West perished within the walls of the monastery; some of them may have been too tattered when they arrived to be of practical use, and there was no respect for rags, however venerable. Texts perished, not because pagan authors were under attack, but because no one was interested in reading them, and the parchment was too precious to carry obsolete text. (Reynolds & Wilson, 1974, p. 73)

6. The Caroline minuscule was the precursor of our lower case letters; we continue to teach cursive writing in our schools. In short, the appearance of our alphabet today is the product of manuscript technology.

7. Morrall (1967) calls the minuscule an "intellectual technology" (p. 76).

8. According to Clanchy (1979),

> Cursive script is thus a product of the shift from memory to written record: the demand was no longer primarily for elaborately copied monastic books, but for documents written economically yet legibly. Saving the scribe's time was a paramount consideration, because labour costs were the principal element in the price of a manuscript. Fine manuscripts in book hand continued to be produced, however, until they succumbed in the Sixteenth Century to the joint attack of printing and the destruction of monasticism. (p. 101)

9. See Alexander Neckham, *De Nominibus Utensalium*; cited in Clanchy (1979), p. 90.

10. Evidence suggests that monks did not consider themselves authors until as late as the twelfth century, when for example, Eadwine, monk of Christ Church Canterbury, composed the inscription: "Prince of writers; whose praise and fame will not die" (*scriptorum princeps ego; nec obitura deinceps laus, nec fama*, cited in Clanchy, 1979, p. 89; full text in C. R. Dodwell, *The Canterbury School of Illumination*, 1954, p. 36).

11. According to Boorstin (1985),

> The book was not expected to be, nor dared it be, a vehicle for new ideas carrying messages from contemporaries to contemporaries. Instead it was a device to preserve and amplify the treasured revolving fund of literary works—the sacred Scriptures and their commentators, ancient classics of Greece and Rome, and a few established texts in Hebrew and Arabic. (p. 493)

12. According to Drogin (1983), "In 1331 King Edward III paid the equivalent of 80 oxen for an illuminated volume"; in 1057 Diemude of Wessorbrunn (a nun) traded a Bible she penned for a farm; in the eleventh or twelfth century a book was traded for a vineyard; in the ninth century, a book was traded for enough land for eight families (pp. 31-32). But evidently the scribe was more expensive than the parchment, as printing was developed in part as a money-saving device:

> It was not dissatisfaction with the work of the best scribes that had stimulated the quest for other ways to reproduce books. The original effort was to find how to multiply manuscripts in larger quantity and at lower costs, but as good as the scribes' and illuminators' best work. The early printers called their craft the art of artificial writing—*ars artificialiter scribendi*. (Boorstin, 1985, p. 515)

Ironically, the medieval monk received little pay for his work; the monastic community gained the wealth. According to Drogin (1983), the scribe earned in three to seven days what a foot soldier in King Edward's army earned in one (p. 30).

13. Chaytor (1950) quotes from the *Rites of Durham*:

> In the north syde of the Cloister from the corner over against the Church Dour to the corner over againste the Dorter dour was all fynely glased from the hight to the sole within a little of the grownd into the Cloyster garth, and in every wyndowe iii pewes or Carrells where very one of the old monkes had has Carrell severall by himselfe, that when they had dyned they dyd resorte to that place of Cloister, and there studyed upon there bookes, every one in his Carrell all the after none unto evensong tyme; this was there Exercise every daie; all there pewes or Carrells was all fynely wainscotted, and verie close all but the fore part which had carved wourke that gave light in at ther carrell doures of wainscott; and in every Carrell was a deske to lye there bookes on; and the Carrells was not greater then from one stanchell of the wyndowe to another. (*Rites of Durham*, Surtees Society, Vol. CVII, 1902, p. 83; quoted in Chaytor, 1950, p. 19)

14. For example, since the books were stacked horizontally on boxes, trunks, or wooden cabinets, small legs or *noduli* were placed on the back covers to prevent their rubbing against other surfaces. A clasp or *signaculum* was attached to keep the text firmly closed so the pages would not buckle. A book binding or *chemise* that was large enough to fold and knot was devised so that the knot could be slipped under the monk's belt and prevent him from dropping the manuscript.

15. M. Deanesly argues that a total of 338 books were passed on in 7568 wills (*M.L.R.*, XV [October, 1920], p. 349; in Chaytor, 1950, p. 109).

16. Writing was first thought of as a subsidiary aid to traditional memorizing procedures, not as a replacement of them (Clanchy, 1979, p. 257).

17. See, for example, Augustine, *Confessions*, Bk. VI, Chap. 3, and Chaucer, *The Hous of Fame*, II, p. 148.

18. See also Grimmelshausen, *Simplicissimus*, Bk. 1, Chap. 10; Eduard Norden, *Die antike Kunstprosa*, Leipzig, Dieterich, 1927; Coultom, *Five Centuries of Religion*; and *The Rule of Saint Benedict*, Chap. XLVIII.

19. According to Chaytor (1950), the modern habit of silent reading makes soundproof reading rooms in libraries unnecessary (p. 19).

20. Evidence of the orality of the medieval mind includes the scribes' proclivity for violence and the assigning of texts to be copied. Ong (1982) explains: "oral peoples commonly externalize schizoid behavior where literates interiorize it" (p. 69); "Some societies of limited literacy have regarded writing as dangerous to the unwary reader, demanding a guru-like figure to mediate between reader and text" (p. 93).

21. "It is probable that the expression of a grant in writing was often less important to the parties than the performance of ceremonial acts of which the charter itself makes no record" (from F.M. Stenton, *Transcripts of Chapters Relating to Gilbertine Houses*, Lincolnshire Record S. XVIII, 1922, xxx; quoted in Clanchy, 1979, p. 232). For example, an 1127 writ of Henry I ordered a jury of 12 men from Dover and 12 from Sandwich to settle a dispute between St. Augustine's Abbey at Canterbury and Christ Church about custom dues at the port of Sandwich; each swore on the Gospel that the tolls belonged to Christ Church: "I have received from my ancestors, and I have seen and heard from my youth up until now, so help me God and these Holy Gospels" (from F. Kern, *Kingship and Law in the Middle Ages*, [S. B. Chrimes, trans.], 1939, p. 179; cited in Clanchy, 1979, p. 233).

22. For example, referring to the monastery at St. Gall, Switzerland, 1416, Cincio Romano wrote: "there were in the monastery an abbot and monks divorced from any knowledge of letters" (*Erant in monastrio ilio Abbas, Monachique ab omni litterarum cognitione alieni*); from Walser, *Leben*, 52, quoted in Murphy (1978), p. 257. The fact that Poggio Bracciolini discovered a complete copy of Quintilian's *Institutio Oratoria* in a dungeon, not a library, indicates the monks' lack of respect for the text. "The ability to write well comprised the technical skill of an artist and was not an integral part of the science of letters" (Clanchy, 1979, p. 181).

23. The language and script of the text were determined by its function (Clanchy, 1979). For example, "English, French, and Latin performed distinct social and intellectual functions in Twelfth and Thirteenth Century England" (p. 154)

24. Perhaps the phenomenon of public readings, which downplayed the importance of learning to read, had something to do with writing being considered the superior skill.

25. According to Clanchy (1979), to be *litteratus* meant "to know Latin and not specifically to have the ability to read and write" (p. 149).

26. "Dialectical differences delayed linguistic uniformity until the Fourteenth Century, when grammars, vocabularies, and phrase-books began to appear. . . . But until the written becomes the printed word and education enables a wide public to read for themselves, instead of depending upon recitation, linguistic stability is hardly possible. For print alone can secure the indispensable conditions of standardization, the substitution

of visual for acoustic word-memory" (Chaytor, 1950, pp. 33, 34). As late as the fifteenth century, English understood in one part of England was not understood in another (Chaytor, 1950, p. 31).

27. "But there was little common training in writing or anything else for either monks or secular clergy before about 1200. Monasteries with great scriptoria, like Christ Church Canterbury, were exceptional" (Clanchy, 1979, p. 102).

28. When Bishop Gerardo Landriani found a manuscript containing five of Cicero's treatises in the cathedral of Lodi, he could not read the handwriting and sent them to Barzizza in Milan (Murphy, 1974, p. 360).

29. According to Boorstin (1985), "the decline of Roman authority dissolved the standards in calligraphy as in everything else. The idiosyncracies of isolated [scribes] were dividing the culture of Latin Europe" (p. 496).

30. According to Clanchy (1979), "Some scribes, like Eadwine, were supreme artists in calligraphy and presumably considered themselves superior to composers or clerks who wrote from dictation, whereas others were copyists who scarcely understood the exemplar in front of them" (p. 97). For example, a charter for Poulton abbey (c. 1146) was "written on an irregularly shaped piece of parchment in a shaky hand which cannot keep the lines straight" (p. 101). "There were thousands of authentic charters without dates or places of issue, some of them written by scribes who seem never to have wielded a pen before" (p. 234).

31. See, for example, Rosalind Horowitz, "Orality and Literacy in Bilingual-Bicultural Contexts," *Journal for the National Association for Bilingual Education*, 8 (Spring, 1984), pp. 11-26; Marcia Farr and Mary Ann Janda, "Basic Writing Students: Investigating Oral and Written Language," *Research in the Teaching of English*, 19 (February, 1985), pp. 62-83; Thomas Kochman, "Orality and Literacy as Factors of 'Black' and 'White' Communicative Behavior," *Linguistics*, *136* (September 15, 1974), pp. 91-115; Thomas J. Farrell, "Literacy, the Basics, and All That Jazz," *College English*, *38* (January, 1977), pp. 443-459; Thomas J. Farrell (1974), "Open Admissions, Orality, and Literacy," *Journal of Youth and Adolescence*, *3* (3) pp. 247-260; Thomas J. Farrell, "Scribes and True Authors," *ADE Bulletin*, *61* (May, 1979), pp. 9-16.

REFERENCES

Bishop, T. A. M. (1961). *Scriptores regis*. Oxford: Clarendon Press.

Boorstin, D. J. (1985). *The discoverers: A history of man's search to know his world and himself*. New York: Random House/Vintage Books.

Brandt, W. J. (1966). *The shape of medieval history*. New Haven, CT: Yale University Press.

Chaytor, H. J. (1950). *From script to print: An introduction to medieval vernacular literature*. Cambridge, UK: W. Heffer.

Clanchy, M. T. (1979). *From memory to written record: England, 1066-1307*. Cambridge, MA: Harvard University Press.

Crosby, R. (1936). Oral delivery in the Middle Ages. *Speculum*, *11*, 88-110.

Curtius, E. R. (1953). *European literature and the Latin Middle Ages*. New York: Bollingen Foundation.

Daly, L. S. (1967). *Contributions to a history of alphabetization in antiquity and the Middle Ages*. Collection Latomus, Vol. XC. Bruxelles: Latomus, Revue d'etudes latines.

Drogin, M. (1983). *Anathema!* New Jersey: Allanheld & Schram.

Havelock, E. A. (1982). *The literate revolution in Greece and its cultural consequences*. Princeton, NJ: Princeton University Press.

McLuhan, M., & Fiore, Q. (1967). *The medium is the message*. New York: Bantam.

Morrall, J. B. (1967). *The medieval imprint*. New York: Basic Books.

Murphy, J. J. (1971). *Three medieval rhetorical arts*. Berkeley: University of California Press.

Murphy, J. J. (1974). *Rhetoric in the Middle Ages*. Berkeley: University of California Press.

Murphy, J. J., (Ed.). (1978). *Medieval eloquence*. Berkeley: University of California Press.

Ong, W. J. (1967). *The presence of the word*. New Haven: Yale University Press.

Ong, W. J. (1982). *Orality and literacy*. London: Methuen.

Reynolds, L. D., & Wilson, N. G. (Eds.). (1974). *Scribes and scholars* (2nd ed.): Oxford: Clarendon Press.

Workman, H. B. (1913). *The evolution of the monastic ideal from the earliest times down to the coming of the friars*. Boston: Beacon.

7

Rhetoric, Truth, and Literacy in the Renaissance of the Twelfth Century

JOHN O. WARD

PROLEGOMENA

Every society establishes both a general consensus of opinion in regard to what is "true knowledge" and an institutional structure designed to preserve, extend, teach, or otherwise control that knowledge. Both knowledge so established and the institutions associated with its preservation and transmission may be described as powerful in that they are normally dominant, protected against intrusion, disturbance, deviation, fragmentation, or collapse by a variety of internal and external mechanisms varying in their strength and efficacy. When the homogeneity of the literate groups and classes that produce and consume society's knowledge and sustain its institutions is disrupted—as seems to have occurred in Western European history during the eleventh and twelfth centuries—we may speak of the collapse or disruption of the political economy of truth in that society. Sensitive elements within a collapsing economy of truth will be the arts of dialectic and rhetoric which emerge variously as the discoverers, arbiters, and persuaders of

AUTHOR'S NOTE: I owe thanks to John Tinkler for many stimulating discussions on the subject of the present chapter, and, above all, to David McRuvie, without whose thorough appraisal and revision (of the original, much lengthier, version), the paper would have been far less comprehensible than it now may be.

new truths. Both dialectic and rhetoric, of course, play different roles, and the role of the former in the eleventh and twelfth centuries is better understood nowadays than is the role of the latter, with which this chapter is concerned.

There are two formal tendencies or directions that seem evident from time to time in Western culture: the scholastic/scientific/logical and the humanistic/impressionistic/rhetorical. These ideal types of discourse, established and accepted by many scholars (for example M. Charles [1985], or Samuel Ijsseling [1976]), imply an ideal type of relation to society that this chapter will explore. With the former ideal type of discourse we may, for example, associate a mentality appropriate to institutions and stable cultural traditions in which a group or class have long been in authorized, validated, licensed possession of knowledge in the form of established curricular disciplines, to which access is carefully monitored and controlled. Such a mentality may well—to use some phrases of Brian Stock's—assume "a radical separation between sense and reference", "between expression and indication", between "surface and deep structure," between language and truth or reality (p. 28). With the latter ideal type of discourse we may associate those groups or individuals with less stake or investment in the institutions and structures of knowledge and curricular disciplines, who may seek a place therein and be denied it or be accepted, but as "different" or less well connected or inferior, or else who may reject the dominance of institutions and their representatives. Such persons or groups will cast around for and make banners out of cultural or intellectual resources that serve to distinguish or mark themselves off from the established institutions and structures or literary/cultural habits, genres, and/or fashions. Thus they may stress the classical past, or poetic language, or the satiric mode of Jerome, or parody, or the humanities, or vernacular composition against dialectic, logical positivism, scientific or empirical discourse, plain prose or similar (Thomson, 1980; Ward, 1988; Wiesen, 1964). Oscillations between one and the other tendency/direction/ideal type of discourse will be essentially short-term, a matter of a generation or a decade or so, and will only be noticeable to the historian when a particularly extended process of change and adjustment serves to push larger than normal numbers of literate persons into the second category

with the result that a sufficient volume of literary traces is left behind
for later historians to detect what they—for the wrong reasons—dub a
"Renaissance." Such a development, it is argued here, took place in
Western Europe in the eleventh and twelfth centuries. These years are
"coming to be seen as one of the most fecund and exciting periods in
the history of western thought" (Dronke, 1974); a period that for almost
a century has enjoyed the status of a "Renaissance" in view of its
alleged anticipation of certain key features of modern cultural patterns,
features which first became evident during the later Italian Renaissance
(see, for example, Benson & Constable, 1982; Burckhardt, 1860;
Chastel, 1982; Haskins, 1927/1958; Helton, 1961; Morris, 1972; Ralph,
1974; Weimar, 1981).

ARGUMENT

The growing relevance or status of texts in the eleventh and twelfth
centuries, and the expanding demand for people equipped to use and
create them (emanating from increasingly archival governments and
from the newly polemicized chanceries/*scriptoria* of church and state,
monasteries and cathedrals, courts, and *cenacoli*) divided and widened
tensions in society, resulting in what can be termed, following Foucault,
the collapse (and then the reconstruction) of the political economy of
truth. The entire process seems to have been at its most intense between the time of the Eucharistic and Investiture Controversies of the
eleventh century and the later twelfth century, although this may well
be a false impression created by the selective sensitivity of historians,
or the nature of surviving documents. Without wishing, however, to
gloss over the individual features of the European cultural scene prior
to c. A.D. 1000, or to ignore oscillations in the political significance
of literacy associated with the experience of the bishops and major
literati in later Visigothic Spain (Ward, 1972b) or the Carolingian
"Renaissance" (Ullmann, 1969), it is, perhaps, defensible to propose
that before c. A.D. 1000 the upper clergy in European society maintained a reasonably tight hold on what passed for truth and knowledge
in society. Debates were in the nature of infighting, whether between

Gunzo of Novara and his detractors (Manitius, 1958), between confused academics (Lindberg, 1978; Stock, 1983), or between monks and bishops (Duby, 1980). The eleventh century, however, saw the emergence of several systems of truth, several social contexts in which these systems flourished, and several seamy areas in which they conflicted, often violently. Party lines were drawn between clerics and heretics, dialecticians and theologians, rhetoricians and occultists, and advocates of *regnum* and advocates of *sacerdotium*. Persons from nonliterate backgrounds were thrust into literacy; persons used to oral modes of communication were confronted with texts in which charismatic orators found new and vital "authority"; persons with uncertain social connections and status found themselves thrust by their precocious grasp of the new techniques vital to the archival, textual age into close proximity with socially better connected (but textually less trained or gifted) persons; people found themselves seduced from the world of primogeniture, *militia*, feudal marriage, lineage, and sword-and-horsemanship into a new world offering new kinds of dominance, mastery, and power, a world in which—as Abelard put it—tournaments were conducted with written words, texts, and *rationes* rather than with horses, swords, and heraldry (Muckle, 1954).

Competing contexts sprang up for the use of new techniques that ministered to thinking and writing about written words and the systems that governed them. Most of these contexts displayed paradoxical aspects indicative of the unresolved play of forces evident in the period. Thus, the new monasticism (Evans, 1983; Leyser, 1984) sought to play up oral meditative rumination and play down the importance of *rationes* about the functioning of words and inferences based upon them. Yet this new monasticism set shrill production records for the composition and circulation of written formulations (the letters and treatises, for example, of St. Bernard of Clairvaux, William of St. Thierry, and Ailred of Rievaulx). The poets and humanists of the schools and *cenacoli* concentrating on Latin authors, grammar, the *colores* and arts of poetry—the veil or *integumentum* of (written) words that cloak truth impenetrably—proclaimed the primacy of speech, eloquence and the need to embed wisdom in social and practical utility (Evans, 1980; Jeauneau, 1973; Paré, Brunet, & Tremblay, 1933; John of Salisbury,

1962; Thierry of Chartres' *Heptateuchon* in Ward, 1972a). Yet their very practice canonized texts: Bernard of Silvester pondered the meaning of the *Aeneid* and a pseudo-Quintilian declamation, transferred some insights to a written *Aeneid* commentary (perhaps via the initial orality of the classroom), and then worked them all up anew in a elegiac, poetic text (the *Mathematicus*—see Dronke, 1974; Stone, 1988). The new emphasis upon speech immediately bogged itself down in the textual complicities of the *Ad Herennium* and a growing series of meticulous webs for untangling them (the *glosae* or *commenta* that entered class-room practice from the later eleventh century, and which the needs of successive generations of users caused to be entrusted increasingly to parchment; see Ward, 1978). Text and commentary emerged supreme on all sides: texts and glosses on the *Timaeus* of Plato (Gibson, 1969), on the *Organon* of Aristotle, on the works of Ovid, Lucan, Virgil, Cicero, Macrobius, Martianus Capella, and others proliferated. New texts emerged in a bewildering succession of fashions and layers to cater to new arts of the day, such as the art of prose composition in epistolary and business communications (*dictamen*—see Murphy, 1974), or the systems of dialectic that emerged to help control theo-logical debate (Evans, 1980). Everywhere a complicated world, still strongly oral, spawned texts in a bewildering plethora, all the more bewildering because users did not yet have suitable procedural and methodological skills to handle them (systems of author labelling, indexing, cataloging, filing, alphabetizing, digesting and excerpting, highlighting on the page, and the like; see Rouse). Modern scholar-ship—in this respect at least—has come to the aid of hard-working contemporaries who try to keep texts in usable order, but there is still much that has escaped us irretrievably because of the unreadiness of the twelfth-century world to associate thought, ideas, novelty, innova-tion, operating systems, and the like firmly with written texts.

Even the highly unstable world of the court began to spawn manuals: the discord between what people could say or write, and what could be held by others (even themselves) to be true was alarming. To protect oneself against the social consequences of placing some abstract idea of "truth," well guaranteed by chosen texts, ahead of what passed for truth in some expedient context where power, resources, rank and status, even survival, were at stake required manuals, and these manuals took odd forms. They might expose and explore creatively the dilemmas facing people or groups, and hope to produce useful insights that way (Chrétien's *Romances*); they might try to sort out the rights and wrongs of the new situations and contexts for literacy and literate persons (John of Salisbury's *Policraticus* [1979]); they might provide ambitious social climbers with the right combination of tellable anecdotes, popular wisdom or lore, and technical expertise necessary to attract the attention of their social betters, and to ensure that they would "get on" in good company (Alfonsus, 1969; Map, 1983); they might show how stupid things *really* were (the *Gospel according to St-Mark-of-Silver*, or the *Translation of the Relics of SS Gold and Silver* and similar texts; see Thomson, 1973, 1978), they might set up usable systems of fashionable knowledge (Gervase of Tilbury's *Otia Imperialia* [1707]), they might give the driest and most guaranteed rules of survival in a world where an incorrect *salutatio* or an unprofessional phrase might mean social or professional failure (*dictamen, artes poetriae*— see Murphy, 1974). All kinds of persons tried their hands at controlling, or at least viewing, the unstable world they inhabited through a variety of compositions that defy the straightforward genre classifications of modern scholars (e.g., Flint, 1979).

In close association with the consequent devalorization or relativizing of truth just reviewed, rhetoric was thrust into new prominence. As a preceptive discipline well covered in extant authoritative, antique manuals, it broke readily enough into two areas of practice: an inventional system of weighing issues and devising appropriate propositions about them, and a network of techniques designed to make words attractive and effective. The first area of practice has reference to the raw *materia* or *tegma* of things—to use the phraseology of the early twelfth-century rhetorical commentators—shaped and rendered manageable with a view to the making of decisions about them in accordance with specific goals. It took the form of a kind of dialectic, appropriate to probable belief about matters of everyday importance; its original setting within a preceptive system designed to produce long, continuous courtroom speeches was no bar to its popularity in a world where such speeches were not in view. Thus Cicero's *De inventione*, which set the system out without the clutter of further precepts that related primarily to the second area of practice, was a popular text, not least because it presented in its early pages an attractive myth about the role of speech, persuasion, and eloquence in the formation of law and civilization (Ward, 1972b).

The second area of practice needed a text like the pseudo-Ciceronian *Rhetorica ad Herennium*, and ministered primarily to making words attractive. The techniques enshrined in the ancient *dispositio, pronuntiatio, memoria,* and *elocutio* (the *colores*) were primarily geared toward making words persuasive and attractive in a variety of contexts where the ramifications of the ancient inventional system were not particularly relevant. These four skills, when united to some sort of largely homespun technique for locating subject matter, were the best guarantee of survival for the new *literatus* operating in a world in which, frequently, neither social connections nor money nor established institutional power might provide much protection. Thus established, rhetoric was to broaden its compass and achieve considerable status as an indispensable art during the later Middle Ages.

Rhetoric, then, emerged in the eleventh century as a new master discipline for a new age of insecurity. It was promoted by master practitioners against rival systems that also ministered to this new age (the occult—see, for example, Anselm of Besate; Manitius, 1958). It was decried as a discipline of deceit by some (Onulf of Speyer, for example; see Wallach, 1950), and lauded as a tool of power by others who invested heavily in *dictamen*, the *cursus*, and the formalized teaching of authoritative resource manuals (such as the *Ad Herennium*) that lay behind these new arts (Patt, 1978). It was used as a weapon in the new age of polemical controversy—a weapon wielded by parties in the Investiture Contest (Robinson, 1976) and by contenders in the race to stereotype and castigate magic, the occult, and heterodoxy. Finally, it was seen as a tool of quiet heuristic power in the new age of penetrating theological controversy that marked the lifetimes of the monk Rupert of Deutz and the secular (later monk) Peter Abelard, both of whom were fascinated by the apparatus of the *De inventione* (see Evans, 1980; Dal Pra, 1969). Rhetoric gained ground as an *ars* that eventually led to a new network of formalized didactic institutions, structures, curricula, and stipendiary personnel, and also as a resource of verbal metaphor, color and semimagical force with which creative individuals sought to give experimental patterns to a world that they felt had slipped beyond the reach of plain statement and logical method. All this—and to document such developments further would be to write again the cultural history of the twelfth century—followed from the collapse of the political economy of truth in the eleventh century.

How did this collapse occur? It occurred, as has been indicated, amidst the obscure and controversial social, textual, and religious circumstances of the first half of the eleventh century. It then gained momentum as a result of the relatively sudden expansion of courts and bureaucracies, and the consequent upward social mobility on the part of nonliterate groups into literacy and membership of the new aristocracy of the literate (Benson & Constable, 1982; Colker, 1975; Ferruolo, 1985; Hauser, 1951; Jaeger, 1985; Map, 1983; Moore, 1975; Murray, 1978; Peters, 1978; Stiefel, 1985; R. Turner, 1978; Ward, 1972b, 1979). Monarchs and popes were equally to blame. One suspects also a social response to the hardening lines of feudal, bureaucratic, and familial power in the period: Georges Duby has explained how patriarchs were drawing the line of property transmission harder and harder against females and sons other than the first-born (see Barker, 1983; Duby, 1968, 1973, 1980a, 1980b, 1985; Stock, 1983). At the same time, the institutions of the Church were drawing the lines harder and harder against what might be called traditional or unqualified entry into the ranks of the Church: the effect of the Investiture Controversy was to make it more difficult to place spare children into important ecclesiastical positions (though not as difficult as the intellectuals of the day would have liked). For all persons excluded by hardening class lines, the schools were "regarded as a vehicle of upward social mobility to improve one's standing in society" (Benson & Constable, 1982; Ward, 1979, p. 67).

Cohn (1970), Nelson (1972), and others have stressed the marginality inherent in the eleventh- and twelfth-century economies, as economic change in sensitive areas promoted new urban groups and disrupted the tranquility of the countryside (Stock, 1983). Among the new types of fraternities that developed to supply a need for community in these disturbed conditions were the unlicensed school and the heretical following. Both were penetrated by the new intellectuals, and both caused the very activity of the schools to acquire a left-wing taint, which must have increased the sense of marginality felt by those whose family connections were too remote or low-born to provide much security. There was, in fact, a power struggle, but not one seen in the traditional sense of a struggle between those who hold power as a commodity and those who lack it as such. It was a more subtle process, in which the very potential of the mechanisms associated with literacy sorted people into place and determined the nature of intellectual discourse. The key idea is provided, perhaps, by Foucault's (1980) analysis of power as evident only in a continuous relationship, in acts, rather than as a commodity in the abstract: "between every point of a social body, between a man and a woman, between the members of a family, between a master and his pupil, between every one who knows and every one who does not, there exist relations of power" (p. 187). Power is "not that which makes the difference between those who exclusively possess and retain it and those who do not have it and submit to it" (as over the earth and its products in feudal power), but is "something which circulates . . . functions in the form of a chain . . . is employed and exercised through a net-like organization" (p. 98), is based on "the production of effective instruments for the formation and accumulation of knowledge—methods of observation, techniques of registration, procedures for investigation and research, apparatuses control . . . power, when it is exercised through these subtle mechanisms, cannot but evolve, organize and put into circulation a knowledge, or rather apparatuses of knowledge which are not ideological constructs" (p. 102). This kind of power, which Foucault (1980) distinguishes from sovereignty, can be traced to the fact that

> from a particular point in time and for reasons which need to be studied [the mechanisms of power] began . . . to reveal their political usefulness and to lend themselves to economic profit, and . . . as a natural consequence, all of a sudden, they came to be colonized and maintained by global mechanisms and the entire state system. (p. 101)

Foucault is dealing with "mechanisms of the exclusion of madness, and of the surveillance of infantile sexuality" (p. 105), but, by analogy, it is possible to view the mechanisms of intellectual control of the twelfth century as the crucial forerunner of the kind of disciplinary power ("this non-sovereign power, which lies outside the form of sovereignty, is disciplinary power") that underlies "the powers of modern society" (pp. 105-107). To study this kind of power, "we should direct our researches . . . towards domination and the material operators of power, towards forms of subjection and the inflections and utilisations of their localised systems and towards strategic apparatuses" (p. 102). The "material forms" of this power are "institutions such as prisons, clinics, schools and universities," and "medicine, jurisprudence, psychology, philosophy and literary criticism" are examples of its "authorized knowledge and forms of research" (Bové, 1980, pp. 29, 33).

Put simply, literacy (in all its senses) created mechanisms of power, which came to operate in the areas of sexual and religious attitudes (homosexuality [Boswell, 1980], heresy [Peters, 1978], intellectual inquiry and state omnicompetence [Baldwin & Hollister, 1978]). What created literacy? This is in part a false question, as literacy had long existed in Western society, but the following seems clear: the dimensions of competition in society from c. 900 on were in successful process of continuous enlargement, and the processes of admission to literacy—seen as a mode of control of discourse the potential for which had always been present and had indeed been utilized by the church and, through the church, sporadically by the state—were at hand as a complex of mechanisms in process of effervescence attributable to the scale of intellectual dispute and controversy that reached a high-water mark in the eucharistic, nominalist, and investiture controversies of the eleventh century. This phenomenon of controversy must itself be placed in a framework to which the multiplication of the number and size of knightly families from c. A.D. 1000 on, and perhaps also primogeniture, contributed important elements (Barker, 1985; Droogers, 1980; Le Goff, 1980).

The collapse of the political economy of truth in the eleventh century ushered in a period of instability, ferment, and relocation. The first three quarters of the twelfth century, in fact, formed a crucial transitional period in which such institutions of truth as existed were inchoate, in process of relocation and transformation.

> For a short time broadly corresponding to the first half of the twelfth century, there was a wide opportunity for individual enterprise and for ruthless competition which was never again so uncontrolled . . . quite suddenly there were many individuals who wanted new skills and new knowledge, which few masters could supply and which traditional institutional schools were by their nature and functions not well adapted to provide. (Southern in Benson & Constable, 1982, p.115)

It is the very unsuitability of the existing educational institutions that created a good part of the sense of dislocation and alienation that affected the "losers" in this competitive enterprise: the cathedral schools "by the mid-twelfth century . . . were accepting pupils who had no intention of progressing beyond minor orders into the priesthood" (R. Turner, 1978).

The unsuitability of the cathedral schools was based on the following factors:

1. Their parent institutions (the Cathedrals) were not primarily educational institutions, and, as a consequence, control of learning and education proved initially difficult.

2. The education the cathedral schools offered, being geared initially for a career in major orders, was frequently too theoretical or drawn-out or broadly based for the emerging bureaucratic/administrative theaters of employment for literacy, with the result that cathedral school alumni (though some certainly continued to find employment in major orders) found themselves overeducated or "socially displaced," "ambivalent . . . envious . . . critical" (Jaeger, 1985) in lay employment, or else were beaten to employment by persons less elaborately and more appropriately trained for the administrative jobs (less than 10% of the total force of justices under Henry II, it seems, were products of the cathedral schools—Benson & Constable, 1982; Jaeger, 1985; R. Turner, 1978; cf. John of Salisbury's (1979) remarks on his time in court: "I am filled with regret and shame, that, trained for a far different

sphere, I have already wasted almost twelve years. It were more fitting that one suckled by a holier philosophy had, when weaned, passed into the ranks of philosophers rather than into the guild of courtiers" [p. 7]).

3. As Southern has shown (Benson & Constable, 1982), the very curriculum of study within the cathedral schools was already, during the first half of the twelfth century, warping the emphasis of teaching and study in the direction of specialized, theoretical research in the *artes* and theology. Thus, the emergence of institutions of education better geared to the different, specialized needs of the time was inevitable (Ward, 1979; R. Turner, 1978; Benson & Constable, 1982).

An important aspect of this latter phenomenon was the so-called "rise of the universities" as machines or engines of truth (Haskins, 1923/1957; Southern, 1979). In the struggle to develop and shelter behind these machines, those of the sycophantic disposition and few principles, or with established social connections and power ("good birth and wealth"—Ferruolo, 1985, p. 96) may have done best; those who did less well formed a generation of marginal intellectuals, whose only claim to privilege was their intellectual capacity. As their poetry makes clear, such claims were hard to bring to the attention of the wielders of power and privilege in society (Ward, 1979). Morris (1972) speaks of the "satirists who write as outsiders" in the twelfth century "as men who have lost hope in the cause of reform and confidence in their own prospects," of "a failure of nerve among the men of letters, as they realized that they were losing at once the power to influence policy in church and state, and the hope of promotion for themselves" (p. 125). Gramsci (Joll, 1977) speaks of

> exceptionally refined and sensitive temperaments caught up between the iron contrasts of modern life . . . when the environment is superheated to extreme tension and gigantic collective forces are unleashed which press hard on single individuals [who] are incapable of arriving at a new . . . equilibrium between the impulse of the will and the ends which the individual can reach. (p. 88)

For Morris (1972) "the problem of alienation and order was central in the literature of the twelfth century" (p. 122). For Ferruolo (1975) "satire usually thrives in the context of rapid social change" and in the twelfth century became "an effective means of protest against growing specialization and professionalism both in the schools and in society" (p. 103). The satirists were "rebels radically alienated from society and intent upon undermining established institutions and ideas" (p. 128).

Ferruolo (1985) and Jaeger (1985), in fact, have recently emphasized the contrast between the broadly, even inappropriately, trained clerical "courtier-by-default" class of the twelfth century, and the more appropriately trained specialists in administration and law of the succeeding period. "What these masters offered their employers was not the specialized training in administration or law that would later become desired credentials, but basic literacy, the ability to read and write Latin, which was still a rare and precious commodity" (Ferruolo, 1985, p. 94). It is the former or "courtier-by-default" group who claim a general brief to comprehend, reform, and improve society, and hence, a right to occupy the most influential and lucrative positions in that society; it is the latter or specialists-by-choice group who put personal profit and advancement first. The former were philosophers, the latter professional courtiers (Ferruolo, 1985; note also the "Cornifician movement," Tacchella, 1980; Tobin, 1984; Ward, 1972a). The inevitability of the movement towards specialization and professionalism was a poor panacea for its effect on the old curriculum of study and agenda for world improvement espoused by those now considered humanists. Peter of Blois, for example, "had neither the good birth nor the powerful friends and patrons nor the practical expertise that might have assured his success" (Ferruolo, 1985, p. 167). Even those *magistri* who secured a permanent place in the institutions of truth (the universities) felt the weight of a rapidly expanding volume of written learning with which they were bound to cope—though at least one, using the metaphor of a burdensome vestment, took refuge in a counsel of despair and advocated abandonment of the whole burden for the simplicity of the cloister and the Gospel (Ferruolo, 1985). If the position of the professional university theologian/preacher is more narrowly concerned with the *via salvationis* offered by the Scriptures than with the *farrago* of things classical and contemporary that interested the generalist-courtier-cleric, we can lay the blame on the stronger institutional affiliation and valorization enjoyed by the former, whose castigation of rival professional preoccupations reflects the minor measure of marginalization we may detect in the world of theologian/preacher versus that of the lawyer/medico (see Ferruolo, 1985).

May we not see here some sort of parallel to the contrast Michel Foucault (1979) draws in our day between the disappearing "left intellectual [who] spoke and was acknowledged to have the right of speaking in the capacity of master of truth and justice, [who] was heard or purported to make himself heard as the representative of the universal" (p. 41), and the "specific" intellectual, the specialist, the expert? The "specific" intellectual is the specialist in the fields of science and technology that have come to constitute the post-Darwinian world. The intellectual par excellence had hitherto been the writer: "the 'universal' intellectual . . . finds his fullest expression in the writer, the bearer of values and signification in which all can recognize themselves." The age of the specific intellectual, however, is one in which the intellectual is "no longer the singer of eternity, but the strategist of life and death. We are living through, right now, the disappearance of the great writer" (pp. 43-44).

It was thus toward the end of the twelfth century that the arts and humanities "died," that the "great writers" of Latin cosmographical and epic poetry disappeared, defeated by the successful specialists (the lawyer, the doctor, the theologian, the dialectician, the government bureaucrat, the student of Aristotelian "science" and the "strategists of life and death"—see Whetherbee, 1972; Jaeger, 1985). As the successful priest of the new age said in a late twelfth-century satire (Ferruolo, 1985): "I have prebends and preside at the altar. I have power and prestige" (p. 115; see also Baldwin, 1970; Evans, 1980; McKeon, 1975). The common denominator of aspirant priest, scientist, humanist, and satirist was the prebend, the benefice, the "altar." Few of our aspirants had the skills, inherited wealth, or family connections to survive without it for any length of time, but not all had the necessary combination of opportunism and expediency or friends in the right places, to submit easily to the regimen, *mores*, modes, and behavior that led to the benefice—or, for those who like Walter Map or Gerald of Wales had benefices enough, but aspired to the benefice of benefices, a bishopric.

To the "humanists" of the day, it seemed self-evident that the "great writers" had disappeared. Gerald of Wales asks:

> Where are the divine poets? Where are the masters of the Latin tongue? Who nowadays in his writings, whether they be poetry or history, can hope to add new lustre to the art of letters? . . . In earlier times the man of letters stood on the topmost step of the hall of fame. Now those who devote themselves to study, which is toppled deep in ruin, or so it seems, and sunk in disrepute, are no longer there to be emulated, they earn no respect; on the contrary they are disliked and despised. (Ferruolo, 1985, p. 175)

This chapter is concerned less with the truth of this statement, or its value as an indication of the end of a "Renaissance," than with its status as an article of faith for marginalized intellectuals, who—in every age that creates and marginalizes them (in relation to money and power)—castigate their contemporaries for ethical, moral, and aesthetic bankruptcy, for gross inattention to the values and principles contained within the corpus or theoretical academic writings it was their lot to study and assimilate and then use in an effort to rewrite their own lives as exemplary (Ferruolo, 1985).

If we were to reconstruct the identity of our marginalized intellectuals, or *intelligentsia*—to use a word not normally applied to groups prior to the eighteenth century—we might have them saying, with Foucault (1979), "that truth isn't outside power, or deprived of power . . . the child of prolonged solitudes, or the privilege of those who have been able to liberate themselves" (pp. 45-46; compare the celebrated remarks of John of Salisbury, 1962, pp. 9-11). We could portray them as seeing that

> truth is of the world: it is produced there by virtue of multiple constraints . . . each society has its own regime of truth, its "general politics" of truth: that is, the types of discourse it harbours and causes to function as true; the mechanisms and instances which enable one to distinguish true from false statements, the way in which each is sanctioned; the techniques and procedures which are valorised for obtaining truth; the status of those who are charged with saying what counts as true. (Lacapra, 1980, p. 270)

For the twelfth century each of these phrases hits its mark. The scholastic commentary, *sententia* and *quaestio* (Benson & Constable, 1982), representing discourse validated by the *licentia docendi* and the emergent machinery of the cathedral school/*studium*/*universitas*, manifest the valorized techniques and procedures for obtaining truth: Abelard's *Sic et Non* elaborated the mechanisms and instances which enabled one to distinguish true from false statements, and the progressive incorporation of the new logic into the twelfth-century schools confirmed such techniques and explained them more thoroughly. The status of those who were charged with saying what counted as true was a vital issue: witness the struggles over the *licentia docendi* in the first half of the twelfth century, the papacy's determined attempt to dominate the schools and nascent universities, and the progressive tendency to let the special fields of law and theology determine the nature of truth.

We are dealing here with the invention of truth, the invention of rules of exclusion: "in every society the production of discourse is at once controlled, selected, organized and redistributed according to a certain number of procedures, whose role is to avert its powers and its dangers" (Foucault, 1972, p. 216). The "will to truth" manifested in the twelfth century "relies on institutional support: it is both reinforced and accompanied by whole strata of practices such as pedagogy . . . the book-system, publishing, libraries . . . learned societies . . . laboratories . . . it tends to exercise a sort of pressure, a power of constraint upon other forms of discourse" (p. 218-219). This "will to truth" invented competing techniques for control of discourse: the commentary, the idea of the author, and disciplines (Foucault, 1979). Later manifestations of the will to truth were to alter the medieval emphases among these techniques.

Yet there was no certainty about any of this at the time; in fact, there were many competing mechanisms and statuses; there was much awareness of the relativity of truth and truth mechanisms, much tension between the "universal intellectual" outside the established institutions of power, and the "specific intellectuals" of the incipient departments of truth in the nascent universities. In this context, writing functioned as both discourse and as antidiscourse. As a discourse it functioned in the sense sanctioned by the nascent institutions of truth—*sermo, commentum, sententia, distinctio, quaestio, disputatio, summa,* and *glosa.* As an antidiscourse it functioned as a web designed to confound and obscure scholastic meaning (Charles, 1985, pp. 138ff; cf. p. 86, "le commentaire est centripète et la rhétorique centrifuge"); it imported ambivalences from the humanist literary rhetoric of Graeco-Roman antiquity, it made use of a rich inheritance of Latin poetic style, rhythm, and metre, it delved into the marvelous resource of late antique hermetic lore, and it hid "truth" behind the *involucrum,* the *integumentum* of discourse. It meant, in some contexts, a shift analogous to that from medieval Gothic (or vertical) structure (the feudal, religious, macrocosmic epistemology) to carefully motivated, naturalistic, narrative structure (the capitalist, materialist, microcosmic epistemology in the fourteenth century—see Jeauneau, 1973; Knight, 1976; Knight & Wilding, 1977).

Antidiscourse kept alive what were progressively to be seen as "discontinuous, disqualified, illegitimate knowledges against the claims of a unitary body of theory" (Foucault, 1979, p. 83) which would filter, hierarchize, and order them in the name of some true knowledge and some arbitrary idea of what constitutes a science and its objects. This antidiscourse is implicitly opposed "to the effects of the centralizing powers which are linked to the institution and functioning of an organized scientific discourse within a society. . . . embodied in a university or, more generally, in an educational apparatus" (p. 84; cf. Williams, 1981, p. 182, institutions of "cultural reproduction").

The antidiscourse of the nonestablishment intellectuals of the twelfth century, situated outside or on the margins of the developing nodes, centers, and institutions of truth and authority is what we have come to know as "humanism," as the so-called "Renaissance" feature of twelfth century society. This is not the humanism of R. W. Southern (1970), or the "Renaissance" of C. H. Haskins (1927), but a reaction to a process of marginalization characterized by patterns evident also in the later Italian Renaissance: a mixture of Latin classicism, polemic, linguistic and stylistic experiments, intellectual precocity, and the beginnings—if accidental—of philological acumen. The key to this humanism, however, is not so much a shift in the content of intellectual life, not so much a shift of consciousness on the part of an age as a whole, not so much a swing of the pendulum of fashion or whim as the collapse of the political economy of truth, the breaching of the monopolistic domination of literacy that was exercised by the established institutions of truth (episcopacy and monastery, together with their schools and traditional aristocratic recruitment fields).

It is at this point that we may link our exposition with the two interpretive responses to texts discussed (perhaps obscurely) by Brian Stock (1984-1985; cf. Evans, 1980): the logical and the rhetorical. The reader may have already detected their presence behind the exposition of the preceding few paragraphs, which have been deliberately couched in the suggestively resonant (if translated) phrases of Foucault. The logical interpretive strategy we may characterize as marked by "overcoding" (Eco, 1979), by "rules," by what Victor Turner (1969) calls "structure," by strong institutional authorization/validation—deriving support from new modes of institutionalizing the control of texts (corporations of *magistri*, the *licentia docendi ubique* [cf. Muckle, 1954], for example), by clear audience projection and minimal authorial self-reference. This is the "winning" environment of *universitas, studium*, dialectic, and scientific *rationes*, though its ultimate status as victor should not obscure its controversial birth pangs in the polemics surrounding the careers of (for example) William of Conches or Roscellin or Abelard, in the latter's own brand of rhetorical, topical dialectic, in the bickering between dialecticians and upholders of the tradition of the Latin grammatical *auctores*, or between the vocationally minded professionals, careerists, or utilitarians, and the humanists (Ferruolo, 1985; McKeon, 1952; Paré, Brunet, & Tremblay, 1933; Poole, 1920/1960).

The rhetorical interpretive strategy we may characterize as the "liminal" discourse of the seams, interstices, and margins that emerged as the systems of knowledge and power evolved (Douglas, 1978; V. Turner, 1969). Here magnification and mystification of the text *per involucrum, per integumentum* prevailed, here we may speak of "undercoding" (Eco, 1979), here texts survive in small numbers, here audiences are problematic, here authorial self-reference *may* compensate for the absence of a "hard" institutional, disciplinary point of reference or source of validation. Other sources of validation were called forth by the rhetorical strategy in the "weak" or "soft" environment in which its texts were produced and consumed: the authority of the ancient stylists, systems of magical/occult *sapientia* (Hermeticism—and note that Cicero's rhetorical teacher was usually felt, in the twelfth century, to be Hermes himself [e.g., MS Oxford CCC 250 fol.9ra line 41; Marx, 1964]), allegorical/poetic code systems (Lewis, 1967; McKeon, 1952; Wetherbee, 1972), adherence to the emerging crown as an agent of reform and change to replace a discredited church (compare the loyalties revealed in Map, 1983; cf. Marshall, 1977; Wilks, 1979). We must not fail to observe that some areas within the rhetorical strategy *did* secure institutionalization, whether longterm or shortlived (the arts of preaching, poetry, *dictamen*, prayer, etc.—Ferruolo, 1985; Murphy, 1974), though never on a scale or to a degree that would invite comparison with the success fields of law, medicine, theology, or dialectic (Evans, 1980; Leff, 1968; Rashdall, 1936/1938; Ward, 1972a, 1979). Nor can we hope to analyze at close range why some literate personalities of the time found themselves in weak environments and why some found themselves in strong ones, why some displayed encapsulated personality structures and some "amoebic modes of perceiving the world and organizing the self" (Newbold, 1981, pp. 72ff), or why some were thrown to the newer areas of literate consciousness (the courts), and some secured places closer to the older core of Latin textual learning (the *studia*, *universitates*, *scholae*).

However we choose to read the lines of demarcation that emerged during the confused decades of the late eleventh and twelfth centuries, and however inevitable, both at this period and at all others, the triumphs of the "hard" disciplines may have been, it is important to at least acknowledge the element of competition and marginalization that accompanied the collapse of the political economy of truth in the eleventh century. Equally as important was the process of reconstruction of the political economy of truth that had gained visible momentum by the last quarter of the twelfth century, and the disappearance or receding of those polyvalent counterstrategies that were thrown up, and to the wall, during the first three decades of the century. Without realizing it, the editors of a recent monumental publication commemorating the older philological conception of the "Twelfth Century Renaissance" have put their fingers, so to speak, upon the crucial moment in time for the reconstruction of the political economy of truth: "for reasons and in ways that are . . . not entirely clear, the phenomena which scholars identify collectively as the twelfth century renaissance began to recede during the third quarter of the century, and their supersession appears to mark the beginning of a new period in cultural history—a period dominated by universities, high scholasticism, developed Gothic styles, and so forth" (Benson & Constable, 1982; De Ghellinck, 1954, on the decline of Latin culture in the twelfth century).

In an earlier paper I wrote as follows of this reconstruction of authority, and of truth, in the years following the middle of the twelfth century:

> This probing, unstructured world of the earlier twelfth century, which coincides with the earliest growth of secular and ecclesiastical bureaucracies and research staffs, leads inexorably to the world of the later twelfth century, in which intellectual activity expanded to papal, episcopal and royal courts, and the university emerged to supply and regulate the flow of tertiary trained clerics to these courts. In a competitive situation characterized by more applicants than posts available, the university functioned to control competition by measuring, grading and rejecting applicants for tertiary employment. With this development, the marginality of intellectuals became less pronounced and finally disappeared, taking with it that efflorescence of "humanist" literature so characteristic of the twelfth century "Renaissance." When institutions of tertiary training were operating in the margins of the cathedral churches, whose main tasks lay elsewhere, and when the alumni of such institutions could find employment in areas only marginally related to monastic and ecclesiastical routine, then intellectuals could only be acutely conscious of a clash of values between their training, their literacy and their environment. The emergence of the universities normalized tertiary training and effected some congruence between educational input and the ultimate social milieu of the tertiary trainee. (Ward, 1979, p. 70)

In the thirteenth century we can observe the consequences of strong institutional monopoly of writing: the university-trained elite dominates, writing reaches a peak of institutional validation or authorization, there is an evident concentration on aids, concordances, alphabet-ization, paragraphing, *florilegia* and other writing devices that stress language as a means of access to truth, that stress the structure of truth behind language, rather than through or in language. Rhetoric is re-duced to Boethius' *De differentiis topicis*, grammar becomes the study of how words convey an impression of beyond-language reality, ser-mons employ a denuded apparatus of classical rhetorical theory in order to bring an audience to a perception of beyond-language truth. It is worth noticing, though, that even this latter employment of consciously rhetorical devices is occasioned by the location of a dominant literate class in a frontier area of tension and interface with the lay world of the unbeliever, the nonbeliever, the lapsed believer, the intermittent believer, or the unorthodox believer. Sermon manuals, with their strong tendency toward prescriptive didacticism, and collections of models flourish—and the same phenomenon can be observed for *dicta-men* in the thirteenth century Italian world, where communal bureau-cracies continued to burgeon but where the growing dominance of the new professionally trained dictaminal and notarial class produced a retreat from rhetorically sensitive literature into didactic codifica-tion. "Humanist" literature in this period is reduced to areas of vernac-ular marginality—Wolfram von Eschenbach's *Parzifal*, Gottfried von Strassburg's *Tristan*, Jean de Meun's *Romance of the Rose*, and the growing volume of vernacular writing in the Italian communes from the mid-thirteenth century onward (Jaeger, 1985; Whetherbee, 1972).

The impact of the reconstruction of the political economy of truth can be observed in the very manuscripts in which our authors have come down to us, both old authors copied during the twelfth century and new authors transcribed for the first few times. In the first half of the twelfth century, texts were spawned by small-scale, competing circles and "foyers." Such texts tended to lack authority, a steady audience, and institutional relevance. They circulated informally among groups that recognized them and were unused to the mature literate habits of author labeling. As groups dissolved or lost relevance, as fast-moving intellec-tual frontiers rendered old beachheads outmoded, texts that were at the peak of their usage ill-labeled and without approachable format were abandoned or lost. Such conditions of text production continued into an era when formalization and institutionalization of texts and learning contexts began to require some regular exposure to curricula, regular texts to support curricula, labels to identify such texts, and a host of lesser aids and classificatory techniques that have been well documented by R. H. Rouse and M. A. Rouse (1979). Writings such as Gervase of Melkley's *Ars Poetica* (1965), or the anonymous commentary on the *Rhetorica ad Herennium* preserved in MS Oxford Corpus Christi College 250 folios 1-17 (Ward, 1972b)—to take two random examples—represent an early phase in the use and application of formalized or institutionalized author labels, when such labels gave identity and status to texts that were now required to circulate beyond their initial oral usage/genesis, contexts, and which consequently ran the risk of being without easily recognizable and transferable validating authority. This phase in which authored texts began to create, in their own right, academic patterns, institutions, and contexts is, preeminently, the phase of the scribal *auctor* + *glosa/glosula*. Not by any means a new distinction or phenomenon, the *auctor* + *commentum/ glosa* (Benson & Constable, 1982) pattern—appropriate to the slow rhythms and immature authority patterns of scribal culture—nevertheless expanded unprecedentedly in the twelfth and thirteenth centuries and familiarized those generations with a rudimentary twofold author-labeling pattern, the original and the (subsequent) commentator. Our manuscripts suggest the slow process whereby the latter becomes a full identity, from an initial status as—literally—marginal and interlinear remarks. The evolution of the *auctor/glosa* pattern occurred wherever and whenever formalized learning contexts had imposed a degree of routinized continuity upon text production/reproduction and audience consumption. The heyday, however, of the *auctor/glosa* pattern is the twelfth and thirteenth centuries, although the emergence of independent commentary-replacement texts is progressively important. In the period of genesis of universities and *studia*, status as a professional within the new institutions of learning derived from an ability to manipulate the new author-labeled texts. In this period authors were literally created and given vague profiles—for example, *Alanus de Insulis*. Once the validating educational institutions got underway, texts were produced that conformed to the new conditions and were generally labeled and given appropriate format upon production—rudimentarily but more systematically than twelfth-century texts, which regularly circulated without author ascriptions and often without titles or other aids to identification.

What happened to texts that were *not* required by the new institutionalized ("hard") utilization contexts? In the first place they were lost. Alternatively, they survived as flotsam without evidence of much supporting audience interest, and often without indication of authorship. In the third place they found "soft" utilization markets in courts, lay reading circles, and the like that led to their survival in low numbers. Such circles often implied new resonance contexts such as, for example, befell Abelard's *Historia Calamitatum*, which seems—together with its companion letters—to have been attracted into new relevance contexts such as the debate over monastic usages at the Paraclete or the marriage-versus-love debate, which led to the survival of the letter collection in the late thirteenth and fourteenth centuries rather than twelfth-century manuscripts (cf. the paper by J. F. Benton in *Colloques*, 1975). Another illustration of a changed resonance context is the survival of epistolary materials from the eleventh-century investiture contest (Robinson, 1976).

Viewed in this way, the humanist/scholastic or medieval/Renaissance problem becomes a question of monopolist versus pluralist control of the location, production, and consumption of writing. The twelfth century represents, in this respect, a problematic liminal period because the institutional control of thought and learning was momentarily loosened when a world unaccustomed to extensive textuality was suddenly confronted with it: the newly literate, coming from outside the customary learned environment, demanded access to it, demanded *rationes* much as the bourgeoisie dispatched euphuism in the sixteenth century; much as Buoncompagno in his mature teaching years called for a severe and straightened practicality in *dictamen* studies rather than the *colores* of *Ad Herennium IV* (Howell, 1956; Stock, 1983, 1984-1985; Witt, 1986; for "liminal" see V. Turner, 1969). New departures in writing types and styles were stimulated within traditional cadres (for example, Cistercian spiritualism), within turbulent, developing cadres (the cathedral schools of northern France), and within novel and expanding cadres (the courts). Thirteenth-century routinization took the form of a more thorough imposition of the university stamp upon writing. By the same token, much of the humanism evident both north and south of the Alps between the twelfth and fifteenth centuries, but especially from the time of Dante onward, took the form of a progressive pluralizing of the institutional control of writing: lay schools, lay centers of government and administration, lay poetic *cenacoli*, and the like.

The novel and unstructured nature of these latter (early Renaissance) poetic *cenacoli* suggests a further train of thought. Individuals, like groups, divide into those with and those without a strongly routinized living pattern and set of social expectations. For the former type social conduct is prescribed by convention and custom, and the sense of boundary between individuals (sexual, social, vocational) is conventional and intuitively developed. For the latter type, social identity is fluid, the sense of boundary is weak, social relations are polemical, exaggerated, or intimate, and the speech code is elaborated (Bernstein, 1973). The latter type will be characterized, where literacy is strongly developed, by events of writing effected in close conformity with the ideal model of the ordinary intelligibility of speech, and literary forms and rhetoric will emerge as a personal identity-locating resource. The former type will rest its personal literary anonymity behind an impersonal façade of gloss, *florilegium*, tractate, *summa*, though such a façade will mask different projects and personal situations. While some will attempt to impose order on the flux of things through the tools of scholasticism, from the vantage point of an agonized and insecure outlook on life, others will wield the same tools from the vantage point of the comfortable and relatively prestigious faculties of respected disciplines such as law and theology. One cannot overcategorize or overdichotomize the kaleidoscopic panorama of literate life; it is a question of identifying trends and directions, confrontations, and resolutions (Douglas, 1982, McRuvie, 1981; Oldroyd, 1986; Stock, 1983).

Future research, if it is to make much of this, will have to concentrate on isolating social situations productive of unusual numbers of weak-boundary personalities in situations of loosely controlled extrainstitutional literacy. Another approach to these phenomena is that, already mentioned, of R. F. Newbold (1979), who writes of the impact of the products of foveal vision—bureaucracy, linearity, literacy—and a corresponding decentralizing peripheral vision countercurrent against it. This antimony, originally elaborated to explain certain features of late Roman imperial culture, is suggestive of the interaction in the twelfth century between the forces of linearity (orthodoxy, specialization, government), and the countercurrent against them: heresy, alienation, and the poetic antidiscourse of the disaffected scholars Colin Morris (1972) talks about in his *The Discovery of the Individual*. It is, in fact, the eternal oscillation between the Apollonian and the Dionysian of Nietzsche, but set in a socioeconomic context in which the social experience of the individual in an age of "soft" (i.e., unstablilized) institutional development, determines which side of the fence he or she will fall upon.

What this chapter proposes therefore, for any interpretation of cultural change between antiquity and the sixteenth century, is not a fixed model seen in terms of the growth over a millenium—whether continuous or by stages, towards a modern or Renaissance episteme—but a behavioural, sociological model of a series of oscillations from one pole or axis to another. The word *oscillation* is that of Victor Turner (1969), whose model of oscillation between liminality and structure is persuasive in the present context. The implications of these remarks for any new perspective on the problem of cultural change in the period between Augustine and Ramus cannot be pursued here, although the pattern of developments evident in the twelfth and thirteenth centuries can be recognized repeatedly in later times.

To sum up the gist of the present inquiry, we may observe that the "Renaissance phenomena" noted by Benson and Constable (1982) are not characteristics of an age as a whole, or benchmarks in the movement of cultures towards the patterns of the present, but types of discourse that occur periodically when sociopolitical and economic forces draw unprecedented numbers of persons into the field of texts, creating competition for literate livings and for systems of control of textual interpretation. The element of competition is reflected in literature at a variety of levels: high-level scholastic disputes, disputes between proponents of orthodoxy and heterodoxy, disputes between and among humanists and cosmologists on the one hand, and on another the competition for courtly livings, benefices, and patronage that spills over into the goliardic verse of the time. The predominant emphasis in these types of discourse is rhetorical because their participants lack a secure institutional foundation to provide authority, to take responsibility for their identity, and to give them the confidence upon which to base an objectification or reification of textual knowledge. When the dislocations that promote these types of discourse pass, tensions are to some extent reduced, imbalances of supply and demand of literate personnel are redressed (Mizruchi, 1987; Murray, 1978), rhetorical discourses are themselves institutionalized or marginalized even further (for example, onto the vernacular). Hence, perhaps, the decline, disappearance, or formalization of such genres as the goliardic stanza, rhetorical history, and letter collections of the humanist pattern, and hence the so-often-noticed "decline of the classics" in the thirteenth century. At the same time, we may surmise, a measure of social conformity developed: the intake from nonliterate to literate classes was reduced, the sons of *clerici* themselves became clerics, or at least the families from which clerics were drawn came to be those from which they were continually drawn. Some cultural and literary traditions are established anew, more appropriate institutions of replication and transmission of the new literate knowledge systems are established; in short, we have the phenomenon of "routinization," leading to the devaluation—even the disappearance—of the marginal and the rhetorical and a new surge of the scholastic and the logical (Bouwsma, 1976; Struever, 1983; Weber, 1964). Such oscillations are, it is true, less marked after the twelfth century because the pluralization of a complex, partially literate society spread across a region as diverse as Europe was to make permanent the coexistence of a variety of discourses; nevertheless, these oscillations *are* visible and are intrinsically more interesting than the paradigms of the classicists, the philologists, and others who maintain a restricted view that notes only the attainment of forms of modernity during the Italian renaissance, appropriately anticipated in some areas by the Renaissance of the twelfth century.

Thus we have given the relativism of the modern age its due and underlined the role of rhetoric, the science of the relative. Use of the term "renaissance" for the twelfth—or for any other—century should alert us to the presence of an oscillation in favor of rhetoric and the relative, rather than to the quest for a single, absolute, simplistic, privileged pattern of modern culture of which we wish to read the evolution back specifically into the past. We should be keen to isolate identifiable patterns of behavior, thinking, writing, funding, authorizing, and undermining; we should be sensitive to ebbs and flows of power through the veins of society, and to the recognition of different features of such ebbs and flows in different periods, albeit within an inevitably more complicated general social pattern. It may be true, to adapt a remark the pre-Socratics made in reference to change in general, that we can never step into the same past twice, but it is equally true that the patterns of the present are arbitrary and derive from the victories of successful groups, individuals, and systems in the past. It would not do, as far as the twelfth century is concerned, to mistake what was, in fact, a series of power struggles for the predestined accomplishment of an inevitable progression.

REFERENCES

Alfonsus, P. (1969). *The scholar's guide*. (J. Jones & J. Keller, Trans.) Toronto: Pontifical Institute of Medieval Studies.

Baldwin, J., & Hollister, W. (1978). The rise of administrative kingship: Henry I and Philip Augustus. *American Historical Review, 83*, 868.

Baldwin, J. W. (1970). *Masters, princes and merchants: The social views of Peter the Chanter and his circle* (2 vols.) Princeton: Princeton University Press.

Barker, P. (1985). The politics of primogeniture: Sex, consciousness and social organisation in North Western Europe (900-1250 A.D.). In E. Leach, S. N. Mukherjee & J. O. Ward (Eds.), *Feudalism: Comparative studies*. Sydney Studies in Society and Culture, No. 2, 87-104.

Benson, R. L. & Constable, G. (Eds.). (1982). *Renaissance and renewal in the twelfth century*. Cambridge, MA: Harvard University Press.

Bernstein, B. (1973). *Class, codes and control* (Vol. 1). London: Paladin, St. Albans.

Boswell, J. (1980). *Christianity, social tolerance and homosexuality: Gay people in Western Europe from the beginning of the Christian era to the fourteenth century*. Chicago: University of Chicago Press.

Bouwsma, W. J. (1976). Changing assumptions in later Renaissance culture. *Viator, 7*, 421-40.

Bové, Paul (1980). The end of humanism: Michel Foucault and the power of disciplines. *Humanities in Society, 3*, 23-40.

Burckhardt, Jacob (1860). *The civilization of the Renaissance in Italy.* (Trans., 1960). New York: Mentor.

Charles, M. (1985). *L'Arbre et la source.* Paris: Editions du Seuil.

Chastel, A., et al. (1982). *The Renaissance: Essays in interpretation.* London: Methuen.

Cohn, N. (1970). *The pursuit of the millenium.* London: Paladin, St. Albans.

Colker, M. L. (1975). *Analecta Dublinensia.* Cambridge, MA: Mediaeval Academy of America.

Colloques Internationaux du Centre National de la Recherche Scientifique (1975). *Pierre Abelard, Pierre le Venerable: Les courants philosophiques, littéraires et artistiques en occident au milieu de XIIe siècle.*

Dal Pra, M. (1969). *Pietro Abelardo, Scritti di Logica.* Florence: Nuova Italia.

De Ghellinck, J. (1954). *L'Essor de la littérature Latine au XIIe siècle.* Paris: Desclee de Brouwer.

Douglas, M. (1978). *Purity and danger: An analysis of the concepts of pollution and taboo.* London: Routledge & Kegan Paul.

Douglas, M. (Ed.). (1982). *Essays in the sociology of perception.* London: Routledge & Kegan Paul.

Dronke, P. (1974). *Fabula: Explorations into the use of myth in medieval Platonism.* Leiden: Brill.

Droogers, A. (1980). Symbols of marginality in the biographies of religious and secular innovators. *Numen, 27*, 105-121.

Duby, G. (1968). In Northwestern France: The 'youth' in twelfth century aristocratic society. In F. L. Cheyette (Ed.), *Lordship and community in Medieval Europe, selected readings,* (pp. 198-209). New York: Holt, Rinehart & Winston.

Duby, G. (1973). *Hommes et structures du moyen Age, recueil d'articles.* Paris: Mouton.

Duby, G. (1980a). *The Chivalrous Society.* (C. Postan, Trans.). Berkeley: University of California Press.

Duby, G. (1980b). *The three orders, feudal society imagined.* (Arthur Goldhammer, Trans.). Chicago: University of Chicago Press.

Duby, G. (1985). *The knight, the lady and the priest: The making of modern marriage in medieval France.* (B. Bray, Trans.). Harmondsworth: Penguin Books.

Eco, U. (1979). *A theory of semiotics.* Bloomington: Indiana University Press.

Evans, G. (1980). *Old arts and new theology: The beginnings of theology as an academic discipline.* Oxford: Clarendon.

Evans, G. (1983). *The mind of St. Bernard of Clairvaux.* Oxford: Clarendon.

Ferruolo, S. C. (1985). *The origins of the university: The schools of Paris and their critics 1100-1215.* Stanford, CA: Stanford University Press.

Flint, V. I. J. (1979). The *Historia Regum Britanniae* of Geoffrey of Monmouth: Parody and its purpose. A suggestion. *Speculum,, 54* 447ff.

Foucault, M. (1972). *The archaeology of knowledge.* New York: Pantheon.

Foucault, M. (1979). In Morris, M. & P. Patton (Eds.), *Michel Foucault: Power, truth and strategy.* Sydney: Feral.

Foucault, M. (1980). In Gordon, C. (Ed.), *Power/knowledge: Selected interviews and other writings 1972-77.* Brighton: Harvester.

Gibson, M. (1969). The study of the *Timaeus* in the eleventh and twelfth centuries. *Pensamiento, 25* 183-194.

Haskins, C. H. (1923 [1957, 1979 etc.]). *The rise of universities.* Ithaca, NY: Cornell University Press.

Haskins, C. H. (1927 [1958 etc.]). *The Renaissance of the twelfth century.* New York: Meridian Books.

Hauser, A. (1951). Renaissance, mannerism, baroque. *The Social History of Art.* New York: Knopf.

Helton, T. (Ed.), (1961). *The Renaissance: A reconsideration of the theories and inter-pretations of the age.* Madison: University of Wisconsin Press.

Howell, W. S. (1956). *Logic and rhetoric in England 1500-1700.* Princeton: Princeton University Press.

Ijsseling, S. (1976). *Rhetoric and philosophy in conflict.* The Hague: Nijhoff.

Jaeger, S. (1985). *The origins of courtliness: Civilizing trends and the formation of courtly ideals 939-1210.* Philadelphia: University of Pennsylvania Press.

Jeauneau, E. (1973). *Lectio philosophorum: Recherches sur l'ecole de Chartres.* Amster-dam: Hakkert.

Joll, J. (1977). *Gramsci.* Glasgow: Fontana.

Knight, S. (1976). Some aspects of structure in Medieval literature. *Parergon, 16,* 3-17.

Knight, S., & Wilding, M. (Eds.), (1977). *The radical reader.* Sydney: Wild & Woolley.

Kristeller, P. O. (1955, 1961). *Renaissance thought: The classic, scholastic and humanist strains.* New York: Harper Torchbook.

Kristeller, P. O. (1965). *Renaissance thought II: Papers on humanism and the arts.* New York: Harper Torchbook.

Kristeller, P. O. (1969). *Studies in Renaissance thought and letters.* Rome: Edizioni di Storia e Letteratura.

Kristeller, P. O. (1980). *Renaissance thought and the arts: Collected essays.* Princeton: Princeton University Press.

Lacapra, D. (1980). Rethinking intellectual history and reading texts. *History and Theory, 19.* 245-76.

Le Goff, J. (1960). *Les intellectuels au Moyen Age.* Paris: Editions du Seuil.

Leff, G. (1968). *Paris and Oxford universities in the thirteenth and fourteenth centuries.* New York: John Wiley.

Lewis, C. S. (1967). *The allegory of love: A study in medieval tradition.* New York: Galaxy.

Leyser, H. (1984). *Hermits and the new monasticism: A study of religious communities in Western Europe 1000-1150.* London: Macmillan.

Lindberg, D. C. (Ed.). (1978). *Science in the Middle Ages.* Chicago: University of Chicago Press.

Manitius, K. (Ed.). (1958). *Gunzo epistola ad Augienses und Anselm von Besate Rhetorimachia.* Weimar: MGH.

Map, W. (1983). *De nugis curialium.* (M. R. James, C. N. L. Brooke, & R. A. B. Mynors, Ed. and Trans.). Oxford: Clarendon.

Marshall, L. (1979). The identity of the "new man" in the *Anticlaudianus* of Alan of Lille. *Viator, 10* 77ff.

Marx, F. (1964). *Ad herennium.* Leipzig: Teubner.

McKeon, R. (1952). Poetry and philosophy in the twelfth century: The Renaissance of rhetoric. In R. S. Crane (Ed.), *Critics and criticism: Ancient and modern*, pp. 305ff. Chicago.

McKeon, R. (1975). The organisation of sciences and the relations of cultures in the twelfth and thirteenth centuries. In J. E. Murdoch & E. D. Sylla (Eds.), *The cultural context of medieval learning*, pp. 151-192. Boston: Reidel.

McRuvie, D. J. (1981). *Changes in the intelligibility of writing in late Medieval, early Renaissance Italy: An aspect of the origins of Italian humanism.* Ph.D. Dissertation, University of Sydney.

Melkley, Gervase of (1965). *Ars Poetica*. In Hans-Jürgen Gräbner (Ed.), *Forschungen zur romanischen philologie, 17.* Münster: Aschendorffsche Verlagsbuchhandlung.

Mizruchi, E. H. (1987). *Regulating society: Beguines, bohemians and other marginals.* Chicago: University of Chicago Press.

Moore, R. I. (Ed.). (1975). *The birth of popular heresy.* London: Edward Arnold.

Morris, C. (1972). *The discovery of the individual 1050-1200.* London: Society for the Promotion of Christian Knowledge.

Muckle, J. T. (1954). *The story of Abelard's adversities.* Toronto: Pontifical Institute of Medieval Studies.

Murphy, J. J. (1974). *Rhetoric in the Middle Ages.* Berkeley: University of California Press.

Murray, A. (1978). *Reason and society in the Middle Ages.* Oxford: University Press.

Nelson, J. (1972). Society, theodicy and the origins of heresy: Towards a reassessment of the medieval evidence. *Studies in Church History, 9,* 65-77.

Newbold, R. F. (1979). Boundaries and bodies in late antiquity. *Arethusa, 12,* 93-114.

Newbold, R. F. (1981). Centre periphery and eye in the late Roman Empire. *Florilegium, 3,* 72-103.

Newbold, R. F. (1981-2). Perception and sensory awareness among Latin writers in late antiquity. *Classica et Medievalia, 33,* 169-190.

Newbold, R. F. (1984). Personality structure and response to adversity in early Christian hagiograhy. *Numen, 31,* 199ff.

Newbold, R. F. (1986). Non verbal communication and parataxis in late antiquity. *L'Antiquité Classique, 55,* 223-244.

Oldroyd, D. (1986). Grid/group analysis for historians of science. *History of Science, 24,* 145-171.

Paré, G., Brunet, A., & Tremblay, P. (1933). *La renaissance du XII* e *siécle: Les écoles et l'enseignement.* Ottawa: Institut d'Etudes Medievales d'Ottawa.

Patt, W. D. (1978). The early *ars dictaminis* as response to a changing society. *Viator, 9,* 135-155.

Peters, E. (1978). *The magician, the witch and the law.* Philadelphia: University of Pennsylvania Press.

Pike, J. B. (1938). *Frivolities of courtiers and footprints of philosophers.* Minneapolis: University of Minnesota Press.

Poole, R. L. (1920/1960). *Illustrations of the history of Medieval thought and learning,* 2nd ed. London: Constable.

Ralph, P. L. (1974). *The Renaissance in perspective.* London: Bell.

Rashdall, H. (1936, 1958). *The universities of Europe in the Middle Ages* (3 vols.). In F. M. Powicke and A. B. Emden (Ed.). Oxford: Oxford University Press.

Robinson, I. S. (1976). The *colores rhetorici* in the Investiture Contest. *Traditio, 32*, 209-238.

Rouse, R. H. & Rouse, M. A. (1979). *Preachers, florilegia and sermons: Studies on the manipulus florum of Thomas of Ireland.* Toronto: Pontifical Institute of Medieval Studies.

Salisbury, John of (1962). *Metalogikon.* (D. D. McGarry, Trans.). Berkeley: University of California Press.

Salisbury, John of (1979). *Policraticus: The statesman's book.*

Southern, R. W. (1970). *Medieval humanism and other studies.* Oxford: Blackwell.

Southern, R. W. (1979). *Platonism, scholastic method and the School of Chartres.* Reading: University of Reading Press.

Stiefel, T. (1985). *The intellectual revolution in twelfth-century Europe.* Croom Helm.

Stock, B. (1983). *The implications of literacy: Written language and models of interpretation in the eleventh and twelfth centuries.* Princeton, NJ: Princeton University Press.

Stock, B. (1984-85). Medieval literacy, linguistic theory and social organization. *New Literary History, 16*, 13-29.

Stone, D. M. (1988). *The* Mathematicus *of Bernard Silvestris.* Ph.D. Dissertation, University of Sydney.

Struever, N. (1983). Lorenzo Valla: Humanist rhetoric and the critique of the classical languages of morality. In J. J. Murphy (Ed.), *Renaissance eloquence: Studies in the theory and practice of Renaissance rhetoric*, pp. 191-206. University of California Press.

Tacchella, E. (1980). Giovanni di Salisbury e i Cornificiani. *Sandalion, 3*, 273-313.

Thomson, R. M. (1973). *Tractatus Garsiae or the translation of the relics of SS gold and silver.* Leiden: Brill.

Thomson, R. M. (1978). The origins of Latin satire in twelfth century Europe. *Mittellateinisches Jahrbuch, 13*, 78-79.

Thomson, R. M. (1980). The satirical works of Berengar of Poitiers: An edition with introduction. *Medieval Studies, 42*, 89-138.

Tilbury, Gervase of (1707). *Otia imperialia.* In G. G. Leibnitz (Ed.), *Scriptores Rerum Brunsvicensium I*, pp. 883-1006. Hannover.

Tobin, R. (1984). The Cornifician motif in John of Salisbury's *Metalogicon. History of Education, 13*, 1-6.

Turner, R. V. (1978). The *miles literatus* in twelfth and thirteenth century England: How rare a phenomenon? *American Historical Review, 83*, 928-945.

Turner, V. (1969). *The ritual process: Structure and anti-structure.* Chicago: Chicago University Press.

Turner, V. (1974). Liminal to Liminoid, in play, flow and ritual: an essay in comparative symbology. *Rice University Studies, 60*, 53-92.

Ullmann, W. (1969). *The Carolingian Renaissance and the idea of kingship.* London: Methuen.

Wallach, L. (1950). Onulf of Speyer: A humanist of the eleventh century. *Medievalia et Humanistica, 6*, 35-56.

Ward, J. O. (1972a). The date of the commentary on Cicero's *De inventione* by Thierry of Chartres (ca. 1095-1160?) and the Cornifician attack on the Liberal arts. *Viator, 3*, 219-273.

Ward, J. O. (1972b). *"Artificiosa Eloquentia"* in the Middle Ages. Ph.D Dissertation, University of Toronto.

Ward, J. O. (1978). The commentator's rhetoric: From antiquity to the Renaissance: Glosses and commentaries on Cicero's *Rhetorica*. In J. J. Murphy (Ed.), *Medieval eloquence: Studies in the theory and practice of medieval rhetoric*. Berkeley: University of California Press.

Ward, J. O. (1979). Gothic architecture, universities and the decline of the humanities in twelfth century Europe. In L. O. Frappell (Ed.), *Principalities powers and estates, studies in medieval and early modern government and society*. Adelaide: Adelaide University Union Press.

Ward, J. O. (1988). Magic and rhetoric from antiquity to the Renaissance: Some ruminations. *Rhetorica, 6*, 57-118.

Weber, M. (1964). The routinization of charisma and its consequences. *The Theory of Social and Economic Organization*. (A. M. Henderson, Trans. and Talcott Parsons, Ed.). New York: The Free Press.

Weimar, P. (Ed.). (1981). *Die renaissance der Wissenschaften im 12 Jahrhundert*. Zurich: Artemis Verlag.

Wetherbee, W. (1972). *Platonism and poetry in the twelfth century: The literary influence of the School of Chartres*. Princeton: Princeton University Press.

Wiesen, D. S. (1964). *St. Jerome as a satirist: A study in Christian Latin thought and letters*. Ithaca: Cornell University Press.

Wilks, M. (1977). Alan of Lille and the new man. *Studies in Church History, 14*, 137ff.

Williams, R. (1981). *Culture*. Glasgow: Fontana.

Witt, R. G. (1986). Boncompagno and the defense of rhetoric. *Journal of Medieval and Renaissance Studies, 16* 1-31.

8

Quintilian's Influence on the Teaching of Speaking and Writing in the Middle Ages and Renaissance

JAMES J. MURPHY

This chapter is a study of the promotion of literacy in the West. It is common today to regard any interest in noncontemporary works as merely "antiquarian" and therefore not worthy of modern attention. The notions of Auguste Comte and John Dewey, coupled with the native American pragmatism which de Toucqueville so admired more than a century ago, have led to a modern realism which has forged an admirably progressive society on this continent. A remarkably flexible Constitution has provided legal support that is enabling rather than restrictive. Yet, there is an American aphorism which declares that "there are no free lunches." Everything has a cost. Enthusiasm for the future has often led to the despising of the past. Concern for process can sometimes lead to rejection of experience.

In the field of writing instruction this has had a high cost. Some pragmatisms of the past are overlooked—not because they do not work, but because they are "of the past." It is probably accurate to say that such ideas are not *rejected*—since rejection implies consideration and deliberate choice—but are simply ignored. No serious chemist today would attempt to secure a federal grant to study phlogiston, it could be argued, so why bother to look into ideas about writing that are even older than Lavoisier? Nevertheless, writing instruction was carried on until fairly recently in a coordinated, systematic fashion, employing principles that were generally accepted throughout Western culture regardless of the language employed. That same mode still generally applies outside of North America, while to the wonderment of many European colleagues the system here has been first fragmented (Stewart, 1982), then factionalized (Berlin, 1981), and then finally allowed to evaporate into eclectic bits no longer qualifying as a viable program.

The radical inability of interested scholars to translate this older system into modern terms is at least one of the causes of this development. The comparative success of writers like E. P. J. Corbett and Frank D'Angelo demonstrates that translation is possible, but even a cursory look over the book exhibit area at any modern conference will also demonstrate that the vast majority of current composition authors are engaged in other types of approaches.

This is not the place to debate the virtues of pluralism versus consensus. Rather, this chapter proposes to set out the principles and processes of an earlier approach as typified by one of its principal adherents—the Roman educator Marcus Fabius Quintilianus—and to show how this system worked out over the first millennium and a half of his influence. This in turn may enable us to determine whatever values that system may have for modern writing. To do that we must first begin with the concept of *school*.

THE CONCEPT OF SCHOOL
IN ANCIENT GREECE AND ROME

Greek writers originated most of the ancient teaching methods, but it was the Romans who correlated them into a system. One of the first writers to argue that it was possible to transmit compositional skill systematically from one person to another was the Greek sophist Isocrates (436-338 B.C.). He declares that every person has a natural talent but that this talent needs to be enhanced by education and then concentrated by practice. While Isocrates did not leave us a formal manual outlining his principles, his ideas are laid out in two speeches, "Against the Sophists" and "Antidosis." It is clear that he used imitation of selected models as the core of his curriculum; this involved both the analysis of models—the evaluation of good and bad points of a text—and then the reconstitution or re-doing of the models by students in their own words. Memorization of models was also used as a means of cementing stylistic features in the student's mind. Isocrates (1954-1956) argues that this use of models not only teaches skills of form and language but also acquaints the students with a wide range of ideas found in the best models; thus he says that while virtue itself cannot be taught, students will see examples of virtue in histories or speeches of the past and will therefore have a better opportunity to be virtuous themselves. Moreover, he says, "I do think that the study of political discourse can help more than any other thing to stimulate and form such qualities of character" ("Against the Sophists," p. 22). When coupled with intensive practice in composition, both oral and written, the plan of Isocrates would produce men who "never speak without weighing their words" ("Antidosis," p. 293).

Other teachers of ancient Greece developed a wide range of teaching methods, among them the *progymnasmata* or graded composition exercises, yet for the most part their teaching was highly personalized. Gorgias of Leontini (485-380 B.C.), for example, apparently relied heavily on his own personal speaking ability to demonstrate before his pupils his theory that the sound patterns of oral language are persuasive by themselves, though he undoubtedly used models in connection with his dictum that "poetry is prose with meter." Socrates' method is especially individualized. The contributions of various Greek teachers have been studied extensively (e.g., Marrou, 1964; Russell, 1981). Plato's attack on writing ("Phaedrus," p. 275) would seem to indicate that his contemporaries were teaching writing skills as well as oral facility.

Isocrates' unique contribution, however, was the concept of what we now call *curriculum*. It is difficult to reconstruct every detail of his school, but the overriding principle is clear enough: that a set of particular activities is designed to achieve a given objective for a stated purpose. Methods are neither random nor pupil centered, but instead

are made into a patterned whole. This principle results in the establish-
ment of the pedagogical structure that depends not on the individual but
on the plan. (This same factor was responsible for the longevity of other
Greek "schools" based on philosophical systems, such as the Academy
following Plato or the Peripatetic tradition following Aristotle and
Theophrastus; these too were based on method rather than personality.)
For Isocrates, language is the essential element in effective citizenship.

His success is attested by several factors. One was that he was
accused of being rich—his "Antidosis" is ostensibly a defense against
this charge—and another was the fact that Aristotle apparently decided
to add a third book to his *Rhetoric* around 347 B.C. to counteract the
success of his rival across town in teaching about style and delivery.

But his greatest influence was to come much later, in Rome. The history of Hellenistic education—that is, for the period between Theophrastus
and about A.D. 100—is not completely known. What is clear is that by
the time of Cicero (born 106 B.C.) the Romans had evolved a coherent,
complex school system which was to operate with near uniformity
around the Western world for all of antiquity, which survived in substantial form throughout the Middle Ages, which inspired Renaissance
education with even greater enthusiasm, which continued into the
nineteenth century in America, and still persists into the twentieth in
Europe. Fragments continue in contemporary America unrecognized by
their users.

The concept of school had been well cemented into Roman culture
under the Republic nearly a hundred years before Christ, as even Cicero
attests, but under the Empire the support of schools became a matter of
public policy. Where the armies went, the schools went also to train the
young of the permanent garrisons all over the Roman world. Vespasian
(A.D. 9-79) was the first of many Emperors to grant subsidies and
special tax benefits to teachers, and municipalities throughout the
Empire followed suit.

The Romans were as systematic about schools as they were about
military and political matters. Henri Marrou observes that is it is fair to
use the term "system" to describe the homogeneous curriculum used for
hundreds of years. For example, the young Aurelius Augustinus was a
schoolmaster before he became a Christian and saint of the Church; he

describes in the late fourth century a teaching pattern that Cicero and Quintilian would have recognized.

The schools in fact survived the Empire itself. Under the Empire the parents of children in Cologne or York or Beirut or Marseilles could expect the same educational program available in Rome itself. Rome fell in A.D. 410, but many of the schools continued to function for a long time thereafter; for example, there is record of a Roman school in Marseilles as late as the sixth century. Eventually the barbarian invasions swept away the whole system of schools as the Romans had developed them.

But what is more important for the Middle Ages is the fact that the teaching methods of the Roman schools outlasted the schools themselves. The original purpose of the Roman schools was to prepare young men for public life, so the central subject was rhetoric. Grammatical study was a preparation for rhetoric. Perhaps the best description of the system is that of Marcus Fabius Quintilianus (c. A.D. 40-c. A.D. 95), one of the Rome's most successful teachers, and one of the first to be subsidized by the Emperors. His *On the Education of the Orator (De Institutione oratoria)* was published about A.D. 95 after a 20-year teaching career. The volume is divided into 12 books: two deal with elementary education, one with the continuing self-education of adults, one with the ideal orator, and the remaining books with the precepts of rhetoric divided into the traditional five parts of invention, arrangement, style, memory, and delivery.

The teaching methods described in the *Institutio* had been inherited from the Greeks, but had been systematized to a high degree by the Romans (Murphy, 1987). Quintilian describes five types of methods:

1. *Precept*: A set of rules that provide a definite method and system of speaking. Rhetoric as precept occupies 8 of the 12 books of the *Institutio oratoria*:
   a. Invention
   b. Arrangement
   c. Style
   d. Memory
   e. Delivery

2. *Imitation*: The use of models to learn how others have used language. Specific exercises:

   a. Reading aloud (*lectio*)

   b. Masters detailed analysis of a text (*praelectio*)

   c. Memorization of models

   d. Paraphrase of models

   e. Transliteration (prose/verse and/or Latin/Greek)

   f. Recitation of paraphrase or transliteration

   g. Correction of paraphrase or transliteration

3. *Composition exercises* (*progymnasmata* or *praexercitamenta*): A graded series of exercises in writing and speaking themes. Each succeeding one is more difficult, and incorporates what has been learned in preceding ones. The following 12 were common by Cicero's time:

   a. Retelling a fable

   b. Retelling an episode from a poet or a historian

   c. *Chreia*, or amplification of a moral theme

   d. Amplification of an aphorism (*sententia*) or proverb

   e. Refutation or confirmation of an allegation

   f. Commonplace, or confirmation of a thing admitted

   g. Encomium, or eulogy (or dispraise) of a person or thing

   h. Comparison of things or persons

   i. Impersonation (*ethologia, ethopoeia, prosopopeia*) or speaking or writing in the character of a given person

   j. Description, or vivid presentation of details

   k. Thesis, or argument for/against an answer to a general question (*quaestio infinita*) not involving individuals

   l. Laws, or arguments for or against a law

4. *Declamation* (*declamatio*), or fictitious speeches, in two types:

   a. *Suasoria*, or deliberative (political) speech arguing that an action be taken or not taken

   b. *Controversia*, or forensic (legal) speech prosecuting or defending a fictitious or historical person in a law case

5. *Sequencing*, or the systematic ordering of classroom activities to accomplish two goals:

   a. Movement, from the simple to the more complex

   b. Reinforcement, by reiterating each element of preceding exercises as each new one appears

Above all, Quintilian insists, this education in literacy must be carried on through the constant interrelation of writing, speaking, reading, and listening. Knowledge of precepts is not enough. He states this clearly in a famous passage at the beginning of Book Ten of the *Institutio oratoria*:

> But these rules of style, while part of the student's theoretical knowledge, are not in themselves sufficient to give him oratorical power. In addition he will require that assured facility (*facilitas*) which the Greeks call Habit. I know that many have raised the question as to whether this is best acquired by writing, reading, or speaking, and it would indeed be a question calling for serious consideration, if we could rest content with any one of the three. But they are so intimately and inseparably connected, that if one of them is neglected, we shall but waste the labour which we have devoted to the others. For eloquence will never attain its full development or robust health, unless it acquires strength by frequent practice in writing, while such practice without the models supplied by reading will be like a ship drifting aimlessly without a steersman.

Later in the same book he declares that "speaking makes writing easy; writing makes speaking precise." Since all reading of written texts was vocalized, of course, the injunction to "read" also meant to "hear the reading voice."

The ancient purpose of these methods, of course, was to prepare young men to be orators in public life—that is, to be public speakers in the forum, Senate, or law court. The training in writing, including the use of models for *imitatio*, was therefore not included for its own sake but was offered as an additional means of learning how to use language in speaking. The entire aim of the school program (to use Quintilian's term) was *facilitas*, or the ability to improvise appropriate language use in any speaking situation.

Nevertheless, writing was an integral part of the ancient program even if speaking was the ultimate objective. The composition exercises (*progymnasmata*) demanded increasingly complex skills as students progressed through them (Clark, 1957). It was the process of imitation (*imitatio*), however, that provided the elements of literary analysis as a preparation for the reapplication of a text's form or style by a student through paraphrase or transliteration.

The ancient process of imitation is much misunderstood today. But because its use continued in schools throughout the Middle Ages and into the Renaissance, and thus became an important segment of Western literary culture, any modern student of writing will need to understand this process. Imitation in the schools was divided into two main operations—first the analysis of a model text, than the reconstitution of the model in new language. As we have seen, each of these two operations had several aspects.

A famous example of the detailed analysis of a model text is that of the grammarian Priscian (c. A.D. 550), whose examination of the first 12 lines (72 words) of Virgil's *Aeneid* is so exhaustive that it covers 56 printed pages in the modern edition of Henry Keil. The object of such analysis in his *Partitiones duodecim versum Aeneides* is to uncover for the student every useful feature of content, organization, and style so that the student will know which features of the model should be included in his own paraphrase or transliteration. The process also introduces the student to matters of authorial intention and choice— why this word instead of that, why this structure or plan as against another. The opening section of Priscian's *Duodecim*, which is in catechism form, may illustrate the method:

Priscian, *On the First Twelve Lines of Virgil's Aeneid*

Scan the line:

Arma vi/rumque ca/no Tro/iae qui primus ab/oris
How many caesuras are there?
Two.
What are they?
The penthemimera and the hephthemimera [*semiquinaria, semiseptenaria,* Priscian says in his barbarous Latin].
Which is which?
The penthemimera is *Arma virumque cano,* and the hepthemimera *Arma virumque cano Troiae.*
How many "figures" has it?
Ten.
Why has it got ten?

Because it is made up of three dactyles and two spondees. [Priscianus takes no notice of the final spondee.]

How many words ["parts of speech"] are there?

Nine.

How many nouns?

Six—*Arma, Virum, Troiae, qui* [sic] *primus, oris.*

How many verbs?

One—*cano.*

How many prepositions?

One—*ab.*

How many conjunctions?

One—*que.*

Study each word in turn. Let us begin with *arma.* What part of speech is it?

A noun.

What is its quality?

Appellative.

What kind is it?

General.

What gender?

Neuter.

How do you know?

All nouns ending in -*a* in the plural are neuter.

Why is *arma* not used in the singular?

Because it means many different things. (Marrou, 1964, pp. 279-280)

This method, of course is simply carrying out the directions that Quintilian gives the grammarians. For instance, in *Institutio oratoria* I.8.13:

In lecturing on the poets, the grammarian must attend also to minor points. Thus, after taking a verse to pieces, he may require the parts of speech to be specified, and the peculiarities of the feet, which are necessary to be known, not merely for writing poetry, but even for prose composition. He may also distinguish what words are barbarous, or misapplied, or used contrary to the rules of language.

A medieval use of this method is pointed out by Saint Anselm, writing in the twelfth century to one of his monks staying for a time in Canterbury. Anselm urges him to "decline" at every opportunity:

I have learned that Dom Arnoul is giving you lessons. If this is so I am delighted; as you may have noticed, I have always wanted to see you make progress, and now I desire it more than ever. I have also heard that he excels in declensions; now, as you know, it has always been a hard chore for me to decline with children, and I am aware that in this science you made less progress with me than you should have. I send you, then, as my dearest son, this word of advice, this plea: everything you may read with him, or in any other way, apply yourself to declining it with care. And don't think you need to, as if you were just a beginner. For, with him, you are consolidating in yourself, as you hear them, things you already know, so as to remember them the more firmly; and, under his instruction, if you do make an error, you will correct it and learn what you do not as yet know. If he is not reading anything with you, and this through any negligence on your part, I am grieved; I want this done, and wish you to work at it as much as you can, particularly with regard to Virgil and the other authors whom you didn't read with me, avoiding those that contain any obscenity. If for some reason you are prevented from attending classes, make every effort to decline, as I have told you to do, completely from the beginning to the end with the utmost concentration and whenever you can, the greatest possible number of books you have already read. (Murphy, 1980, p. 168)

The key term in this passage, of course, is the word *decline*. What does Saint Anselm mean by it? Anselm, as the author of the famous *De grammatico* and a well-known teacher in his own right, would surely use any technical term as precisely as possible. Obviously the word means a great deal more than our narrow modern usage.

Dom Leclercq (1960) offers us this explanation: he defines *declinatio* as an oral explanation of the grammatical forms of the words in a given text. To "decline" then is to produce the "derived" forms of each word subject to varying inflections in the different moods, cases, numbers, and tenses. This declination in other words includes both what is called today "declension" and "conjugation."

Clearly this kind of close reading of a text—any text—could be applied as well to scripture. Richard and Mary Rouse have shown, for instance, that detailed verbal significations (*distinctiones*) found in Scripture became a useful tool for preachers; Beryl Smalley and others have discussed various modes of Scriptural exegesis, but the full impact of school-based methods on this exegesis remains to be explored. Arabic scholars from the eighth Christian century onward made an

explicit connection between grammatical analysis and the study of the
Koran, and devised school curricula specifically for this purpose; the
situation in the West was far more complex, especially after the rise of
universities with their professional schools of theology. To the extent
that large numbers of Europeans were introduced to textual analysis in
the mode inherited from Roman schools, that mode surely needs to be
considered as an element in the exegetical tradition.

Ultimately, of course, this kind of close textual analysis was intended
not for its own sake but as a preparation for future composition by the
student. The progymnastic program—graded exercises in a variety of
modes of composition—was easily coupled with the two steps of *imitatio*, namely the analysis of texts and the paraphrase/transliteration of
models. The effect was to inculcate a poetry without genres, and a prose
capable of many variations. As in the Roman schools, the objective was
to achieve *facilitas* by enlarging the creative capacity of the student,
regardless of the form or genre in which he was to work.

David Thomson (1979) has shown that even though medieval
schools taught a complex set of grammatical doctrines which underwent
significant theoretical changes over time, the basic elementary system
of Donatus and Priscian provided a continuity of instruction throughout
the Middle Ages. And when vernaculars began to flourish it was usually
the Latin grammar of Donatus and Priscian which became the model
for new grammars.

Unfortunately the history of visible changes in grammatical *doctrina*—
Realism, Nominalism, Speculative Grammar—have often obscured the
fundamental continuity of what actually went on in the classroom.
Young men first of all had to be brought from a vernacular base to some
level of Latin literacy—Latin was everywhere a second language (Murphy, 1980)—and then drilled in the various ways that language could
be used. The formal *praecepta* of grammar were of course a part of this
operation—the eight parts of speech, the declensions and conjugations,
and all the rest of the lore brought into the Middle Ages by Donatus and
Priscian and later refined by Alexandre de Villedieu. But the young
cannot learn from precepts alone.

All the available evidence indicates that medieval language instruction in the schools was based on a close, systematic analysis of

texts using methods inherited from ancient times. This analysis made composition possible. From the time of Bede to that of Boccaccio and Chaucer, and beyond that into the eras of Erasmus and Shakespeare, European youths learned the rudiments of language through a co-ordinated process of reading, derivation, recitation, imitation, and memorization.

It might be noted also that formal disputation (*disputatio*) was a feature of elementary language training until the end of the twelfth century, when the university curriculum began to take over the teaching of Aristotelian logic. William Fitzstephen, the biographer of Thomas Becket, describes a scene he witnessed in a London schoolyard in the year 1170:

> The scholars dispute, some in demonstrative rhetoric, others in dialectic. Some "hurtle enthymemes," others with greater skill employ perfect syllogisms. Boys of different schools strive against one another in verse, or contend concerning the principles of grammar, or the rules concerning past and future. There are others who employ the old art of the crossroads in epigrams, rhymes, and metre. (quoted in Orme, 1973, p. 131)

The boys he described are apparently 12 to 14. Another twelfth-century figure, Hugh of St. Victor, describes in his *On the Vanity of the World* a scene in which the youths study not only grammar but "dispute on graver matters and try to trip each other with twistings and impossibilities." But dialectical disputation soon became a university matter, and the study of logic generally disappeared from elementary instruction by the early thirteenth century. Aristotle's *Topics* and *On Sophistical Refutations* became the basic texts in dialectic at Paris with the official curriculum approved by Robert de Sorbonne in 1215, and in fact the process of oral *disputatio* became such an integral part of the classroom instruction at the university level that its use continued in some places into the eighteenth century. Paris, "The Mother of Universities," set the pattern for virtually every other foundation of the Middle Ages, and thus dialectic moved from the elementary curriculum into a permanent place as the organizing principle for higher studies. Law, medicine, and theology as well as the "arts" were all studied dialectically.

The impact of *disputatio* on medieval literature is yet to be assessed, but certainly the dialectical habit of contrariety—the constant matching of opposites—has a bearing on such literary forms as the dialogue and on certain "topics" of literary invention of the type discussed by Ernest R. Curtius in his *European Literature and the Latin Middle Ages* (1953). Aristotelian dialectic brought hundreds of topics (Greek *topoi*, Latin *loci*) to the attention of thousands of medieval university students, and it would not be surprising to find these ideas influencing the literary culture of the period. Nevertheless, there has been little direct investigation of this phenomenon. Curtius points to the use of topics by theologians—not surprising, since theologians were by definition university trained—but four decades after his suggestive study the subject of literary influence remains largely unexplored. What remains after the twelfth century, then, is a pattern of schooling which is "grammatical" in the sense that medieval writers understood that term. It is an education in literacy.

It must be remembered that in ancient times the grammatical/rhetorical education of the schools achieved its ends through a combination of reading, speaking, listening, and writing. Saint Augustine argues in his *De doctrina christiana* (A.D. 426) that this system of linguistic training should be employed for understanding the language of Scripture, and for transmitting the Christian message to others based on that understanding. His argument was decisive, in that it legitimized Christian use of pagan educational processes. Training for public oratory was no longer to be the central concern of schools, of course, but the language-skill base that was originally designed to support oratory proved to be equally valuable for the quite different purposes of Christian schoolmasters whether in monastery, parish, or cathedral schools of the Middle Ages.

The medieval "grammar" school therefore offered a great deal more than the simple *doctrina* of the eight parts of speech named by Donatus and Priscian. About 1174, Matthew of Vendome (1980) criticizes some students because "In school exercises (*in scolastico exercitio*) they grind out stories, ransacking poems word for word for images, just as if they were setting out to write a verse commentary upon their authors" (*Ars versificatoria* IV.1). In that single sentence of Matthew's there is a wealth of information about medieval teaching. Clearly there are verse models being analyzed, and the students are asked to present compositions based on the models—the double process of analysis and reconstitution which the ancients called *imitatio*. It is taken for granted that exercise (*exercitio*) is well known, and in fact so well known that Matthew assumes that his readers will recognize the progymnasmatic sequence that is involved. His *Ars versificatoria* is a book for teachers, not for students, so complete enumeration of the obvious is not necessary. If we were able to re-create the daily regimen in Matthew's classroom it would undoubtedly reveal a pattern which would have been familiar to ancient teachers like Quintilian and Augustine; no doubt, too, poets like Horace and Virgil would recognize the ways in which they were made acquainted with form and genre so they could later set forth on their own creative activity.

Perhaps the most frequently quoted medieval description of this learning process is that of John of Salisbury in his *Metalogicon* (1159). Even though some scholars have argued that the schooling described by John is peculiar to twelfth-century France and therefore cannot be treated as typical of the Middle Ages as a whole, virtually every other surviving record of classroom work down into the seventeenth century shows substantially the same methodological pattern. Henry Osborne Taylor (1949) translates the passage as follows:

> This method was followed by Bernard of Chartres, *exundissimus modernis temporibus fons litterarum in Gallia*. By citations from the authors he showed what was simple and regular; he brought into relief the grammatical figures, the rhetorical colours, the artifices of sophistry, and pointed out how the text in hand bore upon other studies; not that he sought to teach everything in a single session, for he kept in mind the capacity of his audience. He inculcated correctness and propriety of diction, and a fitting use of congruous figures. Realizing that practise strengthens memory and sharpens faculty, he urged his pupils to imitate what they had heard, inciting some by admonitions, others by whipping and penalties. Each pupil recited the next day something from what he had heard on the preceding. The evening exercise, called the *declinatio*, was filled with such an abundance of grammar that any one, of fair intelligence, by attending it for a year, would have at his fingers' ends the art of writing and speaking, and would know the meaning of all words in common use.

But since no day and no school ought to be vacant of religion, Bernard would select for study a subject edifying to faith and morals. The closing part of this *declinatio*, or rather philosophical recitation, was stamped with piety: the souls of the dead were commended, a penitential Psalm was recited, and the Lord's Prayer. For those boys who had to write exercises in prose or verse, he selected the poets and orators, and showed how they should be imitated in the linking of words and the elegant ending of passages. If any one sewed another's cloth into his garment, he was reproved for the theft, but usually was not punished. Yet Bernard gently pointed out to awkward borrowers that whoever imitated the ancients (*majores*) should himself become worthy of imitation by posterity. He impressed upon his pupil the virtue of economy, and the values of things and words: he explained where a meagreness and tenuity of diction was fitting, and where copiousness or even excess should be allowed, and the advantage of due measure everywhere. He admonished them to go through the histories and poems with diligence, and daily to fix passages in their memory. He advised them, in reading, to avoid the superfluous, and confine themselves to the works of distinguished authors. For, he said (quoting from Quintilian) that to follow out what every contemptible person has said, is irksome and vainglorious, and destructive of the capacity which should remain free for better things. To the same effect he cited Augustine, and remarked that the ancients thought it a virtue in a grammarian to be ignorant of something. But since in school exercises nothing is more useful than to practise what should be accomplished by the art, his scholars wrote daily in prose and verse, and proved themselves in discussions. (vol. 2, pp. 157-158)

It will be noted that both prose and verse are practiced. Actually, rhythmics in both prose and verse was also taught. When John of Garland wrote what he considered a compendious treatment of writing in the 1220s, he titled it *De arte prosaica, metrica, et rithmica*. Also, rhythmical language was important both to the art of letter-writing (*ars dictaminis*) and to the art of preaching (*ars praedicandi*), but as an alternate mode of composition rhythmics naturally was important as well to the schoolmasters engaged in acquainting their students with manifold types of composition.

About 1160, Peter of Blois, in writing to a friend about the education of the friend's sons, quotes Quintilian directly several times, then adds this personal note about the value of doing imitative exercises in both verse and prose :

I know that it was of great use to me that, when as a boy I was trained in the art of versification, at the suggestion of the master I took my material not from fables but true history. It was of advantage to me that as an adolescent I was forced to memorize the letters of Hildebert of Le Mans, noted for their elegant style and suave urbanity. Besides certain other books which are celebrated in the schools, it was advantageous to me to inspect frequently Trogus Pompeius, Josephus, Suetonius, Egesippus, Quintus Curtius, Cornelius Tacitus, Titus Livius, who will insert in their histories much for the edification of morals and the perfecting of literary style. I read others too who do not deal with history, whose number is legion, in all whom the diligence of moderns can pluck flowers as it were in a fragrant garden and make for itself the honey of suave urbane speech. (Thorndike, 1944, p. 17)

This combination continues throughout the Middle Ages. In England the codification of teaching practice into statutory form reveals the longevity of the system. In 1308, for example, candidates for the M.A. degree in grammar at Oxford were required by statute to pass an examination in the writing of both verse and prose (*de modo versificandi et prosandi*). Both Oxford and Cambridge created a Faculty of Grammar; one statute from Oxford around 1344 provides another revealing insight into specific teaching exercises which the schoolmasters were expected to administer:

Every fortnight they [i.e., the students] must present verses and prose compositions (*literas*) put together with fitting words, not swollen or half a yard long, and with rhythmical sentences (*clausulae*) concise and appropriate, displaying metaphors, and, as much as possible, replete with *sententiae*; which verses and compositions, those who are given the task should write on parchment on the next free day or before, and then on the following day when they return to school they must recite them by heart to the master, and hand in their writings. (Anstey, 1868, vol. 2, p. 437)

This echo of Quintilian is a far more arduous program than many modern readers would expect of a medieval school, but it reveals once more the writing-directed nature of instruction which goes far beyond basic grammatical doctrine. Samuel Jaffe has shown that this kind of teaching tradition continued into the fifteenth century in Germanic areas, while in Italy the teachers of the *ars dictaminis* commonly make grammar their parallel subject—and the typical pairing of model letter collections with treatises on *dictamen* indicates a teaching process analogous to the use of literary models in other fields. France, of course, was the home of the major *artes poetriae* that most clearly demonstrate the use of the teaching methods under discussion. Again, the continuity of teaching method is evident. "At the heart of the system," as one recent study (Murphy, 1980) has observed, "is a program of Christian (or Christianized) *progymnasmata*" (p. 172).

A final evidence of this set of learning exercises is the survival (Murphy, 1980) of a number of manuscript collections that can only be described as "teaching anthologies." These were anthologies for the teachers, not the students. It is important to note that the concept of *textbook* as we know it today is a product of the post-printing, mass production period. In ancient and medieval times any text under discussion was first listened to by the students, then studied orally word-for-word under the direction of the master; during the Middle Ages this was true even at the university level, where the master's reading aloud (*lectio*) was followed by his oral commentary and his listing of *quaestiones* for disputation. It was all the more true at the elementary level, for the simple reason that any book was by modern standards enormously expensive. A single book, as one modern scholar has observed, could cost an entire herd of sheep for the parchment on which to write it. As a consequence, medieval students at all levels relied on memory of oral language to an extent difficult for many modern readers to comprehend. The medieval classroom could not afford a written text for every student. Reading was oral, instruction was oral, analysis was oral—and the written compositions in verse or prose which resulted from classroom exercises were vocalized by the reader so that the ear as well as the eye took in the form of language used.

Under these circumstances it was clearly useful for the teacher to have available a set of models to present in the classroom for study and imitation. Bruce Harbert (1975) has edited one such anthology from the thirteenth century. It is a Glasgow manuscript compiled between 1200 and 1230, containing treatises on verse writing by Matthew of Vendome, Gervase of Melkley, and Geoffrey of Vinsauf, together with 49 poems on a variety of topics and in a number of genres. Some poems seem to illustrate specific doctrines from the treatises, such as the use of particular figures or tropes, while others seem to have no immediate relationship to the accompanying treatises. The whole collection is evidently designed for the kind of instruction common in medieval schools. Brother S. Bonaventure has shown in an article in *Medieval Studies* (1961) that this practice of compilation continued into the fourteenth and fifteenth century in England at least. It is certainly possible that other medieval collections of literary materials, though apparently random, may have been compiled for the same instructional purposes.

The verse-writing manuals of the Middle Ages—the so-called "arts of poetry"—thus grew out of the practical teaching situation, which coordinated rather carefully a set of teaching methods inherited from ancient times and refined over many centuries of experience. These treatises were not composed in isolation. The recognition of the fundamental continuity of this methodology must be a major factor in any modern attempt to understand the literary infrastructure of the Middle Ages. For one thing, it would be difficult to understand the *artes poetriae* without also understanding the role they played within the system. Most importantly, though, any appreciation of a medieval writer in either Latin or vernacular surely must include some consideration of that writer's use of the resources available to him or her. Petrarch was not born literate, nor was Froissart, nor Gottfrey von Strassburg, nor Chaucer. In some way each had to acquire that level of linguistic capability which would enable him to exercise his genius. Schools were one generally available avenue for that linguistic development; private instruction was certainly another. Self-instruction through reading, and through practice in writing, was certainly possible—but likely only after a certain level of capacity was reached. In any case these questions need to be asked about any medieval author if we are to appreciate fully how the basic skills developed into literary artistry.

The continuity of teaching methodology during the Middle Ages is further demonstrated by the appearance of six Latin teaching manuals usually called "Arts of Poetry" today even though most of them deal with prose as well as poetry. They were all written in France, between

1175 and 1280. The most famous was the *New Poetics* (*Poetria nova*) of Geoffrey of Vinsauf (1971), published in the early thirteenth century. It survives in nearly 200 manuscripts (Woods, 1985), a number indicating long-lasting and widespread popularity. Geoffrey (1971) provides detailed advice on such matters as beginnings and endings, arrangement of parts, amplification and abbreviation, and ornaments of style, highlighted by the much-quoted passage with which he begins his introduction:

> If a man has a house to build, his hand does not rush, hasty, into the very doing: the work is first measured out with his heart's inward plumb line, and the inner man marks out a series of steps beforehand, according to a definite plan; his heart's hand shapes the whole before it is an actuality. Poetry herself may see in this analogy what law must be given to poets: let not the hand rush toward the pen, nor the tongue be on fire to utter a word.

Geoffrey and other schoolmasters like Matthew of Vendome and John of Garland clearly participate in the basic teaching methods inherited from ancient Rome. Gallo (1971) has in fact identified a number of passages in Geoffrey's *New Poetics* that he traces directly to Quintilian. For the most part, however, the medieval masters do not acknowledge Quintilian as a source; this is not surprising, given the homogeneity of teaching methods that had long since lost any visible connection with a particular author.

Moreover, copies of Quintilian's *Institutio oratoria* were extremely rare during the Middle Ages, and in fact the only version known at all to medieval writers was the so-called *textus mutilatus*, which had huge gaps and could not easily be understood as a coherent whole.

By the end of the Middle Ages, then, it was clear that the basic teaching methods survived even though their Roman background was not generally recognized. The pragmatic value of efficient instruction was great enough by itself, with no need to seek sources in Quintilian or anyone else. Nevertheless the influence was there, even if not identified. As Clark has pointed out: "The medieval grammar school, at least at its best, was as solidly based on Quintilian as was the renovated educational procedures of The Renaissance" (1948, p. 165).

QUINTILIAN IN THE RENAISSANCE

This situation changed dramatically in September, 1416, when the Italian humanist Poggio Bracciolini discovered a complete copy of the *Institutio oratoria* stored away in the basement of a monastery in St. Gall, Switzerland. He was apparently the first person in nearly 500 years to see a complete copy of the text. His excitement was matched by other humanists like Leonardo Aretino, who wrote Poggio an enthusiastic letter about his discovery:

> We have now the entire treatise, of which before this happy discovery, we had only one half, and that in a very mutilated state. Oh, what a valuable acquisition! What an unexpected pleasure! Shall I then behold Quintilian whole and entire, who, even in his imperfect state, was so rich a source of delight? I entreat you, my dear Poggio, send me the manuscript as soon as possible, that I may see it before I die. (Murphy, 1974, p. 359)

Suddenly, with the rediscovery of the complete Quintilian, there was a humane and comprehensive rationale for an educational program that had lasted for more than a thousand years simply because it worked. Now there was careful justification for the relation between writing, reading, and speaking; justification for the relation of rhetoric to education; justification for the complex patterns of *progymnasmata* and declamation; justification for the process of imitation; above all, justification for making the educational process a programmed sequence in which all the parts played a carefully planned role. In must have been fascinating for the humanists to note Quintilian's usual practice of presenting alternative views to each subject before declaring his own belief—a practice certainly consistent with the reflective habits of the day.

The history of Quintilian's influence in the Renaissance has not yet been written. Perhaps this is because the data is simply overwhelming— every cultural historian cites evidence of his importance—or perhaps because of the opposite reason that no historian has yet made the decision that Quintilian is important enough to warrant the herculean effort that would be required. Moreover, historians of rhetoric like

Howell (1956) deal only with Quintilian's theories, and not his educational program. It is easy enough to cull out citations from any century and any country, but for our purposes it will be necessary to focus on the writing-speaking process and to argue that some specific examples will demonstrate the ubiquity of Quintilianistic ideas in the Renaissance. Since England was the educational parent of America—for example, the founders of what is now Harvard sent to Cambridge for their masters—English examples may be best.

Donald Lemen Clark's *Milton at Saint Paul's School* (1948) provides an interesting set of examples for seventeenth-century England. "The English grammar school," Clark declares, "was firmly based on Quintilian" (p. 132). The poet John Milton went through exactly the same curriculum described by Quintilian and carried on throughout the Middle Ages and into the Renaissance. "The exercises which Milton practiced at St. Paul's School," according to Clark, "were essentially the same as those practiced by every Roman boy from Cicero to Boethius" (p. 128). Clark describes in detail the ways in which Milton learned to write through imitation, *progymnasmata*, and the other means so long employed throughout Europe.

It is especially noteworthy in Milton's case that despite the influence of Ramism and the use of some Ramistic texts at St. Paul's, the Quintilianistic program still held sway. Peter Ramus had in fact written a book in 1549 attacking Quintilian, and made his rejection of Aristotle, Cicero, and Quintilian the basis of his educational "reforms"; nevertheless the pedagogical continuity was apparently so strong that English schools could absorb Ramism and still follow Quintilian (Murphy & Newlands, 1986).

The example of Milton is worth citing first because it demonstrates that the influence of Quintilian was long-lived in England, the poet's experiences at St. Paul's coming a full two centuries after Poggio's discovery at St. Gall. Earlier in England, the story is the same. T. W. Baldwin (1944) has collected a number of passages dealing with teaching; at Shrewsbury School about 1561 the master ordained that students should submit speaking and writing exercises regularly and "declaim" in dramas:

> Every Thursdaie the Schollers of the first forme before they goo to plaie shall for exercise declame and plaie one act of a comedie, and every Satterdaie versifie, and against Mondaie morning ensuinge geve upp their themes or epistles, and all othe exercises of writinge or speakinge shalbe used in latten. (Baldwin, 1944, vol. 1, p. 389)

The Shrewsbury citation points up another element often overlooked—namely, that memorization for recitation was an important part of language acquisition. Both models and original compositions were so memorized. This process, it will be recalled, is seen in Quintilian in the first century, Saint Augustine in the fourth, John of Salisbury in the twelfth, the Oxford grammar masters in the fourteenth, and is still seen here in the sixteenth.

Memorization also reminds us that the spoken voice in imitation continued to be ancillary to the written word. Richard Mulcaster's *Positions* (1581) points out the value of Quintilian for both writing and speaking:

> Quintilianes rule is very true, and the verie best, and alway to be observed in chusing writers for children to learne, to pick out such as will feede the wit and the fairest stuffe, and fine the tongue with neatest speach. (Baldwin, 1947, p. 175)

Imitation itself retains the full flavor of the Quintilianistic school. William Kempe's *The Education of Children* (1588) specifies that children should be turned loose in due course to do their own composition after learning the various modalities through imitation of authors:

> Now, when the Scholler hath been a while exercised in this kinde of imitation, sometime in prose, sometime in verse, let him assay otherwhiles, without an example of imitation, what he can do alone by his own skill alreadie gotten by the precepts and the two former sorts of practice. (Baldwin, 1944, vol. 1, p. 447)

This regime is all the more significant because it is imbedded in a thoroughly Ramistic curriculum that rearranged which subjects should be called "rhetoric" and which "dialectic," but which for all practical purposes succeeded only in adding syllogisms to the list of linguistic forms that students were asked to look for in a text, and in reinvigorating the study of tropes and figures.

So pervasive is the influence of Quintilian in English grammar schools of the period that the noted Shakespearean scholar T. W. Baldwin (1944) devotes an entire chapter of his study of the poet's education (*Smalle Latine and Lesse Greeke*) to "The Rhetorical Training of Shakespeare: Quintilian the Supreme Authority" (pp. 197-238). He notes specific passages in certain plays that he links to Quintilian's *Institutio oratoria*.

We do not yet have a full account of the role of Quintilian's ideas in the major educational treatises of the English Renaissance, works like Roger Acham's *Scholemaster* or Sir Thomas Elyot's *The Boke of the Governour*. Continental works are, of course, so heavily involved in Renaissance English cultural life that such a study would have to include the notions of writers like the German Philip Melanchthon, with his praise of Quintilian's educational program for the new Lutheran regime.

Quintilian shows up frequently as well in sixteenth-century university lectures. Gabriel Harvey's *Rhetor* (1577), based on two Cambridge lectures of 1575, ranks him with Cicero: "Further, let us read Cicero and Quintilian, that is, our leaders and oratorical heroes" (Chandler, 1978, p. 78). (Harvey immediately adds a recommendation for reading Ramus, apparently unaware of Ramus' 1549 assault on Quintilian in his *Rhetoricae distinctiones in Quintilian*; the pairing of Ramus and Quintilian undoubtedly would have been less likely if Harvey had known the book published earlier in Paris.) In Oxford at almost exactly the same time (1573) John Rainold's lectures on the *Rhetoric* of Aristotle—never published, and rediscovered only recently by Lawrence Green—are studded with references to Quintilian, especially when Rainold compares the theories of various ancient writers with those of Aristotle; again, Rainold does not mention the attack of Ramus on Quintilian, even though he comments that Ramus was moved "to assail Aristotle perhaps a little too sharply" (Green, 1986, p. 181).

No doubt examples from other countries could be located without much difficulty. The German Erasmus Sarcer (Dyck, 1983), the French Etienne Dolet (Meerhoff, 1986), the Italian Gasparino Barizza

(Murphy, 1984)—to name some obvious personages—all knew and respected Quintilian's views. In fact, Marc Fumaroli (1980) has observed that Ramus' 1549 attack on Quintilian may have aroused French humanists to what he calls "exceptional interest" (*l'exceptionnel interet*) in Quintilian (p. 733). By the time Ramus printed his attack, 80 years after its first edition, the *Institutio* had already gone through an even 100 editions in seven countries. Even the Hebrew-language *The Book of the Honeycomb's Flow* (*Sepher Nopheth Suphim*) of Judah Messer Leon (1475/1983) ranks Quintilian with Cicero and Aristotle as an authority.

Most modern investigations of Quintilian's influence during the Renaissance have been for the purpose of determining his possible effect on the composition of poetry or other fictional literature. This of course was the motivation for Baldwin's *Shakespeare's Smalle Latine and Lesse Greeke* (1944), which to this day remains the best collection of English sources for teaching in the English renaissance. More recent studies like those of Kinney (1986) and Sloane (1984) continue the same interests. The same is true of Fumaroli (1980) and Meerhoff (1986) for France. As a consequence we still lack a direct, comprehensive study of the teaching itself. Such a study would be an extremely valuable contribution to our knowledge of instructional methods in a period that had such immense effects on the shape of American colonial education.

CONCLUSION

When a modern reader looks over the history of education from Roman times to, say, the year A.D. 1700, a clear pattern can be seen in respect to the teaching of speaking and writing. In ancient times, the typical Roman learning processes outlined by Quintilian were transmitted throughout the known world through the mechanism of schools. In the Middle Ages the processes continued, though usually without reference to Quintilian as a source; the pragmatic success of the methods was sufficient for continuity. With the rediscovery of the text of the *Institutio oratoria* by Poggio in 1416, there was again a sophisticated rationale for what had worked well for so long; moreover, there was ample ground for sweeping reforms in those areas of education that had become sterile and mechanistic in the late Middle Ages. Quintilian thus became a benchmark in the reaction of humanists against "scholasticism."

The full story of Quintilian's place in this movement remains to be told. Thus this is a preliminary account of the systematic use of precept, imitation, *progymnasmata*, and declamation in a sequenced program, using interrelated modes—speaking, reading, writing—to make literacy possible throughout Europe for a millenium and a half. The full history of this development, and of its sequel into our own times, would seem to be a valuable objective for anyone interested in learning the best ways to promote the teaching of speaking and writing in our own times.

REFERENCES

Anstey, H. (Ed.). (1868). *Munimenta academica, or documents illustrative of academical life and studies at Oxford* (2 vols.). London: Rolls Series.

Baldwin, T. W. (1944). *William Shakespeare's small Latine and lesse Greeke* (2 vols.). Urbana: University of Illinois Press.

Baldwin, T. W. (1947). *Shakespere's five-act structure*. Urbana: University of Illinois Press.

Berlin, J. A. (1987). *Rhetoric and reality: Writing instruction in American colleges, 1900-1985*. Carbondale: Southern Illinois University Press.

Chandler, M. C. (1978). *Gabriel Harvey's "rhetor": A translation and critical edition*. Unpublished Ph.D. dissertation, University of Missouri.

Clark, D. L. (1948). *Milton at St. Paul's school*. New York: Columbia University Press.

Clark, D. L. (1957). *Rhetoric in Greco-Roman education*. New York: Columbia University Press.

Curtius, E. (1953). *European literature and the Latin Middle Ages*. New York: Pantheon Books.

Dyck, J. (1983). The first German treatise on homiletics: Erasmus Sarcer's *Pastorale* and classical rhetoric. In J. J. Murphy (Ed.), *Renaissance eloquence: Studies in the theory and practice of Renaissance rhetoric* (pp. 221-237). Berkeley: University of California Press.

Fumaroli, M. (1980). *L'age d'eloquence: Rhétorique et "res literaria" de la Renaissance au seuil de l'epoque classique*. Geneve: Droz.

Gallo, E. A. (1971). *The Poetria Nova and its sources in early rhetorical doctrine*. The Hague: Mouton.

Green, L. D. (Ed. and Trans.). (1986). *John Rainolds's Oxford lectures on the rhetoric of Aristotle*. Newark: University of Delaware Press.

Harbert, B. (1975). *A thirteenth century anthology*. Toronto: University of Toronto Press.

Howell, W. S. (1956). *Logic and rhetoric in England, 1500-1700*. Princeton, NJ: Princeton University Press.

Isocrates (1954-1956). *Isocrates*. (G. Norlin, Trans., 3 vols.) Cambridge, MA: Harvard University Press.

Kinney, A. F. (1986). *Humanist poetics: Thought, rhetoric, and fiction in sixteenth-century England*. Amherst: University of Massachusetts Press.

Leon, J. M. (1983). *The book of the Honeycomb's Flow, Sepher Nopheth Suphim first published at Mantua, 1475/76*. (I. Rabinowitz, Trans.). Ithaca, NY: Cornell University Press.

Marrou, H. I. (1964). *A history of education in antiquity*. New York: New American Library.

Meerhoff, K. (1986). *Rhétorique et poétique au XVIᵉ siècle en France: Du Bellay, Ramus et les autres*. Leiden: Brill.

Murphy, J. J. (1974). *Rhetoric in the Middle Ages: A history of rhetorical theory from Saint Augustine to the Renaissance*. Berkeley: University of California Press.

Murphy, J. J. (1980). The teaching of Latin as a second language in the 12th Century. *Historiographia Linguistica, 7*, 159-175.

Murphy, J. J. (1984). Rhetoric in the earliest years of printing, 1456-1500. *Quarterly Journal of Speech, 70*, 1-11.

Murphy, J. J. (1987). *Quintilian on the teaching of speaking and writing*. Carbondale: Southern Illinois University Press.

Murphy, J. J. (Ed.), & Newlands, C. (Trans.). (1986). *Arguments in rhetoric against Quintilian: Translation and text of Peter Ramus's Rhetoricae distinctiones in Quintilianum (1549)*. Dekalb: Northern Illinois University Press.

Murphy, J. J. (1990). Roman education as described by Quintilian. In J. J. Murphy (Ed.), *A short history of writing instruction* (pp. 9-76). Davis, CA: Hesmagoras.

Orme, N. (1973). *English schools in the Middle Ages*. London: Methuen.

Russell, D. A. (1981). *Criticism in antiquity*. Berkeley: University of California Press.

Sloane, T. O. (1985). *Donne, Milton, and the end of humanistic rhetoric*. Berkeley: University of California Press.

Stewart, D. C. (1982). Two model teachers and the Harvardization of English departments. In J. J. Murphy (Ed.), *The rhetorical tradition and modern writing*. New York: The Modern Language Association.

Taylor, H. O. (1949). *The Medieval mind* (2 vols.). New York: Columbia University Press.

Thomson, D. (1979). *A descriptive catalogue of Middle English grammatical texts*. New York: Garland.

Thorndike, L. (Trans.). (1944). *University records and life in the Middle Ages*. New York: Norton.

Vendome, M. (1980). *The art of versification*. (A. E. Gaylon, Trans.). Ames: Iowa State University Press.

Vinsauf, G. (1971). The new poetics (*Poetria nova*.) (J. B. Kopp, Trans.). In J. J. Murphy (Ed.), *Three medieval rhetorical arts* (pp. 27-108). Berkeley: University of California Press.

Woods, M. C. (Ed.). (1985). *An early commentary on the Poetria Nova of Geoffrey of Vinsauf*. New York: Garland.

9

L'Enseignement de l'art de la première rhétorique: Rhetorical Education in France Before 1600

ROBERT W. SMITH

Scholars have spent a great deal of time on the theory and practice of French rhetoric, but relatively little on the teaching of it. Though the French pulpit in particular has captured the interest of innumerable scholars and writers, the classroom enterprise has germinated little curiosity. Yet France has as rich a rhetorical heritage as any other modern nation in the western world, a tradition with significant implications for both speaking and writing. The intellectual impact of oral and written rhetoric is particularly evident in the history of French education. Social, political, and religious forces shaped—and were in turn shaped by—the pedagogical development of both oral and written rhetoric. The impact of literacy, as will be apparent, is rooted in the evolving sophistication of popularization of the formal study of oral discourse. This chapter examines classroom rhetoric in France from Roman times to the dawn of the modern era (1600), focusing on the theory and teaching of spoken discourse (*la rhétorique*) and its relationship to writing (Jasinski, 1965; Langlois, 1902; Patterson, 1935)[1]; for in French culture, whether ancient, medieval, or renaissance, the one always led to the other. Understanding this complex interaction of orality and literacy requires not only being sensitive to the concurrent,

184

confluent forces of society and culture but the historical factors that institutionalized their study.

EDUCATIONAL DEVELOPMENT IN
ANCIENT FRANCE, PARTICULARLY GAUL

With Julius Caesar's conquest of France in the Gallic Wars (58-51 B.C.), Latin culture, education, and rhetorical training soon followed the troops, notably in Gaul. Here local inhabitants had a natural bent for eloquence; here the most and best Latin inscriptions are found (Haarloff, 1920); and here strong rhetorical schools thrived. Tacitus, in his *Dialogues*, made all his speakers Gaulists (expect Vipstanus Messalla), while Suetonius (1970) and Ausonius (1919-1921) devoted much time and space to the area's teachers. Ancient travelers found rhetorical schools in Bordeaux, Narbonne, Arles, and Toulouse, and good schools they were, as well-paid and respected faculty turned out educated young men (Haarloff, 1920).

The next few hundred years saw both growth and decline. Literary clubs of the second century influenced the rhetorical schools and perpetuated the methods of rhetoricians, but in the third century the barbarian invasion, Caracalla's troops, the emperor's distaste for literature, and civil unrest brought a decline in the schools. Fourth-century Gaul's *l'âge d'or de l'éloquence chrétienne* saw the apogee of rhetorical training in Roman France, particularly in the flourishing city of Bordeaux. Latin dominated the classroom, but here and there the local vernacular made inroads, much to the relief of teenage lads who struggled with the Empire's *lingua franca* six hours a day. A new Bordeaux, one more interested in education, saw rhetoric prosper not only because of the area's interest in the spoken word but also due to the popularity of such preachers as Hilary and Pictavium, both of Poiters, whose *éclat* highlighted public discourse, leading to demands for materials and teachers to improve the oral skills of gentlemen-students in a milieu dominated by orality (Théry, 1958; Haarloff, 1920).

Gallic rhetorical training, following the pattern set forth in Quintilian's *Institutio oratoria*—grammar in the first cycle, rhetoric in the second—led Gaul's professors to read historical and rhetorical works, particularly those of Cicero. They instructed in matters of cause-effect, proofs, divisions of the discourse, style, memory, and, when appropriate, delivery. Style, in the fourth century, played a prominent part in rhetorical education (Haarloff, 1920), though the *digressio* permitted lecturers, like their modern American counterparts, to teach law, history, and moral values, all of which both they and the ancients believed essential for the educated person. The grounding of rhetorical education, a system inherited from antiquity, became the basis for the evolving study and dissemination of literacy within a Christian culture.

In the following century (that of Attila the Hun) as the number of Christian schools increased, the number of pagan rhetorical schools declined, though such nominal Christians as Ausonius (1919-1921) seemed to find no contradiction between their faith and their rhetorical education. Unfortunately, we process neither titles of Bordeauxian declamations nor other classroom data. Why this lack of information? Perhaps teachers and students saw their practice as so much a part of their lives as to merit no special mention, much the way that twentieth-century basketball practice receives little notice in contemporary American high school newspapers. Or perhaps the damp climate could not easily preserve scripted papers. Yet Ausonius (d. 395) mentions about forty *rhetores* and *grammatici* in Bordeaux—no mean roster for one city and for one author to know. Clearly young students need not have depended on the vagaries of trial and error as they sought to understand rhetorical principles.

Elsewhere we know of such teachers as Julianus Pomerius (at Arles), a rhetorician-dialectician who seems to have devoted more time to interpreting Scripture than to teaching the spoken word; of Sapaudus the Gallic orator; and Loup in Agen and Péregueux (Migne; Roger, 1905). All these individuals (and many others like them) probably taught the same classical theory (grammar, rhetoric, and logic), but whether they instructed in private schools run by others or in their own halls and how they went about their work remains a mystery. We do suspect, however, that classical and postclassical authors looked at the *vir bonus* doctrine, the three genera of speeches, the five offices of the speaker, and the six parts of the oration. They said little, however, about delivery (van Ringelbergh, 1545).

Thus, rhetoric as a discipline and tool both waxed and waned from the Caesarean conquest to the fall of the western Empire. Its total commitment to Latin expedited the importation of classical works, particularly those of Cicero, while the early arrival of Christianity— with its emphasis on proclamation—provided an impetus for young men to learn to speak effectively. The importance of oral discourse is understandable in a culture dominated by oral modes of communication. What is not as immediately apparent, however, is that the refinement of principles of effective oral presentation would serve as the precepts for literacy. Nonetheless, the yo-yo history of the rhetorical period, at times problematic, at times assured, would surface again in the 900 years that followed.

MEDIEVAL RHETORIC IN FRANCE: WRITING IN THE SERVICE OF SPEAKING

Rhetoric had fewer periods of ecstasy during the nearly 1000 years from the fall of the Empire to the Renaissance than it had in the previous half-millennium. As spoken discourse in medieval secular French schools, it often found a place in the curriculum, but always secondary to philosophy, theology, and law, and always as a service course to understand Latin more fully. Oratory, with all its problems of self-restraint in an authoritarian society, was one way to learn Latin grammar and language; writing, more easily monitored, was another. Thus, rhetorical principles, those originally designed for the tribune and law courts, were kept alive through writing (de Dainville, 1968). The fact that Latin continued as the medium of instruction attests to the thoroughness of the assimilation of Roman values and culture. The study of rhetoric, combined with the more elementary work of grammar, proved a useful tool for attaining competency in the language. By reading and pondering Latin textbooks, submitting to the question-answer procedure in the classroom, and composing Latin disputations, teenage boys came to understand the world of law, document-writing, and the pulpit.

From the beginning of the sixth century well into the eighth century, intellectual darkness prevailed in France. One finds no great teachers, no outstanding students, no eloquent preachers, no arresting books, hence no great schools. In the seventh century, classical studies in the church did not fare well. Faculties faced a dilemma: on the one hand, students needed rhetoric just as they needed philosophy and logic to speak for virtue, honesty, and salvation; on the other, rhetoric too often led to vanity and sophistry (Roger, 1905). Both Augustine and Jerome had seen value in secular studies, even if St. Paul had questioned the eloquence he heard in the Second Sophistic (I Corinthians 1:17-19). Emphasis on the written word cultivated language learning and gave opportunity to monitor the finished product.

No documentary evidence of classical studies in the churches of seventh-century Brittany has surfaced, but we can assume that teachers did not renounce their study of classical literature. Llan Itud (sixth century) established rhetorical classes in Brittany, while Paul, Bishop of Verduin (d. 649), was educated in rhetoric, grammar, and dialectic. Both Saint Germain (d. 667) and Attala de Bobbio (d. 727) read in the liberal arts, and Saint Dedier de Cahors (d. 654) studied *gallicana eloquentia*. We assume that their studies reflected something of the curriculum in their own areas as well as in the country at large (Michaud, 1811-1862).[2] Unlike the time of Ausonius and the Empire, the schools would all but forget the *Ad Herrenium*, *De Inventione*, and *Topica*.

The ninth century, inspirited by the vision of Charlemagne and the hard work of Alcuin, found learning in a new and vibrant dress. The liberal arts flourished under Charlemagne. For 15 years the British immigrant-scholar Alcuin spurred the revival of rhetoric and other liberal arts which became the curriculum of France and Western Europe. His *Disputatio de Rhetorica et de Virtutibus sapientissimi Regis Karli et Albini Magistri*, the most important rhetorical work in Western Europe of both the eighth and ninth centuries, treats the five *officia* of the orator (with adaptation to the current political scene), moral philosophy, the three genera of speeches, six parts of the oration (exordium, narration, division, proofs, refutation, and conclusion), *status*, and so forth. The nine editions of Alcuin's *Rhetoric*, with its strong emphasis on judicial matters, played their part in developing a forensic rhetoric for canon law, writing on church and legal matters (Howell, 1965), and the grounding of Charlemagne's educational patronage. Later, Remigius (c. 841-c. 908), the Benedictine monk of Auxerne, lectured in Paris on the liberal arts (including, presumably, speaking and writing) and enjoyed a wide reputation as a teacher. Numerous manuscripts of his commentary on Martianus Capella's views of the seven arts have survived (Lutz, 1956, 1957).

The eleventh to thirteenth centuries, called *la grand epoque* because of artistic and literary fortunes during the reigns of Louis VI, Philippe Auguste, and Philippe le Bel (1081-1314), saw a revival of the arts. If for over a century Chartres had earlier dominated the study of classical literature, with its special attention to grammar ("the art of explaining poets and historians, the art of speaking and writing," so Rabanus Maurus; Paetow, 1910), by the mid-twelfth century Orléans, not far to the south, had replaced it. Unfortunately, classical interests in general waned here in the following century.

Orléans, famed for its School of Grammar, Rhetoric, and Classical Literature, familiarized its students with rhetoric, but chiefly through writing and versifying—the *ars dictaminis*. Written style, though an outgrowth of its oral counterpart, became an indispensable adjunct of the latter, but a decline in writing skills produced a corresponding demise in speaking. In addition, the principles of the spoken word had a marked influence on ethics because they honored the useful and dealt with human nature. Cicero, who looked at both of these in his own day and set the standard for Latin usage, served the curriculum well (Delhaye, 1949). In the High Middle Ages rhetoric (both writing and speaking) increased in popularity, at least in the thirteenth century, and continued so to the dawn of the Renaissance—about 1450 in France (Jasinski, 1965; McKeon, 1952). In late fourteenth-century Perpignan, bachelors and masters had to show verbal skills by composing proverbs, reciting daily, and participating at least weekly in disputations on grammatical subjects (Paetow, 1910).

Port Royal, founded as a women's retreat near Paris in 1204 but moving to the capital in 1600, took as a *propositio maxima* to learn *à bien parler et à bien ecrire*, since serving God by defending one's faith required such skills. Its curriculum embraced all the human faculties: speaking, writing, memorizing, analyzing, and experiencing. In time its faculty and textbooks brought renown to the institution. As in other French schools, Port Royal placed heavy emphasis on reading and understanding primary documents, while discouraging simplistic responses of "ceci est bon, cela est mauvais" (Carré, 1887). Such thoroughness should not surprise us, remembering that such writers as Blaise Pascal, and polemical Jansenists Antoine Arnauld and Pierre Nicole—all laymen—studied and lived there. The institution's teachers, moving beyond mindless memorizing and recitation, wanted their students to understand human nature. Probably the renaissance preceptor, like his earlier and later professional cousins, took his students through the text, explained the principles as well as the historical, literary, and mythological allusions, and gave them opportunities in the classroom to put the theory into practice. Some lectured, as did their colleagues, in various disciplines. While they may have utilized models of Demosthenes, Aeschines, and Cicero, any pulpit models probably were reserved for the monasteries and seminaries.

Technological constraints on book production had a direct impact on literacy in medieval France, particularly with respect to textbook materials. No classroom, because of cost and time required for copying, could boast of a plethora of manuscripts. Teachers lectured from their own or school documents, setting forth the ancient principles insofar as they understood them. From 500 to 1450 several books—in addition to the usual fare of Aristotle, Cicero, and Quintilian—were available to them, but surely not to their students. Thus, lectures, based upon professors' reading of manuscripts, prevailed in the classroom. The *De Rhetorica*, of Rabanus Maurus (784-856), borrowing freely from secular literature, defined rhetoric as speaking well on civil questions, recognized three ends of speaking, and noted three kinds of style and the effects of each (Migne).

In a broader vein of the liberal arts, students looked at Martianus Capella's *De Nuptiis Mercuri et Philologiae*. This allegory, while perhaps composed in Carthage prior to the fall of Rome, captured academic interests for centuries. Remigius of Auxerne's (c. ninth and tenth centuries) commentary on *The Marriage* kept both the treatise and the larger subject of rhetoric before students (Lutz, 1962; Stahl, 1971). Later, in the twelfth century, Thierry of Chartres' *Heptateuchon* looked at rhetoric in the larger context of the seven liberal arts. While some academics saw the arts courses as mere preparation for the study of theology, medicine, and law, medieval French students understood well the interdependency of their classroom disciplines (Clerval, 1895)[3]; writing and speaking closely influenced theology, reading, and law.

In the more restricted sense of rhetoric Peter of Blois' *Libellus de arte dictandi rhetorice*, probably written in twelfth-century France, was so broad in scope and theoretical in conception that it never found a significant place in the classroom (Camargo, 1984). Yet the works of Alain de Lille (1116-1202) and Jacques de Vitry (1170-1240) did provide training, though of a limited sort. Alain's *Ars praedicandi* showed the seminary student the need for order and analysis, even if it limited rhetoric to a truncated view of content. The first chapter discussed audiences while the next 37 chapters gave ideas for sermons, including sins on which the sacred orator might preach. Focusing on content and audience adaptation, the author virtually ignored organization, style, memory, and delivery (Evans, 1981). The *Exempla* of de Vitry, himself a masterful raconteur, similarly stressed content, furnishing uneducated priests with stories for their sermons (Crane, 1890).[4] French preaching, both in theory and criticism—if not in practice—took seriously St. Paul's command (I Thessalonians 5:20), "Do not despise prophesying [preaching]." What is evident in the French mode of preaching is the coordination of writing in the service of preaching; that is, the preparation for effective preaching is grounded in principles of composition that were intended to be "performed" to an audience. As oratory had been a type of literature in antiquity, so also was preaching a literature performed before its readership. In such a context, the role and importance of writing is not only apparent but indicative of the instrumental function that writing takes in a society essentially oral in its medium of public expression.

In the thirteenth century the *De eruditione praedicatorum* by Humbert de Romans, general of the Dominicans, examined the pulpit speaker and his qualities, as well as including more than 100 sermon sketches for different kinds of listeners and occasions, showing Dominicans how to handle pulpit responsibilities. A second book by Humbert, *De praedicatione sanctae crucis contra Saracens*, not only described Crusade preaching for the local peasant, it also included the use of hymns for those occasions when volunteers came forward at the *invitatio* to join in the recapture of Jerusalem (Brett, 1984).[5] Humbert's probable contemporary, Thomas de Chabham (fl. 1230), perhaps penned the *Summa de arte predicandi* (1210-1215), instructing the seminarian/priest to read Scripture, debate, and preach, all with the goal of instructing the listener about matters of God and the Church (Murphy, 1974).

A generation after Chabham's work, *Li Livres duo trésor*, an encyclopedic work by Dante's teacher, Brunetto Latini (1230-1294), described rhetoric as oral suasion whose purpose is to secure belief. He acknowledged the five offices of the orator, provided help in refuting arguments, and urged the speaker to prepare for his public appearances. Latini's emphasis on argument contrasted with many of his contemporaries who, borrowing the principles from oral rhetoric, applied them to written composition in their efforts to prepare young men for church administrative careers. With Brunetto Latini, however, we witness a cycle in which rhetoric, originally intended for oral persuasion, is then abstracted in matters appropriate to writing and eventually restated in persuasion but within a society familiar with literary application.

Of lesser concern were treatises by Georgius Trapezuntius (1538)[6], the Cretan-born Greek who quickly learned Latin and both taught and wrote in it; the German scholar Joannis Caesarius (1529); and Pierre de Courcelles. De Courcelles' *Rhétorique* (1557), while appearing a couple of years after Focquelin's French translation of Talon's *Rhetoric*, is more original then Talon's work, but saw only two printings. Each author, however, looked at the scope of rhetoric, the three genera, the parts of the oration, and sundry related materials, providing at least a skeleton of the ancient discipline.

At the same time students could do more than look at elementary postulates. Scholars wishing to study ancient rhetoric could find a catalog of antiquity's sophists and orators in Jean Tixier de Ravisy's (d. 1524) *Cornvcopiae Ioannis Ravisii Textoris epitome* (1572), Book II of which contains the names (with some excerpts) of three to four dozen sophists, as well as many orators. In the *Progymnasmatum* (1520) of Franciscus Sylvius (d. c. 1530) students could ponder the ancient Grecian exercises promoted by Hermogenes and Aelius Theon of Alexandria. Its author noted assignments such as description and narration, then followed them with statements from Cicero, Sallust, and other Romans—no Greeks—who spoke to the points at issue. The book's 100 *capita* show that teachers sought to develop their students' analytical skills. They were not content with childlike repetition of archaic exercises.

While at times we can identify some books and procedures, we know little about rhetorical training in some areas like Montpelier, Orléans, and Angers; we assume that fifteenth-century law professors continued the platform training, but we can find no evidence to support this belief. It is likely, however, given the continued standardization of legal training, the stable role of rhetoric in higher education, and the argumentative nature of jurisprudence, that rhetoric was a standard feature of legal education. At the same time, some of the arts, along with the study of jurisprudence, did command their attention if for no more reason than preparation for later occupations. During the medieval days, then, rhetoric both waned (sixth to eighth centuries) and waxed (ninth, tenth, thirteenth, and later centuries), depending upon the emergence of imaginative teachers, inquisitive students, and the proper political conditions. Here and there schools, teachers, and books kept the discipline alive, but faculty neither conceived, expounded on, nor practiced the theory with the vigor which could have made the universities and the country more exciting places in which to study and live.

THE FRENCH RENAISSANCE: THE CURRICULAR
STABILITY OF ORAL AND WRITTEN RHETORIC

The French Renaissance, rippling toward France in the reign of Philippe VI (1328-1350) and his immediate successors, broke onto its shores like a massive wave in the late fifteenth and early sixteenth centuries. This *ratour a l'antiquité* flourished in a variety of ways: writing, editing, printing, teaching, and in other individual initiatives. In the Renaissance schools rhetorical teachers typically explained (both in the morning and afternoon) principles of invention, organization, style, and delivery, then let students work on assignments. For a five-hour day this meant two hours of group study, one hour of recitation, and two hours for conversation, exercises, disputation, and imitation. Fifteenth-century law students at Angers, however, seem to have had no preparation or training in rhetoric. Unlike classical Greece and Rome, law in Renaissance France overshadowed the study of rhetoric, despite the emphasis on Latin literature (Rashdall, 1895). Conditions in the courtroom and deliberative assembly were more restrictive than they had been in ancient Gaul or later in the eighteenth century. Yet Caen could boast of an endowed chair of rhetoric almost from its beginning in 1437 (Rashdall, 1895).

We should pause here to say something about education of a religious nature. The Council of Trent (1563) had prescribed for the classroom all the belles lettres as well as other curricular offerings. This meant that seminaries not only taught rhetoric by precept and perhaps by writing, but by oral exercises. More important, from early Christian times the Church emphasized education and training, some of which took place in churches and monasteries and some in private schools, as in the earlier schools of Clement and Origen in Alexandria. In Gaul, where rhetoric generally flourished, we can identify no Christian rhetorical school during the first four centuries, perhaps because of the area's antipapal feelings, Christian suspicions of the Second Sophistic's embellishing the truth, and local misgivings regarding secular learning even though some Christians were educated by pagan professors (Haarloff, 1920). Rhetoric's study continued in the monasteries, however, under the watchful eye of the local abbot.

Later we learn of rhetorical training in church-related schools throughout the country. At Chartres, for example, Bishop Fulbert, "le prince des écoles chartraines," in the eleventh century taught rhetoric, grammar, and dialectic, while in the next century Alcuin's earlier *Rhetoric* and Victorinus' commentary on Cicero's *De Oratore* had gained secure places in the curriculum. As rhetoric nourished humanistic and professional studies, wedding reason to expression, it examined rules, looked at selected orators, and encouraged written essays on sacred or secular topics appropriate to the discipline. The Chartraine preceptors seem to have known the *Ad Herrenium, De Inventione,* and *Topica* (and the Verrine and Catalinarian orations) as well as J. Severus' *Syntomata ac Precepta Artis Rhetoricae,* but not, apparently, Quintilian's *Institutes.* These, along with Capella's *Marriage* and Thierry's *Heptateuchon* show that in teaching rhetoric the religious instructor, like his secular counterpart, first cited a passage, then explained it, and finally looked at individual words *ad litteram* (Clerval, 1895). So also the *Rhetorica novissima* (1235) of Boncompagno de Siena, the first systematizer of letter-writing, shows that young Italian notaries who wrote letters based them on the formulae found in rhetorical works (Bolgar, 1982).

In the fourteenth century, Franciscan and Dominican seminarians, excited about the call to proclaim the "Good News," read and pondered rules, and debated ideas (Bonnefant, 1915; Douais, 1884).[7] For the oral disputation the professor read the thesis, which one student attacked and another defended (using syllogisms), then concluded it, all with parents and the public listening for two to three hours (Lantoine, 1919). While the activity of spreading doctrine is inherently a feature of Christian faith, the interrelationship of writing and public reading illustrated by seminarians reveals the compatible relationship of oral and written rhetoric that was a feature not only of the educational life of the period but in the religious activity of the clergy.

Jesuit education mirrored the friars' approach, but in a more thorough way. After Paul III had chartered the Society of Jesus (1540) its schools multiplied rapidly. In time the lustre of their alumni eclipsed that of the graduates of the University of Paris. The *Ad Herrenium*, Cicero's works, and Cyprian Soárez's *Rhetorica* set the pace in matters of content, style, and delivery—all in Latin, which continued as the medium of instruction until about 1700. Textual models, though plentiful, were employed only sparingly (Lantoine, 1919).

With their emphasis on speaking and writing, Jesuit teachers mirrored some approaches of the earlier Chartraine teachers. They (1) noted the passage; (2) pointed out and explained the precepts of searching for ideas, proving an argument, or selecting the right ornaments or gestures; (3) gave the sense of the passage, referring to the historical setting and the author's meaning; and (4) put their students before the class in practical exercises. This regimen permitted students to use poems, passages from Greco-Roman orators (even entire selections from Cicero), or perhaps their own compositions to develop inventional, organizational, stylistic, and delivery skills. Aristotle's *Rhetoric* and *Poetics* and Cicero's works furnished the precepts. The teaching of disposition and style always preceded the teaching of invention, for the Society's professors thought that once ideas started flowing, pruning was easier than adding (Lantoine, 1919). To improve their Latin style, students were asked to do a variety of things, such as describe a garden or storm, or perhaps translate a Greek passage into Latin or Latin discourse into Greek (de Dainville, 1940).

After studying came late-summer vacations, the timing of which depended upon the curriculum. Students in rhetoric began theirs on September 7, those in logic a week earlier, while others remained in school until September 14. All returned on October 1. Rhetoric students sat in class five hours per day, presumably six days per week, while philosophy students endured six hours per day (Lantoine, 1919).

Some sixteenth-century rhetorical writing was obscure, confused, and unbalanced, but Jesuits in part rectified that while planting it more firmly in the curriculum. The Society's teachers found their basis in ancient writers, including their rhetorical works, and returned Greek studies to a place of importance, giving it two hours per day. Aristotle served the older students well, while Cicero and Quintilian held the younger ones. Instructors continued to expound the texts, not so much to teach students the need to search for ideas and to arrange them properly, but to improve their style and adapt to audiences (de Dainville, 1940; Tilley, 1968). An inventory (1522) of a deceased

University of Paris student's books revealed no Ciceronian rhetorical works, though the young man did have the *Letters* and *Tusculan Disputations* of Cicero. Quintilian's *Institutes* ("en un petit volume") was also mentioned. While the catalog of one student's books reveals little, we may say that rhetoric, though alive, was hardly flourishing.

What of female education? Some training of women, and probably in rhetoric, dates from at least the sixth century. Christianity, with its emphasis on the dignity of women, pushed for female education. Moreover, Charlemagne recommended that girls should study letters, gleaning from them all that they could. So, here and there, rhetorical principles captured the interest of girls and young women. Cecilia, daughter of William the Conqueror, learned at the feet of Arnoul Mauclerc, an orator and dialectician who surely taught her at least the Latin orators. If Pierre le Venerable scolded young women for their apathy and for rejecting the literary traditions, perhaps he did so because the frivolous character of female education generated indifference, and ultimately a rejection of the literary tradition. In time, shallow education of men and women alike contributed to the moral corruption of French nobility and society in general (Jourdain, 1874).

Meanwhile the University of Paris, though in some sense a religious institution because it emerged (1170) from the convergence of three church schools, was a secular institution independent of monasteries or convents. Its Faculty of Arts, inferior in quality to those in theology, canon law, and medicine, surfaced near or in the first decade of the thirteenth century, and from the first it included rhetoric in its curriculum (Lacroix & Seré, 1848; Leclercq, 1946; Rashdall, 1895). Service oriented, the course was geared to practical speaking and to preparing students to study philosophy, law, and other disciplines. As in earlier centuries, the scarcity of books necessitated a heavy reliance on oral instruction. Aegidius Romanus (Giles of Rome; 1247-1316), part of a team of scholars at the University, translated Aristotle's *Rhetoric* into Latin and provided a commentary on it useful to Parisian students. These, along with the other arts, were taught in the morning, and for longer periods of time in winter than in summer. Later, in the sixteenth century, the Arts faculty explicated the rhetorical texts of Cicero for both oral and written use. Thus, rhetoric became the servant of writers, speakers, and philosophers (de Dainville, 1940; Rashdall, 1895).

Scholars have uncovered an enormous number of sermon manuscripts, largely exhortative in nature, from the thirteenth and fourteenth centuries (Haskins, 1904),[8] but for many young men the content made little impression in their extracurricular lives. Like university students in any era, some looked for excuses to avoid Saturday exams, were lazy, truant, inclined to socializing, and pined more for graduation than for mastering their studies. The riffraff even mugged people on the street, broke into homes, and violated women (Rashdall, 1895; Théry, 1858).[9] Aristotle's *Rhetoric* is first mentioned at the University in the fourteenth century, a time when students sat on the floor at the feet of their professors—to humble them, said some (Kibre, 1948). Instruction, however, had declined in value and quality to the point that university legislation called for Masters to lecture extemporaneously rather than read from their written manuscripts.

The French Academy also played its role in stabilizing oral and written rhetoric in the French curriculum, particularly through those members who showed an "imperieux dogmatisme fondé sur les principes d'Aristote et la pratique des écrivains de l'antiquité." Moreover, their love of nature—the product of a transcendent Creator—and their desire to learn to write "naturally" prompted their desire to study and use the principles of Latin rhetoric (Cousin, 1933).

Prior to 1600 a small band of humanists renewed the University of Paris' Faculty of Arts' interest in classical rhetoric, so that by the dawn of the seventeenth century the University's statutes mandated older students to peruse Ciceronian speeches, and professors to read aloud in the classroom Latin selections from the *Brutus*, *De Oratore*, *De Partitione*, and others, along with Quintilian's *Institutes*. All this was calculated to improve the young men's skills in the ancient language of Rome (Lang, 1956). Rhetoric then remained basically healthy, though in a service capacity, in Renaissance France, but at times in a writing more than an oral mode.

Some textbooks or manuscripts that one could find in specific institutions have been noted. What other books were available? Several come to mind. The first rhetorical work printed in France was the

Rhetoricum libri III of Guillaume Fichet (1433-c. 1480), the Sorbonne librarian and professor of rhetoric, Scripture, and philosophy. Because his students were pirating his lectures, he wanted to provide a more accurate account of Greco-Roman principles. Like Samson of biblical times, Fichet tried to pull down the pillars of the opposition—in his time, faltering scholasticism. The *Rhetorica*, divided into three books of about equal size, treats invention and disposition (Book I), demonstrative and deliberative speeches (Book II), and elocution, memory, and delivery (Book III). It defines rhetoric as persuasion, notes the five *officia* of the orator, declares that invention is the discovery of things likely to persuade, looks at the three genera of speeches and six parts of the oration, and in general provides an outline of a basic course in the discipline. Its many lists suggest the author's lecture notes, which he probably amplified in the classroom (Fichet, 1471).[10] Although more complete than *The Art or Crafte or Rhetoryke* (1530) by the Englishman Leonard Cox, the *Rhetoric* did not enjoy great popularity.

The highly popular *Le Grand et vray art de plein rhétorique* (1521) by Pierre Fabri (fl. 1483-1515), the French theologian and literary scholar, set forth the usual principles for speaking, but saw their direct application to writing. It (1) incorporated tenets appropriate for judicial, demonstrative, and deliberative occasions; (2) embodied the five duties of the orator's preparation and delivery; (3) recognized three kinds of style for speaking and writing—the grand, middle, and plain; and (4) devoted 85 pages to letter-writing, setting forth a basis for epistolary rhetoric. Its wide acclaim by scholars led to many reissues over the next three to four centuries.

If Fichet's *Rhetoric* did not flourish, two works by Cyprian Soárez (1524-1593) and Omer Talon (1510-1562), the latter the close friend of Peter Ramus, certainly did. *De Arte Rhetorica libri tres* (1562), by the Jesuit Soárez, like many other textbooks of the era defined rhetoric as the *doctrina dicendi*, noted three genera of speeches, described the five responsibilities of the orator, and discussed in detail the four parts of arrangement. A small book based on Aristotle, Cicero, and Quintilian, it would handily fit into a student's pocket, but would need amplification in the classroom by the instructor. Professors used it widely for more than a century—over 200 editions, revisions, and printings—for the *Rhetoric*, particularly in Jesuit schools, handled classical territory as Latin writers conceived it (Soérez, 1562/1620).

Talon's *Rhetorica* (1548), reflecting Ramean philosophy and analysis, went through more than 100 editions by 1700. The author, who taught at Le Moine College (1544-1562), defined rhetoric as the theory of expressing oneself well, and focused on a truncated view of the discipline: two parts of rhetoric (style and delivery). He believed the orator should take content and arrangement from logic and embellish it, making the whole acceptable by voice and delivery (Talon, 1548). His *Institutiones oratoriae*, not so popular, nonetheless went through 12 editions/printings between 1548 and 1555, even though its separation of content from other rhetorical concerns met some resistance. It borrowed from earlier Latin works, including, presumably, Quintilian's *Institutes* which enjoyed considerable popularity in the sixteenth century (Fumaroli, 1980; Mollard, 1934).

Supporting Talon was, of course, Pierre de la Ramée (Peter Ramus; 1515-1572); In some respects the most important—though not the most popular—rhetorical figure of sixteenth-century France. His greatest crime was slandering Aristotle in an age unprepared to tolerate such insolence. In Ramus' attempts to shore up rhetoric and logic, he removed from each what one could find in the other. This divorcing of content and disposition from style has persisted into some twentieth-century circles. At the same time, he sought to simplify and clarify rhetoric and logic, which he believed Aristotle, Cicero, and Quintilian had obscured with their rules and applications. Enormously prolific— some 60 works flowed from his pen, most for classroom use—Ramus (1574/1970) emphasized writing rather than disputation, placing him squarely in the humanist tradition.[11] He stressed the analysis of simple aphorisms or longer texts, whether of Cicero, Quintilian, or medieval writers. As an educational reformer, he, like his counterparts at Port Royal, wished to make the classroom a place for reflection.

There were other books. Students training in declamation could find help in the *Paradoxes* (1553) of Charles Estienne (1504/1505-1564), which included 25 declamations on topics like poverty, ignorance, human sterility, and war. It would help school boys not only in classroom disputations but in taking a position on controversial topics. On the other hand, the L'Éloquence Françoise (1590) of Guillaume du Vair, the sixteenth-century parliamentary speaker, quickly went through several printings even without corrections, so eager were some to get it into the classroom. Combining Stoic morality with Christian thought, du Vair analyzed Greco-Roman tenets long known in France (Hennebert, 1968).

Models became increasingly popular. Scholars/editors published many editions of Cicero's speeches as well as Greek editions of Demosthenes and Aeschines. Louis LeRoy's (1510-1577) edition and commentary on Demosthenes, Sept oraisons de Démosthène, urged the study of the ancient Athenian's speeches as a means of improving one's vernacular style, refining one's judgments about human nature, and becoming sensitive to what influences people (Leroy, 1575).[12]

CONCLUSION

This chapter ends with 1600, and for good reason. Not only do scholars often speak of the dawn of the seventeenth century as the beginning of the modern era, but more specifically Henry IV (1589-1610) liberalized France with the Edict of Nantes (1598). Education flourished, the Huguenots enjoyed unprecedented freedom and political rights, and the economy prospered. Less than a century later, however, pressures from the Catholic hierarchy led to the revocation (1685) of the Edict, driving French Protestants out of the country, depopulating whole areas, and bringing shame on the Church of Rome. Thus, the seventeenth century took on a character different from what preceded it.

French rhetoric flowered and withered at different times in France during these fifteen hundred years. In the halcyon days of Roman Gaul and the High Middle Ages its fragrance enriched the lives of many, while in early medieval France, and in the fourteenth to early fifteenth centuries, its aroma attracted few serious scholars to study it as one might law and medicine. Chroniclers like Ausonius, educators like Alcuin, pioneer authors like Fichet, and theorists like Ramus significantly contributed to the theory and practice of rhetoric and its resulting place in the educational curriculum. But too often the periods were springlike, never seeing the full blossoms of summer. Centuries divided Fichet and Cicero, Soárez and Quintilian, but the same ideas and principles prevailed—sometimes as oral communication, sometimes as written. French education, both early and late, emphasized clarity in writing, a skill assumed but not directly taught in any other discipline. If the office of writing presupposed the art of speaking, both represented a search for ideas and adapting to them, as well as organizing and stylizing them—exercises which heightened thought and enlarged the soul. This chapter has omitted some personalities, rhetorical books, and other materials it ought to include. The issue, however, is not so much numbers as significance. No one book, no one teacher, no one school tells the whole story. Taken together, however, they reveal the trends, the prosperity, the nature of *l'enseignement de l'art de la première rhétorique* in France before 1600, as well as something about the pulpit, and even the bar.

NOTES

1. Jean Molinet's *L'Art de rhétoricque*, written before 1492, deals with poetry, not oral suasion; together, "la première rhétorique" plus "la seconde rhétorique" equals "pleine rhétorique," the whole field of writing.

2. Data on Loup, Jean (in Languedoc), Felix, Llan Itud, and J. Severus are not available in: Michaud (1933-), *Dictionnaire de biographie français*. Paris: Librairie Letouzey et Ane; the (1907-) *Encyclopedia üniversal ilvstrada*. Barcelona: Espasa; or A. Pauly/G. Wissowa (1893ff), *Real-Encyclopädie der klassischen Altertumswissenschaft*. Stuttgart.

3. This edition by Clerval provides a full description of the *Heptateuchon*. Thierry's view of Creation and the Creator (*Archives d'histoire doctrinale et littéraire du moyen âge* [1955], 137ff) shows an evolutionary process with God behind it all.

4. Collections of *exempla* abound in the thirteenth to fifteenth centuries. Étenne de Bourbon, Étienne de Besancon, and Humbert de Romans were only three of many compilers. See also L. Petit de Julleville (1909), *Histoire de la langue et de la littérature française* (2nd vol.). Paris: Colin.

5. European libraries today contain more than 40 manuscripts of Humbert's *Tractatus*, attesting to its popularity. Jacques de Vitry, an excellent raconteur, seems to have introduced the *exempla* to France of which de Julleville, *Histoire*, II, 242ff, includes a helpful discussion.

6. Guillaume Fichet, though jealous of Trapezuntius, used some of his ideas in writing his own *Rhetoric* (1471).

7. We have no direct evidence for the use of preaching manuals, though surely they had a place in the curriculum. See Georges Bonnefant (1915), *Séminaires Normans du XVI(e) et XVII(e) siècle*. Paris: Picard.

8. Ironically, the author, after expressing his misgivings about the manuscripts, proceeds to extract valuable data from them.

9. Théry quotes Firmin Laferrière (*Histoire du droit civil de Rome et du droit française*) when he says, "Laferrière a réuni toutes les preuves historiques qui fixent au milieu du 1(er) siecle le voyage de saint Paul dans la Gaule Narbonaise."

10. See, also, Michaud, *Biographie universelle* ("Fichet, Guillame"); Anatole Claudin (1898), *First Paris press*. London: Bibliographical Society; and Jules Philippe (1885), *Origine de l'imprimerie à Paris après des documents inédits*. Paris: Charaway Freres.

11. See, also, Peter Ramus (1574/1959), (Trans. by Roland MacIlmaine and Ed. by Catherine M. Dunn), *Logike of the most excellent philosopher P. Ramus martyr*. Northridge, CA: San Fernando Valley State College; Pierre Albert Duhamel (1949), "Logic and rhetoric of Peter Ramus." *Modern Philology (46)*, 163-171; Walter J. Ong (1971), *Rhetoric, romance, and technology*. Ithaca, NY: Cornell University Press.

12. See, also, Abraham H. Becker (1896), *Un humaniste au XVI(e) siècle, Loys Le Roy*. Paris: Lecene, Oudin; and Werner L. Gundersheimer (1966), *Life and works of Louis LeRoy*. Geneve: Droz.

REFERENCES

Ausonius (1919-1921). *Commemoratio professorum burdigalensium*. (H. G. E. White., Trans., 2 vols.) Cambridge, MA: Harvard University Press.

Bolgar, R. R. (1982). Teaching of rhetoric in the Middle Ages. In *Rhetoric resolved* (pp. 79-86). Binghampton, NY: Center for Medieval and Early Renaissance Studies.

Bonnefant, G. (1915). *Seminaires Normans du XVI(e) and XVII(e) siècle*. Paris: Picard.

Brett, E. T. (1984). *Humbert de Romans*. Toronto: Pontifical Institute of Mediaeval Studies.

Caesarius, J. (1529). *Rhetorica*. Cologne: J. of Aich.

Camargo, M. (1984). Libellus de arte dictandi rhetorice. *Speculum, 59*.

Carré, I. (1887). *Les pédagogues de Port Royal*. Paris: Librairie Ch. Delegrave.

Clerval, A. (1895). *Les écoles de Chartres au moyen-âge*. Paris: Picard.

Cousin, J. (1933). Rhétorique latine et classicisme française. *Revue des Cours et Conférences (34)*, 502-518, 589-605.

Courcelles, P. de (1557). *La Rhétorique*. Paris: S. Nyvelle.

Crane, T. F. (1980). Exempla . . . of Jacques de Vitry. *Publications of the Folk-Lore Society, (25)*.

Dainville, F. de. (1940). Naissance de l'humanisme modern. *Jesuites et l'éducation de la société francaise*. Paris: Beauchesne.

Dainville, F. de. (1968). L'Évolution de l'enseignement de la rhétorique au XII(e) siècle. *Dix-septième siècle*, nos. 80-81.

Delhaye, P. (1949). L'Enseignement de la philosophie morale au XII(e) siècle. *Mediaeval Studies, 11*.

Douais, C. (1884). *Essai sur l'organization dans l'ordre des fréres prêcheurs*. Paris: Picard.

Estienne, C. (1553). *Paradoxes de sont propos contre la common opinion . . . en causes difficiles*. Paris: de Roy.

Evans, G. R. (Trans.). (1981). Art of preaching. *Cisterian Studies, 23*. Kalamazoo: MI: Cisterian Press.

Fabri, P. (1521). *Le Grand et vray art de pleine rhétorique*. Rouen: Simon Gruél.

Fichet, G. (1471). *Rhetoricum libri III*. Paris: Ulricus Gering.

Fumaroli, M. (1980). *L'Âge d'éloquence: Rhétorique et "res literaria" de la Renaissance au seuil de l'époque classique*. Geneve: Droz.

Haarloff, T. (1920). *Schools of Gaul: A study of pagan and Christian education in the last century of the western empire*. Oxford: Oxford University Press.

Haskins, C. (1904). University of Paris in the sermons of the thirteenth century. *American Historical Review, 10*.

Hennebert, F. (1968). *Histoire des traductions françaises d'auteurs grecs et latins pendant le XVI(e) siècles*. Amsterdam: B. R. Gruner.

Howell, W. S. (1965). *Rhetoric of Alcuin and Charlemagne*. New York: Russell & Russell.

Jasinski, R. (1965). *Histoire de la litterature française*. Paris: A. G. Nizet.

Jourdain, C. (1874). Memoire sur l'education des femmes au moyen âge. *Memoires de l'institut nationale de France, 28*. Paris: Imprimerie Nationale.

Kibre, P. (1948). *Nations in the mediaeval universities*. Cambridge, MA: Mediaeval Academy of America.

Lacroix, P., & Sere, F. (1948). *Moyen âge et la Renaissance*. Paris: n.p.

Lang, R. A. (1956). Rhetoric at the University of Paris, 1500-1789. *Speech Monographs* (now *Communication Monographs*), *23*, 216-228.

Langlois, E. (1902). *Recueil d'arts de seconde rhétorique*. Paris: Imprimerie Nationale.

Lantoine, H. (1919). *Oeuvres de Henri (Eugéne) Lantoine*. Paris: Hachette.

Laclercq, J. (1946). Le magistére de prédicateur au XIII(e) siècle. *Archives d'histoire doctrinale et litteraire du moyen âge*.

Leroy, L. (1575). *Sept oraisons de Démosthène, prince des orateurs, à scavoir trois, Olynthiaques et quartre Philippiques*. Paris: Morel.

Lutz, C. E., (1956). Remigius' ideas on the classification of the seven liberal arts. *Traditio, 12*.

Lutz, C. E. (1957). Commentary of Remigius of Auxerne on Martianus Capella. *Mediaeval Studies, 19*.

Lutz, C. E. (1962). *Remigii autissiodorensis commentum in Martianum Capellam*. Leiden: Brill.

McKeon, R. (1952). Rhetoric in the Middle Ages. In R. S. Crane, (Ed.). *Critics and criticism*. Chicago: University of Chicago Press.

Michaud, J. F. (1811-1862). *Biographie universelle*. Paris: Delagrave.

Migne, J. *Patrologiae Latina, 59*, 411-519.

Mollard, A. (1934). La diffusion de l'institution oratoire au XII(e) siècle. *Moyen Age, 3*.

Murphy, J. J. (1974). *Rhetoric in the Middle Ages*. Berkeley: University of California Press.

Paetow, L. J. (1910). Arts courses at medieval universities with special reference to grammar and rhetoric. *University Studies, 3*(7).

Patterson, W. F. (935). *Three centuries of French poetic theory* (3 vols.). Ann Arbor: University of Michigan Press.

Pollard, A. W. (1924). *Short-title catalog of books printed in France* . . . *1470-1600*. London: British Museum.

Ramus, P. (1574/1970). *Peter Ramus: The Logike*. Menston, UK: Scolar.

Rashdall, H. (1895). *Universities of Europe in the Middle Ages*. Oxford: Clarendon Press.

de Ravisy, J. T. (1572). *Cornvcopiae Ioannis Ravisii Textoris Epitome*. Lugudni (Lyon): S. Honoratus.

van Ringelbergh, J. S. (1545). *Rhetorica*. Paris: S. Colinaeum.

Roger, M. (1905). *L'enseignement des lettres classiques d'Ausone à Alcuin*. Paris: Picard.

Soárez, C. (1562). *De arte rhetorica libri tres*. Coimbra, Portugal.

Stahl, W. H. (1971). *Martianus and the seven liberal arts*. New York: Columbia University Press.

Suetonius (1970). *De rhetoribus*. (J. C. Rolfe, Trans., 2 vols.). Cambridge, MA: Harvard University Press.

Sylvius, F. (1520). *Progymnasmatum in artem oratoriam centuriae tres*. Paris: Vaenundantur I. Badio.

Talon, O. (1548). *Rhetorica*. Paris: M. Dauidis.

Théry, A. F. (1858). *Histoire de l'éducation en France*. Paris: Dezobry, E. Magdeleine.

Tilley, A. (1968). *Studies in the French Renaissance*. New York: Barnes & Noble.

Trapezuntius, G. (1538). *Rhetoricorum libri quinque*. Paris: J. Roigny.

du Vair, G. (1590). *De l'éloquence française*. Paris: A. L'Angelier.

10

Technological Development and Writer-Subject-Reader Immediacies

WALTER J. ONG, S. J.

Research examining oral and written communication over the last 25 years has not only revealed an interest from scholars across a number of disciplines (Havelock, 1986) but demonstrated that relationships between thought and expression—long considered to be elementary and stable—are much more complex and interactive than previously thought. Notions long fixed in the minds of researchers, and hence rather intolerant of alteration, are now under re-examination. In this instance, the notion of *text*, and its plasticity when subject to various forms of mediated communication, is one such concept in need of more sensitive examination. Since we have burrowed further and further into questions of textuality, we have become increasingly aware (mostly in backhanded ways) that an inscription is not fully a text until someone reads it, that is, until someone produces from the writer's text something nontextual, a sequence of sounds, exterior and audible or in the imagination—or, as in the case of congenitally deaf persons, some kind of sensory temporal sequence related, however indirectly, to sound. To do this requires a code that the text itself does not provide. Texts, as texts, are dependent on something nontextual. All text is pretext. Unless someone has this extra textual code which makes reading possible and applies the code, the physical inscription remains forever no more than a visible pattern on a surface. The one who has the code and uses it is

206

a reader. (This is not at all to say that everything in writing is merely a transcription of actual speech, but only that writing is ultimately based, if in a variety of ways, on speech.)

The fact that a text is a text because it can be read means, in short, that a text as text is part of discourse. Physically, the text appears *not* to be. Discourse moves. The text is immobile. But by putting words into a text we do not freeze them, remove them from dialogue. We only suspend the dialogue with the writer until a reader chances along. The impression a text creates, that words are fixed because the visible signs are fixed, has wrought havoc in philosophy, theology, jurisprudence, literary and critical theory, and who knows where else. No word can be present all at once, as words seem to be on a visible surface. The word *nevertheless*, for example, is not a thing, but an event: by the time I get to the *-theless*, the *never-* is gone, and has to be gone or I cannot make out the word. Thus, while written texts have a stable quality, they only appear to have whole, fixed meaning and actually lack features of momentary communication that would provide additional, more complete understanding.

But discourse calls for the presence of two or more persons to one another. (Here lies the basic sense of presence: person-to-person relationship, not thought-to-word-to-thing relationship.) Such direct personal relationship texts do interfere with, for normally the writer and reader are not present to one another. Often, and indeed more often than not in the case of the book texts on our library shelves, when the reader engages the text, the writer has long been dead. This absence calls for fictionalizing. Someone has to play a role: writer or reader or both. And, since the reader has to be alive to read, his or her roles are more proximate to us, and in some ways easier to discuss, more urgent. They call for special attention.

Out of such considerations has grown, in the words of George L. Dillon, the "literary theorizing extending from Wayne Booth and Walker Gibson through Walter J. Ong, Wolfgang Iser, Walter Slatoff, and Umberto Eco to the recent work of Peter Rabinowitz, all of whom speak of the reader as playing a role" (1986, p. 139). The roles that readers play can be categorized in an almost limitless number of ways. Dillon reviews various "ideal, implied, model, or intended" readers, pretending readers, submissive readers and resisting readers, suspicious readers, innocent readers, congruent and incongruent readers, mistreated readers, precisional and wishy-washy readers, and so on and on and on (pp. 138-143).

Umberto Eco has deliberately mixed readers' roles in his lengthy narrative *The Name of the Rose*, which has had an extraordinarily wide appeal for so recondite a work, an appeal suggesting that sensitivity to reader-writer relationships has roots deep in the psyche at our present stage in the evolution of consciousness, roots deeper than the explicit, exfoliated theories that *litterateurs* play with. These deep, inarticulated, subconscious or unconscious roots help give *The Name of the Rose* its surprisingly strong appeal even to those who have never heard reader-writer relationships discussed. Deliberately weaving an arabesqued intertextuality at all sorts of levels, Eco's remarkable work creates a new kind of narrative density, supported in part by the author's earlier theorizing about semiotics, which posits interpretive codes used by his "model reader" as against generative codes used by writers (Sallis, 1986). Eco distinguishes two kinds of texts generated by authors, *closed* texts (calculated to elicit a specific response from readers) and *open* texts (designed in a maze-like structure for readers to labor through), although he wisely notes that the "closed" text is open to more than one interpretation and that the "open" text is not open to random interpretation.

The fictionalizing of readers is a coefficient of the relationship of the writer to his or her own life-world. This relationship develops or shifts for many reasons. Today we are hyperconscious of the ways in which the electronic media, notably television, have altered the way persons relate to one another and to the world around them (Gumpert & Cathcart, 1986). Now consider briefly a change in relationship in a work on the technological border of the coming electronic age. The work is, perhaps surprisingly, Gerard Manley Hopkins's "The Wreck of the Deutschland," which has been treated in somewhat different perspective in *Hopkins, the Self, and God* (Ong, 1986). Through such a work we have the opportunity to examine the introduction of a new medium to the communication of thoughts and sentiment, as well as how such a form shapes the text, the relationship between author and audience, and the technology for inducing a presence of mediated immediacy.

Hopkins was not yet in the world of electronics in the strict sense of electronics, which has to do not simply with the use of electricity, but with the emission of electrons as in electronic tubes and transistors. But Hopkins lived in a world of electrically implemented communication. The American Samuel F. B. Morse had exhibited a genuine telegraph instrument in 1837, and his famous message "What hath God wrought" was sent by telegraph from Baltimore to Washington in 1844, the year of Hopkins's birth. A telegraph company was formed in the United States in 1845, and in the same year the Electric Telegraph company was organized in England. The first transatlantic cable, running between Newfoundland and Ireland, was completed in 1866.

Moreover, Hopkins grew up in a family milieu concerned with rapid transmission of information, and of information about disasters. His father, Manley Hopkins, was a marine insurance average adjuster (or, as we would say today, a marine insurance actuary) keeping account of shipwrecks, among other things, to adjust marine insurance rates—just as modern insurance companies adjust automobile insurance rates according to the number of accidents one has or, we hope, does not have. The Hopkins household was certainly more sensitive than most households to recent—even ongoing—shipping disasters. Hopkins knew the communications milieu on which marine insurance companies relied: in a letter of May 21, 1878, to Bridges he brands insensitive readings of "The Loss of the Eurydice" as "mere Lloyd's Shipping Intelligence." His family background is hardly irrelevant to the fact that his two long poems are about shipwrecks.

In "The Wreck of the Deutschland" Hopkins was relying for details on the current *Times* reports, many of which are explicitly identified by the *Times* itself as coming by telegraph (Weyand, 1949). The result is a poem not simply about a disaster and suffering, but about *ongoing* disaster and suffering, evoking new kinds of writer and reader responses. Hopkins's relationship to his subject matter differs strikingly from that of Milton's in "Lycidas," the only other poem in English about a ship foundered off the coast of England to have generated a corpus of commentary comparable to the corpus concerned with Hopkins's poem. The difference reflects the differing states of the communication media in the mid-seventeenth century and the late nineteenth century. The difference is particularly interesting because Hopkins had read and re-read Milton, rating him the best of all poets in English, and perhaps in any language. It appears, as John J. Glavin (1980) has circumstantially argued, that in his composition of "The Wreck of the Deutschland" Hopkins was reckoning, consciously or unconsciously, with Milton's achievement in "Lycidas" (Ong, 1986).

Edward King's death was an event well past, and felt as past, when Milton wrote about it, and an event about which Milton had rather scant details. (The scantiness of detail in pre-electric and pre-electronic cultures, not to mention oral cultures, as compared to the avalanche of details in such electronic-age displays as the Watergate case, deserves more attention than it has been given. Scant details foster common-place treatment—for want of specificities one has to fall back on tried and true generalities, whether in poetry or in law court rhetoric.) Setting Edward King in a pastoral elegy (to the annoyance of Dr. Johnson), Milton involves him in the classical world of the past (laurels, myrtles, nymphs, watery bier, remorseless deep, Tempe, the Muses, and so forth), even while assigning him current relevance to seventeenth-century ecclesiastical disputes. Milton's concluding line is "Tomorrow to fresh Woods, and Pastures new." The line is a kind of foreclosure. The past is past. King is dead and gone.

For Hopkins, the German nun's death he celebrated—there is no more apt word—in "The Wreck of the Deutschland" was a distant but far more immediate experience. Far from detached and past, the sense of presence, immediacy and (consequently) reader interaction is not merely "captured" but entwined as part of its meaning. In short, those concepts of intimacy which one associates with momentary communication are features of the text and facilitated by new technological advances. The *Deutschland* struck on the sands of the Kentish Knock on Monday, December 6, and the *Times* accounts (Weyand, 1949) run from Tuesday, December 7, through Saturday, December 11 (when the German nun's cry "O Christ, come quickly" was reported among other details), on through the following Monday, December 13. The

British people, Hopkins among them, were aware of the wreck and its sequels as ongoing events, distant but pressing on them. Among the *Times* stories, as just noted, are telegraphed news reports, identified by the *Times* as such. Hopkins's sense of immediacy is indirectly reflected in his reference to the storm as "electrical horror" (in "The Loss of the Eurydice," Hopkins also refers explicitly to electricity: "deadly electric"). The near-synchronicity effected by the telegraph, abetted by the railroad tying together the east coast of England, off which the ship foundered, and the west coast near which Hopkins was living in Wales, leads Hopkins to reflect on exactly what he was doing at the very time the *Deutschland* was breaking up and some 78 of her 213 (or 223) passengers and crew were being cast to their deaths in the North Sea.

> Away in the lovable west,
> On a pastoral forehead of Wales,
> I was under a roof here, I was at rest,
> And they the prey of the gales.

With Hopkins, the reader shares the press of the events with which the poem is involved. The reader, who of course is typically not reading the text while the writer is writing it—most certainly not in Hopkins's case here—is nevertheless caught up in the immediacy of the writer's experience when he or she later enters into the text. The synchronic sense with which he experienced the *Deutschland* disaster was not strange to the world Hopkins lived in: other persons read the *Times* and profited from telegraphed news. Yet, the rapidity of communication relative to the normative standards of conventional technology provided a response so rapid that it presented for readers a proximity to the event that approached the spontaneity, and hence degree of imminence, associated with speech. Electric technology, facilitating the rapidity of print, provided an immediacy readers today take for granted. A few generations before Hopkins, readers knew nothing of this pressure within the present.

We are concerned not only with writers, but also with readers. Does Hopkins's electrically implemented relationship with his subject establish any special relationship with his readers? It does establish a new kind of directness in the relationship, a new intimacy, a participatory intimacy. This is not an intimacy of the sort that Hemingway readers are often made to feel, a kind of buddy-buddy relationship, so that the reader is made to feel like the writer's boon companion, and a very understanding companion (Ong, 1977). Rather, it is a kind of immediate personal involvement.

A paradox is at work here, as always when we are dealing with the application of technologies to the word, from writing on. Electricity means generators, machinery, and mechanical equipment. It interposed a great deal that is not directly human between the written verbalization of the events by reporters (whom the *Times* still identifies as "correspondents"; Weyand, 1949, p. 355) off the east coast of England and the reception of this verbalization on the west coast of the island in Wales. The interposition is not so massive as in the case of the technologies at work in the more nearly instantaneous electronic communication, but it is massive enough. Sending a telegram is not the same as sending a messenger. Yet its rapidity itself brings closeness, dissolving distance.

With Hopkins's close attention to the self and to the relations of one self to another, this immediacy is particularly significant and effective. John Robinson (1978) astutely observes that in some of Hopkins's poems, including the early "Nondum" (1886), "It was not his own fate which caused such a shudder of loneliness but a feeling of the ultimate inaccessibility of others' lives and deaths" (p. 124). Hopkins's poetry and, much more, his prose writings show how intensely he was aware that one person cannot enter into the consciousness of another directly, that the "taste" of one's self as such is incommunicable. But he was also aware that love can bridge the gap. And at the center of "The Wreck of the Deutschland," his intent is to enter into the mind of the German sister at her moment of crisis when she calls out "O Christ, Christ, come quickly" ("The Majesty! What did she mean?"). He discerns her meaning as the welcoming of her death, where Christ was coming to her. The drive to immediacy and to intimacy of interpretation here appears as great as it can well be for human beings. Unlike Milton's classical closing of King's case in the last line of "Lycidas" ("Tomorrow to fresh Woods, and Pastures new"), Hopkins's last lines abide in the present: "Dame, at our door/Drowned, and among our shoals/Remember us." This is not classical apostrophe, but prayer to a real person, still accessible after death to Hopkins's Catholic faith, which here abets the media development to enhance a sense of personal presence.

The reader is caught up into this immediacy-effected-at-a-distance, which is of a new intensity in the history of literature. The reader's role is to penetrate maximally with Hopkins into the interior of another human being's consciousness, physically but not temporally distanced. Earlier literature does not achieve or attempt such intensity in quite this way. Hopkins's closeness is a deep union of self-consciousness. Granted that in Hopkins's day the use of new technologies of communication could paradoxically foster in the reader the sense of immediacy as just explained, what can be said about the effect of still more sophisticated electronic technologies? Do they foster among readers any new roles of intimacy with the writer and his or her subject matter? This is a large and almost impossibly complicated question, and only a few suggestions shall be offered which may move toward answers.

From Hopkins's age on, and with increasing intensity in the age of electronic communication, the old oratorical expectations that for two thousand years and more so largely governed writer and reader, and held writer and reader commonly at a formal distance, have virtually disappeared. Electronic communication on radio, television, and now the computer has done away with the old declamatory tone of the ancient rhetorical tradition and the distances this tone implied. Readers trained by the McGuffey's *Readers* were still very much caught up in rhetorical declamation and distancing; readers were still thought of as reading aloud and their roles were tailored accordingly. Here is a sample of what McGuffey's *Readers* readers read, taken from McGuffey's *Rhetorical Guide, or Fifth Reader* (1844). The passage is from Lyman Beecher's "The Memory of Our Fathers":

> Caesar was merciful, Scipio was continent, Hannibal was patient; but it was reserved for Washington to blend them all in one, and, like the lovely masterpiece of the Grecian artist, to exhibit in one glow of associated beauty, the pride of every model, and the perfection of every artist. (p. 291)

This sounds like an oration, but it was presented by McGuffey as something to read—which meant to declaim, for the *Readers* were largely intended to be used for declamatory voiced reading. The reader's role in this age was still largely associated with oratory. One was likely to read even alone somewhat as though one were declaiming.

People still read on the radio and television from teleprompters, but they do not declaim when they do. They conceal the fact that they are reading, and often pretend to be informal and extemporaneous. A new line of intimacy—or of pseudointimacy—has been established in the close conversational verbalization normal on radio and in the pseudo-face-to-face relationship of speaker and audience on television (Gumpert & Cathcart, 1986). Now oral presentation to millions of persons has been tailored by electronics to appear to break down all artificial borders, although it separates sender and receiver from one another by technologies of Byzantine complexities that reach to outer space and back.

For Hopkins, the innovations of technology provided the opportunity for written communication to increase in the rapidity of expression. Diminishing the temporal distance of the printed word decreased the impersonal distance between reader and writer. Eventually other forms of mediated communication will provide greater, more direct interaction beyond the immediacy of the event and increase the interactive nature of the discourse in ways that artificially simulate (but nonetheless approach) direct verbal communication. Just as the electronic technology of Hopkins's era altered the rapidity and immediacy of the "text" so also will new forms of mediated communication compel us to adopt a more malleable notion of the text than our current predispositions allow. We need continued investigation of the ways in which these new uses of the technologies of the word affect the way we write when we write fiction or essays or scholarly works, and how they affect the roles of readers when readers read such things today.

REFERENCES

Dillon, G. L. (1986). *Rhetoric as social imagination: Explorations in the interpersonal function of language.* Bloomington: Indiana University Press.

Glavin, J. J. (1980). "The wreck of the Deutschland" and "Lycidas": Ubique naufragium est. *Texas Studies in Literature and Language, 22,* 522-546.

Gumpert, G., & Cathcart, R. (Eds.). (1986). *Inter/media: Interpersonal communication in a media world.* Oxford: Oxford University Press.

Havelock, E. A. (1986). *The muse learns to write: Reflections on orality and literacy from antiquity to the present.* New Haven, CT: Yale University Press.

Hopkins, G. M. (1970). *The poems of Gerard Manley Hopkins* (4th ed.). Oxford: Oxford University Press.

Ong, W. J. (1977). *Interfaces of the word.* Ithaca, NY: Cornell University Press.

Ong, W. J. (1986). *Hopkins, the self, and God.* Toronto: University of Toronto Press.

Robinson, J. (1978). *In extremity: A study of Gerard Manley Hopkins.* Cambridge: Cambridge University Press.

Sallis, S. (1986). Naming the rose: Readers and codes in Umberto Eco's novel. *Journal of the Midwest Modern Language Association, 19*(2), 3-12.

Weyand, N. (Ed.). (1949). *Immortal diamond: Studies in Gerard Manley Hopkins.* New York: Sheed & Ward.

11

A Rhetoric of
Mass Communication:
Collective or Corporate
Public Discourse

LYNETTE HUNTER

It has been suggested that the figures of classical rhetoric are archetypes or postures of individual minds (McLuhan, 1962), and that rhetorical study needs to be extended for a collective or corporate theory of written communication. More precisely, there is growing interest in forms of written communication that emphasize its difference from rhetoric in terms of the oral/written divide, in turn mapping that division onto orality/literacy and the individual versus the mass. Since much of this interest derives directly or indirectly from Plato's discussion of writing in the "Phaedrus," this chapter will begin there as a location for many of the issues that arise. Not that the "Phaedrus" holds timeless remedies; indeed, some of the remedies are effective just because they are bound to an historical materiality.

Ever since the writing of the "Phaedrus," it has been argued that mass rhetorics are inevitably manipulative rather than engaging. Specifically, there is the criticism that writing does not address each individual: the individual is denied the response possible to the listener to oral communication. Written communication addresses not only a mass audience but an overtly absent audience. Plato has Socrates worry about this, because the techniques it invariably turns to debilitate readers by depriving them of evaluative processes; and if they debilitate, they may mislead. It is this question of the absent audience that has worried critics and commentators ever since. Recent media theorists center in on the question of new rhetoric by specifically addressing the problem of absence. Yet they invariably concentrate on rhetoric as a set of techniques, as if a new "set" could be manufactured and uplifted wholesale into mass communications. Such a solution depends on separating rhetoric from its social and historical context, and can only perpetuate the idea that an absent audience is a "problem."

This said, the "Phaedrus" itself is rich with contradiction, generating many readings. An overarching direction of the text is that rhetoric is not merely a set of techniques; it is also instruction in the strategy of speaker and audience or *ethos* and *pathos*, and a guide to stance or "goodness" (Hunter, 1984a). Each of technique, strategy, and stance is addressed distinctly, and it is made clear that the discussion of technique in particular—and strategy to a lesser extent—is not focused on a debate between the oral and written as such. Rhetoric in Plato's society was not simply a description of the oral: in the *Republic* the poets are banished and the poets of Plato's time are not writers but real speakers (Havelock, 1963). Rhetoric was a description of oratory.

As a description of oratory, rhetoric may well be considered a description of an early form of mass communication. The word *mass* is used here to take in communication of ideological constructs to a large audience, a definition that will be elaborated on a little later. The writer of "Phaedrus" recognizes this mass element, and spends most of the time criticizing the relationship of two orations to their audiences. But we should not forget that the criticism is enacted in writing, and further that while the techniques and strategies of oratorical rhetoric may not be suited to the written, what is said about stance lies at the foundation of both and provides jurisdiction for the medium Plato is using. Of course Plato did not criticize either the two orations or writing simply because they described communication to large audiences; what he was drawing out were the precise details whereby both orator and writer might produce texts that would debilitate their audience. In other words, issues might be put forward that both formally and structurally tried to disguise or hide their constructed status, thereby "naturalizing" them, making them seem for granted. It is this that is at the root of the mass debate about modes of the presentation or activity of communication: the recognition, and means of recognition, of ideology.

Writing primarily draws forth criticisms of strategy resulting from its absent audience. The most immediate of these criticisms is that the audience cannot ask questions; the texts cannot reply. "If you ask them what they mean by anything they simply return the same answer over and over again" (Plato, 1973, p. 93). And further, because the audience is at a distance, the arguments of writing cannot be shaped with specific readers in mind: "a writing cannot distinguish between suitable and unsuitable readers" (p. 97). The implications of these criticisms have been taken up ever since, not just for writing, but for all systems of mass communication. In terms of technique, writing is criticized because it is a medium that is thought to destroy the need for and the exercise of memory. Readers will become forgetful; "they will rely on writing to bring things to their remembrance by external signs instead of their own internal resources" (p. 97)—again a fear that has accompanied the inception of all technologies ever since because it is related to the fear that wisdom will be superseded by a patina of information. At root, writing is criticized both in techniques and strategy because it deprives its audience of a basis for reasoning and evaluation. It should be underlined that what Plato is specifically attacking is the writing of speeches. At the time of "Phaedrus" this was a new if increasing practice for, generally, writing was not common. The other main area outside commerce where writing was growing and which Plato addresses implicitly, if not explicitly, was philosophy.

The most detailed criticism in the "Phaedrus" is reserved for oral speeches, although this is complicated by the fact that of the two orations studied the first is retold from a written version, and the second (although supposedly direct) reaches us through the written medium of the book. Criticism of the first speech from Lysias is made quite explicit by Socrates, who quickly uncovers the shambles of figuration and illogicality of which it is made up. The course of Socrates' own first speech is technically far more sophisticated, but concomitantly with its own more serious drawbacks (Hunter, 1984a). The second speech ostensibly criticizes the techniques of the first, insisting on precision in figuration, and clear analysis and synthesis within the argument so that the audience need not be told what to think but instead be led to understand. These aspects are the specific contribution of the art of rhetoric to vocal communication, since ambivalence and vagueness are the negative qualities of oral poetic expression (Plato, 1955). But having given the second speech, Socrates stops and criticizes it himself, saying that in his splendid argument portraying a love that manipulates he has purchased "honour with men at the price of offending the gods" ("Phaedrus," p. 44). Despite the sophistication of his technique and the shift of his strategy away from force to manipulative argument, he shows that his stance is identical to that of Lysias. The figures may be clear and the argument logical, but they delineate their own grounds and do not allow the audience to go beyond them and introduce questions that might challenge, disrupt, or seriously question. The speeches deny a full participation and assume the authority of the speaker over the audience.

It is a crushing if rather obvious joke that the centerpiece of the "Phaedrus" is Socrates' second speech, a written mythological poem that is like neither oratory nor writing as criticized elsewhere in the book. What the writer of the "Phaedrus" is doing is presenting the reader with a work constructed in a responsible written rhetoric. The shift in stance underlines the different strategy taken and emerges in the emphasis on a rather different set of technical devices, heavily analogical, that engage the reader in dialectical involvement. In the case both of writing and of oratory, it is the effective fixity of authority which each achieves if the rhetoric is used unwisely that Plato criticizes. In other words, he is criticizing the authoritative stance that is the counterpart to depriving the audience of a basis for evaluative reasoning. For Plato such a basis resides in textual dialectic, which generates participation between reader, writer, and writing—audience, rhetor, and speech.

It is not the absent audience that is a problem, but the deprivation of evaluative reasoning that can apply equally to the individual or the mass, to the spoken or the written. Further, it is not a "new" rhetoric that is needed for mass communication because rhetoric is fundamentally related to stance, which expresses belief. Through the analogy of the lovers which runs throughout the writing, Plato indicates that an understanding of stance is the province of the philosophical lover who also comprehends strategy and technique; the nonphilosophical lover neglects stance, while the nonlover of Lysias' speech is merely a technician. This view of rhetoric as philosophical, sophistical, and technical, addressing itself to materiality, *ethos/pathos*, and device respectively, is most important for a proper comprehension of the scope of rhetoric.[1] It is possible to understand that techniques may vary just as those of Socrates' first speech are of oratory and of his second are to do with writing. Yet in terms of *ethos*, the strategy of the oral simply provides an analogy for the strategy of the written: for example, the authoritative *ethos* of the written speeches is no different from the *ethos* of writing portrayed in the story of Theuth. Stance itself is the root of the "Phaedrus," but it remains an effect of reading the analogies; it is not conceptualized.

While limited to the position of writing and activity of speechmaking within his society, Plato's work allows for a subtle and complex view of rhetoric in each medium. Yet it is ambiguous in addressing the central questions behind this chapter; the question of whether the rhetoric presented here addresses only the oratorical or the growing discipline of writing. Rhetorical studies today are split quite clearly between the two approaches. George Kennedy (1980, p. 5), insists that "primary rhetoric" has to do with oral discourse, and that literature is "secondary rhetoric." Alone, this would leave open the possibility that written discourse might attain to primary rhetoric if its emphasis were persuasion rather than narration. However, when Kennedy goes on to indicate that secondary rhetoric is frequently manifested by "commonplaces, figures of speech and thought, and tropes in elaborate writing" (p. 5), this avenue appears to have been cut off. The literary is held simply to have uplifted the technical devices of rhetoric as a convenient prefabricated and sophisticated description for literary criticism, while neglecting that the oral is an act: "Delivery is an important part of rhetoric. The time, the place, and the immediate reaction of the audience are also important factors, as they are not in the case of literature" (p. 109)—yet again that emphasis on the absent audience. But this is to restrict the scope of rhetoric, despite what Kennedy says elsewhere, to the technical.

In contrast, Walter Ong (1982) claims quite forcefully that rhetoric, while it initially describes oratorical discourse, describes the oratory of a culture that was becoming graphically sophisticated. Further, it does so in a way that would have been impossible without the written making up a substantial part of the approach to oratory. The very linearity of speech that distinguished it from the narrative structures of literature (Kennedy, 1980) is part of the conceptual apparatus Ong (1982) regards as impossible without writing and reading. For Ong, it is precisely because of the written that oratory becomes possible, moving away from preliterate forms of oral poetic expression. Yet even this movement is slow, and the reification of the word into "context-free language discourse which cannot be directly questioned because written discourse has been detached from its author" (Ong, 1982, p. 78) has to wait for the advent of print. Here we are presented directly with the idea that rhetoric is a set of techniques allowing the speaker/writer to address people at a distance, despite the fact that Ong later refers to rhetoric as "an index of the amount of residual primary orality in a given culture" (p. 109), describing it in the terms of oral poetry as agonistic and oppositional.

From either point of view the absence of audience becomes the key factor in the recent criticism that, because of this absence, writing has to become authoritative, imposing its point upon the reader or audience. This emphasis, however, depends upon an understanding of rhetoric primarily as a technical device, and completely abstracts it from the historical context necessary to assess strategy or realize stance. Versions of the "Phaedrus" useful in assessing the pursuit of a "new" rhetoric are found in three areas: first, the language debate over the construction between the oral and the written; second, the literacy debate over modes of cognition; and third, the debate within media studies over the existence of the mass audience and the role of ideology.

VERSION 1:
THE LANGUAGE DEBATE

The "Phaedrus" is central to the language debate over the difference between the oral and the written, because the written is often cast in terms of being a second-order sign system that corrupts the spoken word. Within the history of linguistics during the twentieth century this view is definitely present, but not nearly as consistently or clearly as recent literary critics would have us believe. The concentration by linguists on the spoken word may partly have been due to a belief that writing was corrupt, but was primarily a result of the fact that the written was rule-bound, described and overdetermined by grammar. To study language, linguists needed to escape not the corrupt but the correct state of the written.[2] Whatever the cause, one reaction was the entire endeavor of New Criticism to divorce writing from the potentially corrupting forces of writer and reader: the intention and affective fallacies so dear to first-year criticism courses. Instead they attempted to develop a formalism of the text in itself, parallel to language studies of *langue*; and in this they were negatively encouraged, despite K. Burke and I. A. Richards, by the impoverished reduction of rhetoric to a set of techniques. The result was a theory of literature that excluded material context. This phenomenon strained toward correct writing implicitly, underwriting its potential for corruption. Combined with the enormous influence of J. Derrida's *Of Grammatology* (1974), it is the supposed attitude of both language and literature critics toward the written as "corrupt" that has infused many arguments over the last 20 years.

Derrida (1974) focuses on the arguments of Saussure, whose centrality to twentieth-century studies in language and literature cannot be denied, and in turn on Saussure's debt to Rousseau. First, Saussure specifically thinks of writing as a second-order sign system that "exists for the sole purpose of representing [the spoken word]" (Derrida, 1974, p. 30). Second, as with Plato in the "Phaedrus," "the evil of writing comes from without" (p. 34); in other words, it can stand for real wisdom, rather than expressing the realty of the originator. Writing is for Saussure not merely at one remove but morally impure, "a garment of perversion and debauchery, a dress of corruption and disguise, a festival mask that must be exorcised" (p. 35). Plato, Rousseau, and Saussure are held as examples of a quest for purity, for the natural, for presence within spoken language versus the corruption of the written. Derrida himself is aware that the early twentieth-century attempt to divorce the spoken from the written was partly to do with the limitations of written grammar, the mathematical theories underlying communications, and argues the same for Plato and for Rousseau. The basis of his argument in *Of Grammatology* is that a more reasonable attitude to writing would end by bringing both the oral and the written within the broader field of grammatology or semiotics. But since the burden of his argument is to expand upon the wider implications of writing as *differance*, he goes on to emphasize that the linguists have created their own rule-bound limitations and does not follow up on what they might gain from exploring their own *differance*.

The reaction of other criticism to this eloquent work has been a huge concentration on the differences between the oral and the written, rather than on their similar foundation in *differance*, and of course these critics have made hay of Derrida's use of Plato in particular. Literary criticism has made much of the strong line of oral=pure and written=corrupt by which Derrida (1974) defined language criticism, and has often converted it to the argument that the written text is imposingly authoritative while the oral is dialectically engaging. This in turn has fueled the simplistic attitude that writing is the imposition of power and that the printed word is the root of hierarchical authority, while the oral has to do with democratic power and that the spoken word is more natural. These positions do indeed have some source in language studies, but the avoidance of their history has left them as a kind of demonic idol for critics of the written to destroy in order to expand their own exploration of *differance*.

The pursuit of a correct or pure written language becomes acute when print technology intensifies the issues of an absent audience by making availability more widespread (McLuhan, 1962; Eisenstein, 1979), and it comes to a head in the sixteenth and seventeenth centuries with the communicative aims of modern science. But it has an earlier tradition developed by historians of both rhetoric and writing that turns the initial

oral/written divide into a separation between the debased written, and
the pure or correct. Historians of rhetoric have a particular interest in
the debate partly because the idea of pure writing is anathema to
rhetoric, and perhaps also because of their far greater awareness of the
complications in the oral tradition—that orality is not some "natural"
instinctive skill. At every level it is learned, and of course, particularly
so at the level of public oratory that generates the first recorded—in
other words, written—rhetorics of the Greek classical period. But even
within the study of rhetoric we find yearnings after the more "direct"
communication of the oral. George Kennedy (1980) notes that because
a lot of Greek literature had a public function it tended to take up
oratorical forms, yet the "introduction of writing into Greece tended
to freeze speech into texts" (p. 11). It is not clear whether this is
primarily Kennedy's worry or a comment on that of the Greeks themselves, for although Plato discusses it in the "Phaedrus" we do not know
whether this was a widespread concern—indeed, his commentary indicates that the practice of writing was growing quickly and without
reflection upon its implications. What is quite clear is that Greek, and
later Roman, modes of education happily taught public oration and
writing side by side. Kennedy speaks with anxiety of Quintilian's
importation of "stylistic abundance" and "imitation" from poetics into
rhetoric as part of the crossover, and certainly Quintilian is credited
with the formalization of classical education in both oratory and literature. S. Miller (1982), in "Classical Practice and Contemporary Basics," lays out the three-part structure of classical schooling: *literator*,
grammaticus, and textual study. Even at the ages of 12 to 15, with a
grammaticus boys were expected "to parse sentences correctly, to use
new vocabulary, and to speak with the correct accent and pronunciation
needed to make effective speeches" (p. 48). This combination of the
oral and written continued throughout their education. It is interesting
that Kennedy (1980) claims that Cicero, in contrast to Quintilian, deals
wholly in primary rhetoric, while Ong (1984) points out that "the tight,
analytic organization of Cicero's oral-style effects is possible only to
the mind conditioned by writing" (p. 4).

What becomes important is the shift from the oral=oratory=public to
the oral=popular, with its concomitant shift from the oral to the writ-

ten as the location for power. B. Stock (1983) notes that the connection of the oral with the popular came about "only when culture values were beginning to be associated with literacy" (p. 19) during the Roman conquest of Greece, when Latin acquired the literary forms of Greek. This began the separation between one language for the written and another for the oral that has persisted in Western culture "since wherever Latin improved, the spoken and grammatically written languages grew farther apart" (p. 25). Both Kennedy (1980) and R. Pattison (1982) link the development with the early Christian church. Pattison argues that Christian society in the first century was opposed to "formal systems of written and rhetorical language" (p. 69) because of their alliance with the Latin language of domination, elitism, and paganism. Kennedy suggests that the rejection of classical rhetoric by the early Christians has more to do with its humanist roots in establishing the authority for persuasion in dialectical argument rather than in the revelations of God, and he notes the dependence of the Gospels on story, myth, parable, image, and poem. This kind of written rhetoric which claims to reveal divine grace was finally incorporated into classical rhetoric by Augustine, the classical rhetor converted to Christianity, who states that "Persuasion cannot be accomplished by rhetorical means unless the truth is first known or simultaneously revealed by divine grace" (Kennedy, 1980, p. 152). At the same time Augustine reemphasizes the division between dialectics or exegesis and rhetoric or preaching, which pushes rhetoric toward style and technique away from reasoning, and separates the interpretive from the popular. In contrast, Pattison's (1982) argument stresses that when the Church realized the importance of the written it developed an elite which not only wielded effective power, but also protected the masses against "the deformities of truth believed necessarily to be present in formal written languages" (p. 81). The result was a split literacy, formal from popular, which dealt respectively in "the language of power and the language of the streets" (p. 84). This split was parallel to that within Rome itself, but the Roman divide was between bureaucracy and the populace (Pattison, 1982), while the Christian was overtly a separation between the corruptible written and the purity of the oral.

Whether viewed as corrupt from the start or not, writing certainly became allied by the Church with interpretation, and provided one of the fundamental administrative underpinnings for the priesthood as a necessary mediator between the Bible as the word of God and the laity. But what kind of interpretation? Pattison (1982) would have us believe that it was consistently authoritative, in other words, finding specific meanings that effected social change. However, Stock's impressive *Implications of Literacy* (1983) argues persuasively that interpretation from Augustine until around A.D. 1100 may well be thought of as "interpersonal communication with God" (p. 327); whereas with the shift, particularly of medieval law into church control (Clanchy, 1979), interpretation from the written becomes increasingly textualized. What Stock (1983) means by "text" is a key element in the oral/written debate. Although he concentrates at the start on text as the transition of the written word from mere record to necessary proof from about A.D. 1100, he widens this definition to imply that text in effect is ideology. Texts are the authorities for society, hence an oral society has a textual basis just as much as a written. Yet written texts are consciously formulated and formalized. Oral texts "evolve" by customary law, whereas written texts are only open to reduction and interpretation. And again, the oral text persists to legitimize activities in the popular, while the written underwrites law—particularly property law.

The transition from text=necessary proof to text=ideology is an uneasy one because ideologies can form which are not based on necessary proof, and it is at this nervous juncture that Stock's (1983) ambivalent attitude toward writing shows itself most clearly. He speaks on the one hand of two written "textual models," one presenting an "inviolable standard" and the other "progress through two stages of 'textual community' " (p. 483), and on the other hand of written texts as the location for authoritative interpretations operating "as intermediaries between orally transmitted ideas and social change" (p. 527) which form the basis for scholasticism. The excellent quality of Stock's work is to emphasize the continuing interdependence of the oral and written for many centuries, and to explore why writing in particular became associated with "socially useful rationality" (p. 10) by connecting with the aims of scholasticism. Yet he begins from the position that the oral is based on "individual interchange" (p. 15), and has no recourse to "a 'correct' version of events" (p. 15). In contrast, the written is "less of a subjectively determined performance and more of an objectified pattern within articulated norms" (p. 18). The objectivity allied with writing ties it to developments in science and economics, where the new use of mechanical clocks and of coinage became analogous media for distancing time and exchange; and encourages the sophistication of exegetical exchange or interpretive literary techniques such as allegory. This separation between word and interpretation generates the beginnings of the split between *langue* and *parole*. More important for our purposes here, Stock (1983) allies the oral with direct, interpersonal, individual communication from a standard set of rhetorical techniques, while the written addresses itself to the abstract general and objective. At the same time, the written is related to isolated individual interpretation and bureaucratic order, while the oral is connected with social communities and the popular.

It is an unbalanced equation. In the main, the imbalance derives from the focus Stock needs to take on the unique scholastic endeavor. Ostensibly both oral and written under discussion are forms of media connected to social order, to text: how the scholastic community organizes itself. Yet there are other—less overt, but just as ideological—forms of both media operating concurrently, such as song, drama, epic, and romance, which never cease to interact with the more bureaucratic and theological texts and which have other things to say about the oral/ written divide. Within scholasticism the oral and popular have recourse to rhetoric, but the written is based on "interpretation": exegesis, allegory, philosophy, and theology, all of which are modes of reading. Despite pointing out (Stock, 1983) that the oral epic contains many figures found in early written records, and despite the illumination of descriptive comments on the *cursus* as a conscious mutation of metrics into syllabics, there is no sense that writing as it begins to be used by ever larger numbers of people is acquiring its own set of defined techniques for anything other than ratiocinative, objective interpretation. In other words, it can never achieve direct interpersonal communication. What is not made plain is that techniques in themselves do not enforce a specific *ethos*, let alone a stance. It needs to be underlined that it is the scholastic endeavor within an intellectual hierarchy which provided the ideological context that used these particular techniques in this manner. Just so, the implication is that the rituals of oral communities are not semiotic, that they perform a magical unity with nature and God; and that writing itself, rather than the *use* of writing within this society, is the agent by which semiotics or sign systems emerge as interpretable rather than absolute. However, it is in this transition from the absolute of God to the scholastic absolutes of textual interpretations that writing becomes, for the Renaissance inheritors, simultaneously correct and potentially corrupt.

The split between debased writing and the purity of speech is discussed from a different angle by Pattison in his separation between early reformists such as Wycliff and the humanist world view. Whereas Stock emphasizes the connection of the vernaculars with the oral, Pattison (1982) proceeds to connect written vernaculars with "the eminence of God in the Word," while "the formal tradition argue[d] that language was but a reflection of the divine that required authoritarian interpretation" (p. 99). It is at this point that the idea of pure written popular communication emerges. Until now, the debate has focused on the division between the oral and the written. From this point on, the oral continues to be associated with the pure right up until the present day, lingering on in the eighteenth-century vernacular dictionaries (Ong, 1984), in the shadows of Wordsworth's attempt to revitalize poetic language by turning to the speech of the common man, or in the later dialect writing of the mid-nineteenth-century working class (Beetham, 1987). But writing itself splits into different approaches. The supposed preserve of the oral=pure is taken up by the reformists into the written of the Bible=pure, because the Bible is the word of God. In contrast to this is the tradition that the Bible is written in the words of mankind and therefore needs interpretation to understand the word of God, that it has a correct form which may be corrupted. The tradition of Augustine is severed in two. The purity of the written, essential to reformist religion, and the correctness underwriting scholastic nominalism were neither, according to Augustine, necessary to the Christian tradition. It is as if the scholastics had wrenched classical rhetoric out of probability into interpretation by formal logic, at the same time as the reformists—

who did not have an equally weighty tradition of technical Biblical rhetoric to foreground its persuasion—claimed direct revelation of the word parallel to the purity of oral communication.

Pattison (1982) illustrates the two traditions in terms of the seventeenth-century English inheritors of the severance, Bunyan and Donne, and claims that Milton goes the furthest to bringing the two traditions together (see also Frye, 1982). But however much Bunyan may have appeared to use a simple style, and may have claimed direct access to God's word, the fact remains that his fictional writing is highly allusive and allegorical, often with figures drawn from chapbook literature (Spufford, 1981) and the supernatural tales and ballads that are part of the "other" vernacular written tradition of the time. Donne, as a part of the humanist tradition, inherits an again radically transformed concept of interpretation from the written. Scholastic application of Aristotelian rhetoric had come to be seen as reifying, reductive, and tautologous (Streuver, 1982). Stress is placed on the conventions of discourse rather than logical formalism, on *topos* rather than syllogism, on context rather than analysis as the basis for moral evaluation (see also Sloan, 1974).

It is exactly this kind of rejection of previously accepted rhetorical techniques that reinforces the need for a recognition of history. The syllogism was a potent tool in the hands of scholastic thinkers; only when it became restricted to logic, at the same time that logic was split from rhetoric, was its activity made tautologously abstract and decontextualized. This point is made in a later article by Stock (1984), where he notes that the minority of medieval language theorists who stressed rhetoric criticized inherited logical assumptions and proposed instead an understanding of language "in which the meaning of expressions was inseparable from contexts and conventions which surrounded them" (p. 27). Writing may have attempted the abstract and objective by using certain logical schemes like the syllogism in a particular way, but neither the syllogism nor writing itself was inherently limited to this procedure. Just so, classical rhetoric was criticized by humanists (Streuver, 1982) for the reification effected by means of the "unselfconscious use of trope as deviation from normal use" (p. 193). Yet humanist rhetoric was based on an "ontological interpretation of style" (Platt,

1982, p. 372), mainly from a study of the tropes themselves. At the same time, Platt argues that courtly rhetoric depended upon trope to conceal and dissimulate. It is instructive that Renaissance rhetorics rarely if ever discuss the potentially corrupt schemes of persuasion, claiming always that—because God gave language to mankind—language is uncorruptible, yet a work such as Shakespeare's *Troilus and Cressida* provides what is virtually a guide to corrupt rhetoric in the speeches of its obsessed characters (Vickers, 1982).

Bacon is often attributed with the banishment of trope in the seventeenth century (for example, Miller, 1982) which culminates in the work of the true inheritors of the Protestant reformists, the scientists and philosophers. But Bacon recognized that trope was essential to rhetoric in its scope of applying reason to imagination. He did, however, firmly divide the province of logic from that of rhetoric. The former could discuss the true and the latter the probable; moreover, the former was an intellectual tool, while the latter was a popular device. Here the popular is uniquely bound to tropes and figures, while the intellectual and written is the preserve of the precise and accurate. After the general incursion into English education of the Ramist split between logic and rhetoric in the 1620s and the 1630s (Hunter, 1984a), Bacon's division frequently became restated in terms of correct and corrupt writing, a process possibly exacerbated by an excess of Ciceronian rhetorical exuberance (Croll, 1966). Hobbes, Sprat, and Locke were representative of the general intellectual trend to consider words as potentially corrupting if infected with figures and schemes (Corbett, 1982; Hunter, 1984a). They argued for the "plain style," relegating rhetoric to decorative technique and allowing its study gradually to become divorced from the humanist ends of social order (Johnson, 1982). What they desired was written language with access to Nature, just as the protestant reformers claimed direct access to God. Their ideal of a clear language without figures, a language where words=things, seemed to forget entirely the humanist criticisms of scholastic reification: their "unconscious" use of trope was a massive "deviation" in the history of language. Through them, the written attained three styles: the logical or correct, the rhetorical or corrupt, and the poetic or sublime. The latter category admitting some mystical understanding of the world or Nature through controlled or inspired figuration.

The primary pragmatic end that these language reformers aimed toward was the precise and accurate representation of the phenomena in the world—political, philosophical, or scientific. The demand for such communication was fundamentally linked to the changes in the medium of intellectual exchange that had taken place, and the concomitant changes in the intellectual practice. Ideas were no longer written down to be circulated, read aloud, and debated. Private experiment and observation, eschewing interpretation, was the basis for inquiry; print was the dominant medium of transmission; and individual readers were the primary audience. Suddenly the audience was no longer a small group, but potentially thousands; the medium was no longer oral/aural but tactile/visual; and the onus was on the originator to prove the truth of his observations of Nature. Faced with exactly that potentially corrupting communication of the written to a large audience that Plato had foreseen—and these thinkers would undoubtedly have had the opportunity to read the "Phaedrus" (Kennedy, 1980)—they developed the scientific method and literary style largely still intact today.

The appeal to plain speaking and the end of metaphor has been a common response to the problems that appear to come to the fore when an aspect of the written finds itself with a large audience, and it has often been linked with the oral. Both the claim to correctness and the claim to purity were built on the initial oral/written divide, and attempted to seek for the written what appeared to be the case for the oral: an inherent means of communicating ideas responsibly. In response to the signal difference between the oral and the written, the absent audience, both approaches to writing rejected rhetorical persuasiveness and in doing so also rejected ideological constraint. Twentieth-century interpretations of the oral/written divide present these rejections as the result of a series of elisions in the history of rhetoric and writing, since the oral clearly has its own rhetoric and its own ideological constraints. Furthermore, these elisions are still apparent in other contemporary debates, particularly that of literacy.

VERSION 2:
THE LITERACY DEBATE

It is impossible to study the discussion of oral-versus-written without addressing the question of literacy, particularly because reading and writing have become synonymous with education. During the twentieth century, there has been a tendency to equate the oral/written with uneducated/educated, illiterate/literate, and ultimately primitive/civilized. Although the equation has undergone radical revision over the last 20 to 30 years, its influence is still felt. UNESCO funds a number of projects on literacy dissemination, and has recently directed many of its efforts toward devising a mode of teaching that will mitigate the dangers of cultural imperialism carried with the spread of reading and writing (Goody, 1973; Pattison, 1982; Street, 1984; Wendell, 1982). But the literacy debate also focuses upon the supposed long-range changes that occur in cognition once writing becomes a dominant factor in society, and it is here that research has laid a foundation for considering the techniques and strategies specific to writing as inherent to its mode of communication, perpetuating the concept of writing as correct/corrupt or pure.

Within the field of cognitive psychology, the literacy debate has focused on the question of whether the written or oral effectively changes one's perception of the world (McLuhan, 1951; Whorf, 1956). If so, how does the written affect the oral world-view, and does print exacerbate or change the effects of writing? Much of this work refers to the premise in the work of J. Goody and I. Watt: "The overwhelming debt of the whole of contemporary civilization to classical Greece must be regarded in some measure the result, not so much of Greek genius, as of the intrinsic difference between nonliterate (or protoliterate) and literate societies" (1968, p. 49). The writers base their studies on a broad field of essential and social factors, but despite their comprehension of the latter they still claim that, for example, "the effects of reading are intrinsically less deep and permanent than those of oral conversation" (p. 54), relating this to the "abstractness of the syllogism" and "categorizations of knowledge" that are supposedly inherent aspects of alphabetic writing.

In order to study the effects of writing, writing itself was often contrasted to the oral, possibly because so much well-documented analytical work had already been done on the effects of spoken language; and there has been enormous stress on the absent-audience factor in writing as the major distinction between the oral and the written. D. Olson and W. Chafe provide the signal points of departure for many recent writers in cognitive psychology. Chafe speaks of writing as a "lonely activity" that has "a detached quality that contrasts with the involvement of spoken language" and its "environment of social interaction" (1985, p. 105). Olson and Hildyard (1983) base the article "Writing and Literal Meaning" on the divorce of the speaker from the text. Others refer to the "lonely figure" of the writer in terms that read as a loose translation from the "Phaedrus":

> cut off from the stimulus and corrective of listeners. He must be a predictor of reactions and act on his predictions. He writes with one hand tied behind his back being robbed of gesture. He is robbed too of his tone of voice and the aid of clues that the environment provides. He is condemned to monologue; there is no one to help out, to fill the silences, put words in his mouth or make encouraging noises. (Collins & Michaels, 1986, p. 207)

The emphasis is on speech as interpersonal and writing as detached, but the valuation placed on these strategies is quite different from that found among linguists. Not many commentators would go as far as D. Olson, who, in an early article, "From Utterance to Text" (1977), claimed that both culture and development evolved from utterance to text. Most would, however, agree that writing opens up a broad field of sophisticated devices that according to some few far outweighs what is lost in terms of personal contact, but which according to most others leaves it with inherent communicative limitations because it is not face-to-face.

A central concern of cognitive psychology in this field has been to contest the linguistic idea that writing simply "represents" speech. Research in this area has dealt with the physical acquisition of writing skills, and with orthography and neurology (Martlew, 1983; Olson, Torrance, & Hildyard, 1985), the latter producing some interesting work on the different neurological locations for aphasia and agraphia

(Marcie, 1983). Most research, though, has focused on the need to describe writing as other than a second-order sign system. L. Vygotsky has been as important to this pursuit as Saussure to the linguistic, when he lays the foundation in the 1920s and 1930s for the psychological study of writing as "direct symbolism" (Vygotsky, 1983; see also background in Scribner & Cole, 1981). As such its symbolic mode is detached, leaving it "more objective, distant and equitoned . . . [it] involves the packing of more information into a single idea unit than speech" (Olson, 1982, p. 6). Furthermore, writing is "a slow, deliberate, editable process, whereas speaking is done on the fly" (Chafe, 1985, p. 105). Hence writing is integrated and speech fragmented; writing is concerned with "degrees of truth . . . statistical probability" while speech is concerned with "categorical" truth (p. 122). Chafe makes no secret of the fact that he is comparing conversational speech with academic writing, but the idea that writing is involved with the probable while speech concerns the categorical underlines the vast expanse of oratory and rhetoric that he has chosen to ignore or defer. This would not in itself be problematic, were it not that so many other writers in the field persist in comparing conversational speech with formal writing in order to determine the differences between the illiterate and literate.

The ignoring of rhetoric, either oral or written, by psychologists is quite extraordinary—but then, the linguists do the same. It can lead to the astounding statement that "As researchers and teachers we have, until very recently [1968], assumed that writing, as act and as product, is an indivisible and relatively impenetrable phenomenon which does not vary appreciably from occasion to occasion" (Watson, 1983, p. 123). It has held back, and still holds back, understanding of both processes, because the focus on the absent audience leads virtually all researchers to consider the differences as located in the presence or absence of context. Because speaking is personal and involved, it draws heavily on the context of the communicative act. In contrast, writing is supposed to be context-free. This is the source for its apparent objectivity, which some take to be an effect of cognition itself. The comparison of the intonation and hesitation of speech with the punctuation of writing (Chafe, 1985) indicates the impoverished attitude toward written language. Just so, comments that the "live narrator" of the oral leads to more conventionalization in story elements than in the more distanced narrator of the written, even to the extent of saying that "written stories do not have a conventionalized opening" (Brewer, 1985, p. 184), ignore all the twentieth-century work in narrative analysis. This particular statement comes in a study of the narrative in science fiction, mystery stories, and the western, among others, which together must represent some of the most highly conventionalized writings available (Brooke-Rose, 1981; Scholes, 1979). But a further comment in the same article foregrounds the view of several commentators that there are inherent rhetorical techniques that divide the written from the oral. There is the suggestion that because writing is not performed but at a distance, there is far more discourse characterization. The growth in characterization within English literature from Chaucer onward, however, probably has far more to do with the social shifts of the late Middle Ages, with that ambiguous movement of the "individual" that Stock (1983) attempts to analyze in the context of literacy, than with inherent strategies of communicative media.

Recently, more work has been carried out in an attempt to deal with the sophistication of the written. Some studies combine rhetorical technique with discourse theory, producing elaborate new handbooks of schemes and strategies which are admitted to be problematic because they "imply a linear, almost mechanical, process" (Cooper & Matsuhashi, 1983, p. 36). This kind of work, sometimes emerging from psychologists who have just been converted to the sophistication of writing, overlaps to a large extent with rhetorical theory aimed at the novice writer (Hauser, 1986; Winckler & McCuen, 1978) in its pragmatic and reductionist movement. Other studies focus on the performance of the medium, claiming that the "communicative tasks" for writers and speakers have more consequences for language than modality (Collins & Michaels, 1986, p. 208). This route often leads to a study of cohesion devices, although rarely with the complexity outlined in, for example, Halliday and Hasan (1976). Collins and Michaels compare oral gesture, intonation, and feedback with genre conventions, and contrast oral prosody with lexical devices such as punctuation and italicization because they claim that prosody is not available to the written. They conclude that "the [black] fourth-grader who has an oral discourse style that relies heavily on prosodic cuing has more difficulty expressing himself, in writing, than does the [white] fourth-grader who uses more lexicalized and grammaticalized cohesive ties in his oral discourse" (p. 215). However, they avoid the consistent tradition of prosody in writing and neglect the fact that written prosody is not taught within the first four grades to anything approaching the same extent as lexical and grammatical guides, if at all. Although oral and written prosody may differ, the experimental premises established here do not allow for adequate differentiation.

In a similar way, D. Tannen looks at cohesion in an attempt to sort out the context hypothesis, the absent-audience condition. Here, the paralinguistic and prosodic features of the oral are contrasted with the comparatively impoverished lexical techniques of capitalization, underlining, and italics (Tannen, 1985). Quite sensibly, Tannen notes that the three aspects of the context hypothesis—the absent audience, the fact that the reader "cannot ask for clarification," and the writer's lack of knowledge about the readers' attitudes and beliefs (all, we could note, again identical with Plato's criticism of written speeches in the "Phaedrus")—are related to technological communication of information, not the focus of involvement. Hence, written literary discourse may be interpersonal. However, Tannen connects the three aspects with loss of "immediate context," with an "overloading of background information," and "filling in as many as possible steps of a logical argument" (p. 128), as well as noting that lexical cohesiveness does diminish involvement because it "draws less on the reader's shared social knowledge" (p. 132). The observations foreground the tendency within cognitive psychology to ignore the book as an object and publishing as a social phenomenon, to dismiss the history of rhetoric and logical structures of oral persuasion, and imply (despite a whole tradition of commentary) that analysis is primarily written; and to deny the educational impact and change of grammatical, print, and chirographic skills.

All of which is to use Tannen rather unfairly because the clarity of her argument summarizes much that is going on in cognitive psychology, and to play down the invaluable service the work does in insisting on the interpersonal. The point here is rather that the reasons given for the interpersonal may be displayed because they appear to emphasize a necessary condition for writing: inherent figures, schemes, and strategies. Olson and Hildyard (1983) produce a detailed revision of some of Olson's earlier related work in "Writing and Literal Meaning." They begin by saying that the oral and the written each have their own contexts, and often differ from the "simple consequence of their occasions of use and the purposes to which they are put" (p. 41). Yet they go on to reemphasize the activities of writing as "study" and "memorization"; we "analyze, summarize, paraphrase and evaluate" (p. 42) the authority of the written, because it provides an "original" with literal meaning in contrast to the process of oral transmission, which is rarely word-for-word (p. 46). Literal meaning is defined as the meaning of the sentence as opposed to the speaker's meaning, and the writers call on Searle and Bierwisch to introduce the concept of written context within which a semantic field can yield meaning (p. 50).

In a radical shift of the absent audience or context debate, it is admitted in Olson and Hildyard (1983) that context is vital to the written. Because writing lacks the knowledge of actual shared assumptions necessary to the oral, it constructs its own context by systematically working out "a consistent set of relations between sentence meaning S and speaker's meaning M" (p. 59), which is the writer's style and allows it "to stipulate a possible world which serves as its context" (p. 59). The implication is that writing becomes an "ideal device for the acquisition and expression of new knowledge and new points of view" (p. 59), and that the concomitant aspects of writing are, technically, a decrease in deictic expression of immediate context (this, that, here, there) and, strategically, the construction of common ground precisely and unambiguously to permit "any reader to construct essentially the same meaning" (p. 61). Writing therefore requires "more care in planning and revision than does speaking" (p. 62), because the writer has continually to judge whether the sentence can be read in another way than the one intended, and this also calls upon shared standards of the larger society expressed in (for example) dictionaries or teaching.

What is fascinating about this account, and familiar to rhetoricians at least, is its proximity to the rhetorical theory of argumentation.

Argumentation bases its effectiveness on the construction of common grounds—both, it should be said, for the oral and the written: Many aspects of speech-act theory either derive from, or have emerged at a later date in spite of, the theory of argumentation. But developments in the theory have indicated not only the drawbacks it entails, but also the rather specialized use to which it is actually put. The drawbacks are the classical problems with reification and tautology that follow all too easily upon an argument whose conclusions are implicit in its grounds or premises. As we have seen it is the primary strategy in scientific writing, and it is frequently used in journalism.

The popularly conceived role of journalism is split between the scandal mongers, obvious opinion benders, and the responsible face of objectivity, accuracy, and truth to reported events. The double role has precedents from the early days of personal pamphlets and foreign newsheets in the late sixteenth and early seventeenth centuries, but emerges firmly into newspapers with the government-sponsored "official news" versus the papers of opinion in the eighteenth century. However, newspaper writing was always slightly scandalous—reserved for "hacks"—until the Houses of Parliament were open to a new breed of men, the reporters, whose skill lay in word-for-word transcription of what was said (Smith, 1978). Although their role was changed during the nineteenth century, the possibility of "true" reporting spread throughout the newspaper trade, bolstering the myths of an independent fourth estate necessary to democracy. As the policymaking of newspapers shifted from the editor or publisher-owner to advertisers (Innis, 1947) and corporations (Lee, 1978; Murdock, 1982), this claim to objectivity was carried on willy-nilly. The journalists G. K. Chesterton in the 1920s and G. Orwell in the 1930s both exposed the claim as groundless, in the latter case getting a horrified response when he presented himself, the reporter, as suspect (Hunter, 1984b).

What is interesting is the technical and strategic methods which journalism developed to ensure that "single reading." Both Orwell and Chesterton comment on the need for a single "line" that denies any possible alternative, but most of all they were concerned with the use of supposedly "denotative" language that claims to represent things exactly but is in effect made up of conventional phrases, jargon, euphemism, incantatory repetition, tautological logic, abstractions, and so on.[3] All these devices aim to hide or disguise the basis of their argument in opinion, and claim truth by giving the reader no option but to enter their argument on their own terms. Both these early twentieth-century journalists were acutely aware of the persuasion effected through the mass media by advertising, business, and politicians, but neither suggested that the persuasion could be avoided. Chesterton's answer was self-criticism, correction, and reconstruction, while Orwell's was the constant activity of evaluation.[4] Both perceived the solution in terms of awareness to journalistic technique and strategy through education in writing and reading.

Argumentative rhetoric outlines similar techniques, although restricting the written to the nonimaginative and nonlogical. In a close parallel to Olson and Hildyard, it is stated that "the essence of argumentation is the establishing of a convincing connection between two terms" (Brandt, 1970, p. 24). The means for doing so are syllogism; "sequential, additive" connection (p. 60); and objective language (denotation). But what argumentation stresses is not only this particular set of techniques of writing but the necessity for the author to establish a clear position, an *ethos* so that the argument does not "prove" but "persuade the reader to assent" (p. 197). Brandt also defines reportorial writing as pseudo-argumentation that gives "the illusion that one's subject has the logically related parts of an argument" (p. 23), and notes that such journalism is based on the writer presenting himself "as what he cannot possibly be—an impartial observer" (p. 257). Brandt plays down the fact that it is the very techniques of observation that make the "invisible author" possible, but outlines the implications quite clearly. Within this writing the *ethos* of the writer is one of authority, and the ends of the pragmatic usefulness of this kind of argument depend wholly upon whether the audience or reader understands that *ethos* and how it is constructed.

It is, however, of considerable interest that the strategies described as inherent to writing provide so many parallels with the actual strategies used by specific media addressed to large audiences. It is of further interest that the qualities of "objectivity," rational analysis, and detachment described by cognitive psychologists as a result of writing

transpose easily into the techniques of denotative language, verisimilitude, sequential narration, and unseen writer that those media also
call upon. While Olson and Hildyard (1983) indicate that the single
reading and completely controlling author are desirable, the rhetoric of
argumentation points out that it is unethical. The techniques and strategies are of enormous pragmatic use in achieving short-term ends, or
what cognitive psychology would call the transfer of factual information. But unless the process of that achievement is recognized for the
corporate movement it is, within which individual decision and choice
is temporarily deferred to the authority of the group, then the pragmatic
short term can easily elide into the dictatorial long term.

My point here has been to discuss the features of strategy, particularly those of rational analysis and objectivity that Olson and Hildyard
(1983) present as necessary to the written. In effect our experience of
writing, here illustrated in terms of journalism, lead us to believe that
not only is it only one type of text that is written in this way, but that
these works are themselves open to radical shifts in stance once placed
within an historical context. Indeed, the narrow attitude toward writing
only underlines the concept of writing as correct, and inevitably carries
with it the underbelly of the corrupt in all these figures and schemes
that do not satisfy "correctness." In other words, although it is helpful
to move on to the idea that the written does have a context, to constrain
this to the internal invented context of a possible world is not going
far enough. Writing is just as contextualized as speaking, but in a
different manner. The audience is never absent. A growing amount of
cognitive study is becoming more interested in this, and hence in the
learned rather than inherent aspects of writing. In the process of pro-
posing a more flexible rhetorical model, Scardamalia and Bereiter
(1985) show precisely that writing appears to be an impediment to
communication for many people until they become highly literate;
and that the reflective thought so "characteristic" of writing in some
accounts is not "an automatic consequence. . . . It's an achievement"
(p. 327).

Despite the stress in cognitive psychology on the supposedly inherent aspects of writing dependent upon the context-free or absent-
audience condition, a much referred-to piece of anthropology by

Scribner and Cole (1981) suggests an alternative. Beginning with a suggestion from Goody and Watt (1968) that literacy makes possible "logic, and classificatory schemes," the writers surveyed recent work and comments on writing, concluding that too little had been done in the field of education. In their study of the Vai in Liberia, where writing is taught at home, not in school, Scribner and Cole (1981) looked at the following "properties of writing": that it diminishes the "tendency to confuse properties of words and properties of things" (pp. 134-135); that it emphasizes linguistic units not delineated in speech; that it encourages skill in the handling of logical relationships; and that it encourages "greater understanding of the systematic nature of language" (p. 135). They found no evidence for a direct correlation, except in the case of the last activity. What they did find was that it was easier to learn other graphic skills if you have already got one; that writing affects speaking perceptions; that it fosters "effective instructional communication"; and that memory for oral stories is not affected by literacy education. What Scribner and Cole also suggest is that it may be education itself that encourages the skills in logic previously attributed to writing, a suggestion elaborated and claimed as the case for theoretical logical skills by Tulviste (1979).

The effect of formal schooling on perception moves one away from the cognitive psychologist and toward the history of literacy by way of social history and anthropology. One of the most persuasive efforts has been that of J. Cook-Gumperz in *The Social Construction of Literacy* (1986). Her introductory study of the history of literacy in terms of education from the eighteenth century to the present day argues that the introduction of "schooled literacy" during the nineteenth century was geared to promote the skills and discipline needed by modern industry. Commonplace literacy, a telling phrase in terms of the broad use of commonplace books, was quite widespread even before the eighteenth century. Hence, "the major goal of mass schooling was thus to control literacy not to promote it; to control both the forms of expression and the behavior which accompany the move into literacy" (p. 30). As such it needed to train people in analysis and reasoning, and it is this kind of literacy that is "the fundamental technology on which modern societies are built" (p. 33). The point of the article is to

suggest that the kind of literacy stressed has not only become a supposedly "neutral and objective evaluation . . . of individual abilities"
(p. 39), but that it is also biased in favor of people from a specific social
background, and needs to be broadened to incorporate wider literacy
skills if we are to insist on it being used as an evaluative measure.
The point for this argument here is twofold; first, that literacy in terms
of home-based learning and the earlier focus on letters, diaries, tracts,
almanacs, Bibles, broadsheets, ballads, and so forth is presented as
quite different from the analytical literacy of a school-based grammar;
second, that school-based literacy is held to cut the mass of the people
off from common culture, leaving them with "less control over their
own cultural products" (p. 31).

The social conditions of literacy education are indeed of great importance, but the basis for suggesting that there is a particular kind
of literature appropriate to the "mass" is shaky. There is growing evidence that reading itself adapts to the current ideologically formed
pursuits of literacy, so that (for example) monastic readers would
meditate upon stretches of writing, while scholastic readers became
increasingly involved in commentary, compilation, re-ordering to follow logical patterns, indexing, and so on (Parkes, 1976). This may be
a result of reading skills being picked up willy-nilly from writing skills;
after all, the basis for medieval education was rhetoric, which stressed
composition before interpretation. But many people even now only
read; they do not write. Literacy in terms of reading was far more
widespread than was thought until recently. Several researchers have
now shown that, for example, many medieval guild apprentices had to
be able to read[5]; and that it is probable that a large number of people
from the yeoman class upwards became literate in reading during the
late sixteenth century (Spufford, 1981). However, as has been pointed
out with some acerbity by H. Graff, reading should not necessarily mean
literate. In Sweden during the eighteenth century, reading was a com-
pulsory and tested skill, but it is apparent that many of those who could
read did not show much comprehension of what they could technically
say aloud from a written page (Graff, 1987). The supposed "inherent"
qualities of writing all too often depend upon what and how the reader
reads, as well as how the writer writes.

Here the history of the development of education with that of rheto-ric is revealing. Western European and North American education is based on the influence of Quintilian during the Renaissance (Murphy, 1982), with strong Ramist overtones that separate logic from rhetoric, idea from utterance, and absolute from context (Sloan, 1974). Al-though frequently produced for ten-year-old schoolboys, sixteenth- and seventeenth-century school textbooks in writing were often little more than handbooks of devices with examples. They existed hand in hand with the new science and its devotion to geometry, mathematics, and theoretical syllogism, put to the use of rational, analytical logic. This division curiously allied the teaching of science and logic with ideal, context-free writing and the teaching of eloquent rhetoric with utter-ance and performance, to the extent of Thomas Sheridan's school of eloquence in the late eighteenth century. There are many other reasons for the division (Hunter, 1984a), some of which have already been touched on earlier in this chapter. In terms of education, however, the nineteenth century exacerbated the division with the rhetorics of Whately (logic) and Blair (eloquence) (Johnson, 1982), underwriting the educational tradition that writing was either correct or corrupt. That writing was underpinned by this concept meant that teaching gradually drove out corrupt eloquence, leaving the equation literacy=writing= analytical logic, allowing the social historians and cognitive psycholo-gists of today to think of formal schooled literacy as parallel with, if not identical to, the theoretical syllogisms of modern scientific proce-dure (Cook-Gumperz, 1986; Tulviste, 1979; Vygotsky, 1983).

Part of the problem here is that contrasting this kind of literacy with orality does not yield helpful comparisons. If oral skills were ever taught to a degree proportional with those of writing, specifically the kind of writing described above, useful differences might emerge. But the fact is that we educate people formally in oral skills rarely if at all, whereas written skills are undertaken with intensity for a good 10 years at least. When oral skills were taught with this degree of intensity against the background of scholastic rhetoric, they produced medieval dialectics that were founded on the elaboration of the theoretical syllo-gism. If we want to divorce analytical and categorizing skills even further from writing, we could look at recent work into the classifying systems of preliterate cultures (Berlin, 1977).

Far more significant is the rarely explicit, but frequently implied, underside to the argument that education trains literacy into formal analysis: that the oral is closer to the repository of "mass culture" with its fables, parables, folktales, jokes, and proverbs, as well as its common sense and its empirical syllogism. This sets up a myth of orality as the home for non-analytic reasoning, which underwrites the corollary that the only logic available to writing is linear, analytic, and rational. The implications are often made more explicit when looking at the position of women and literacy, and the proposition that women have retained an empirical, non-analytic, "intuitive" common sense because they are closer to the oral traditions—some would suggest necessarily closer because less rational. But the alternative modes of communication that women developed historically have nothing to do with proximity to the oral, nor even with a lack of schooling, but far more to do with their lack of formal education. If we look for example at domestic manuals, a nonformal didactic mode making up one of the largest areas of popular printing and publishing, we find in the seventeenth century evidence for considerable literacy as in, for example, Hannah Woolley's advice to artisan wives on how to write letters to their husbands (Woolley, 1670). We also find that the instructions in, say, Mary Tillinghasts' *Rare and Excellent Receipts. Experienc'd and Taught by Mary Tillinghast: And Now Printed For the Use of Her Scholars Only* (1690) are indeed a world away in technique from the contemporaneous Newton's *Principia*. Their stress on the empirical, and their lack of rational consistency or specific rigor, however, are not that different from the procedures of John Evelyn's *Acetaria: A Discourse of Sallets* (1699), written by one of Newton's colleagues in the Royal Society. Evelyn and Tillinghast were writing within a recognized genre, for readers with a nonformal education.

Schooling in literacy outside the formal was partly geared to purpose, or what the reader wanted to read, but also to availability, or what the book trade thought the reader should read; and that in turn was closely controlled, as least in the early days, by government licenses. Hence the close ties of such schooling with Bible study, not only an important political tool to the populace but also a steady and dependable seller for the printer/publisher right through from the sixteenth century (Graff, 1987; Spufford, 1981) to the nineteenth (Altick, 1957; Graff, 1987). Effectively, the education of the masses as carried out by church schools, Sunday schools, dame schools, and home-based learning depended upon the Bible; and this in many ways determined what and how the "mass" reader read. As several critics have noted, the Bible is based upon a rather different set of rhetorical techniques than the classical (Frye, 1982; Kennedy, 1980—see also comments on Curtius in Kennedy, 1980), which has not lent itself so easily to the separation into logic, rhetoric, and poetic. Biblical rhetoric is not closer to the oral tradition than classical, but operates with a fundamentally different strategy.

Another main area of popular reading was tied to the widely available chapbooks, broadsides, almanacs, and ballads, and it is this area that some modern critics suggest is not only closer to the oral but also closer to "true mass culture." However, there is a growing body of evidence to indicate that the ties between this kind of writing and orality are as strong or as weak as those between classical rhetoric and orality. Just as with classical rhetoric, the act of writing may change the context, change the techniques and sometimes the strategies, but is as open to assessments of stance as is the oral (Duggan, 1975; Ong, 1984). This is quite apart from other research in publishing history which indicates that, for example, most oral ballads collected in the nineteenth and twentieth centuries derive not from pure oral sources, but from printed ballads circulated in the mid-sixteenth century.[6] These writings do have a different set of rhetorical techniques to those of both classical and Biblical works, but they are not somehow closer to the oral.

As Biblical and popular influences became displaced with Charles Knight's Society for the Diffusion of Useful Knowledge, the vocational schools of the 1840s, and particularly the Education Acts of the 1860s and 1870s, education of the majority of the populace came under state control and took up the structure and emphases of formal education. Certainly the post-Education Act cookbooks of the 1880s with their protoscientific appearances derived from Isabella Beeston's *Household Management* (1861) are radically different from Eliza Acton's

Modern Housewife (1845), which still had much in common with seventeenth- and eighteenth-century works. We are speaking here of books, both Acton's and Beeston's, that went into hundreds of impressions during this period, some of the better known selling literally hundreds of thousands of copies (Hunter, 1987). That writing addressed to women was able to adjust in such numbers from an intuitive "oral" cast to analytic reasoning, within 20 to 30 years, argues as strongly against inherent qualities in writing as against inherent qualities in the female mind.

Research into the history of literacy education has done much to argue against the essentialist notion that rational analysis is inherent to writing and provides its correct form. But when looked at more closely it may be seen simply to reverse the axis of correct/corrupt, claiming that analytical writing somehow corrupts the genuine products of popular communication, which are in turn implicitly valorized. This raises the whole issue of the interconnection between mass communication and mass culture that media studies have been elaborating for some time.

VERSION 3:
MEDIA STUDIES

Whereas for Plato writing significantly enlarged one's potential audience, with today's electronic media writing appears more select. Yet while the elements of power and acquiescence sum up for many the dangers in the largeness of the "mass" audience, the numbers involved do not change the materiality of communication, only its technical effects. For some time media studies of mass communication have ignored this aspect, and have been intimately tied up with the idea of the absent audience occasioned or made necessary by their vast distribution. They derive the following equation: oral/written=individual/mass=immediate audience/absent audience=participation/submission. The standard argument from the early days of mass communications studies is that the mass media, including writing as one of the first, have no individual audience and hence generate less response and encourage the imposition of authority. The concomitant belief in a folk tradition that is closer to the "masses," legitimated in its purity by its proximity to the oral, has generated much work on "mass culture" (Leed, 1980; Zipes, 1980). What both aim toward is an understanding of the way ideology functions in society: how and why the norms of our world come to be accepted, challenged, and changed.

The passive or submissive members of the audience, supposedly descendants of Plato's "unsuitable readers" (1973, p. 97), have often been described—from Q. Leavis in *Fiction and the Reading Public* (1932) to R. Hoggart in *The Uses of Literacy* (1958). Early American communications studies describe the mass media whose "audience are [sic] passive consumers, their participation limited to the choice between buying and not buying."[7] Just so, D. McQuail defines the media in contrast to "face-to-face" communication, as "one-directional and rarely interactional" with little "variability in response" (1983, pp. 34-35) and follows Blumer in outlining the mass as large, widely dispersed, without self-awareness, and acted upon. This absent audience causes the early J. Baudrillard to describe the mass media as "speech without response" (1984, p. 577) where the "power belongs to him who gives and to whom no return can be made" (p. 578).

Although still frequently used as an entity in political and social discussion about for example censorship, the notion of the passive audience has increasingly been resisted or redefined by academic research (Bennett, 1982). Much of this redefinition is connected with the role of the "masses" in the study of politics and ideology. It is a role which, in some versions, continues to cast the masses as a solid group whose actions will obviate what appear to be the inherent effects of the mass media. Some Marxists stress the force of the masses which will eventually break through the capitalist basis of the mass media. Others, such as the recent Baudrillard, put forward the idea that the acceptance of the media is an ironic and antagonistic submission by the masses, who refuse to participate in an ideology they view as oppressive.

The tendency in these theories is still to treat the "masses" as a distinct oppressed entity, and mass culture as a definable, corrupt thing, inducing passivity through inherent qualities of the mass communications media. A. Swingewood (1985), in an argument moving from the Frankfurt School toward Gramsci and Marcuse, suggest that there is no forced or unconscious oppression but consent by the masses to bourgeois ideology, and that the mass media is not inherently corrupting because they are the primary means through which this consent is effected, as they convey the historical knowledge necessary to self-awareness and action. This hegemony theory changes the role of the masses, and Swingewood (1985) echoes the direction of R. Williams (1961) who says that there are "only ways of seeing people as masses" (p. 289) when he says "We are all masses now" (p. 118); but he does not change the role of mass culture. The argument still treats "mass culture" as a corrupt thing, reifying human labor and producing the cultural object as a commodity (p. 120) that denies participation. Perhaps significantly, Swingewood thinks of literacy as necessary to aware political action, calling upon Goody and Watt to support his argument on the importance of analytical reasoning. It is as if the "development of independent institutions" along with "practical activities," which either are or guarantee the existence of analytical reasons, will necessitate participation and the democratization of culture. The suggestion appears to be driving toward Plato's aim of evaluative reasoning, but is diverted into the concept of the analytical=correct.

What is not pursued is the shift made by the Frankfurt School from the absent-audience problem to the enclosed audience that is its other face. To convince an absent audience, the grounds of persuasion must be carefully laid out so that the ensuing argument not only appears logical, but appears to make unnecessary any other interpretation. In order to carry this out the argument usually relies upon an intensely detailed conventional representation of contemporary ideology, to the point where the detail of the argument superimposes on that of experience of the actual and encloses the audience. This enclosure cannot be fully achieved; but attempts can be made—particularly with the extensive technologies of film, radio, and mass publishing (Hunter, 1984b). By focusing on the similarities of the argumentative device, the Frankfurt School moves the debate from the conditions resulting from an absent audience to those resulting from the totalizing systems of the mass media; they proceed to reject the mass media because their sheer size and distribution make possible completeness and enclosure to authoritarian technique (Negt, 1980).

This analysis shifts the responsibility onto the media maker, and underwrites a politics of individual liberty. Within this context, Habermas's politics of consensus and belief in the public use and exploitation of the mass media was a significant challenge. But, as has been pointed out, such a rhetorical agenda for politics never addresses the pragmatic economic limitations on public involvement in expensive mass media. Neither does it address the group rhetoric of fascism that effectively demands a submissive, non-evaluative response. While the mass media are inherently neither positive nor negative, so the "public" or mass rhetor is not intrinsically or "naturally" going to effect a politics of global or community involvement and assessment.

There are some explicit claims, however, for rhetorical analysis and writing as the means by which the ideological effects of the mass media can be changed from corrupt to correct. Baudrillard inaccurately attributes the aim of an achieved transparency of analytical information and communication through the new technologies to McLuhan, but there are certainly those who would argue this (Woodward, 1980). It is perhaps closer to the mark (although again naive) to attribute to McLuhan the strand of communications studies which is attempting to gain for the media another myth from the oral/written debate, that the oral is closer to immediate communication, that it changes the absent-audience condition and hence claims direct access to meaning, a purity of word that is curiously nonideological (Brewer, 1985; Ong, 1985). Both traditions, the analytical writing=correct and the oral=pure, focus on rhetoric merely as technique, isolating it from the materiality of history. The former claims a technique which, if followed correctly, will ensure accurate communication of the boundaries of ideology; the later implicitly claims that because the techniques of its communication do not fall within those of classical rhetoric, neither do they persuade but are pure. Both the technological optimism and the nostalgic yearning simply perpetuate the oral/written divide and its attendant myths.

It is interesting to watch the convergence of work on writing and mass communications that has taken place over the last 10 to 15 years, and which locates the communication of ideology in a rather more useful direction (see Hall, 1980, 1982). The story of the structuralist response to the language studies developing in the early twentieth century, and then the transposition of the structuralist into the semiotics of literature, has often been told (e.g., Culler, 1981), and can be seen as a counterpart to the emerging work on genre studies (e.g., Hirsch, 1967, 1976) in that semiotics has often focused on the reader while genre studies have focused on the writer. Work coming from these studies has tended not to emphasize technique, but what in rhetoric is called strategy: the *ethos* of the writer and *pathos* of the audience in communication.

Much genre theory stresses the activity of writers. There is discussion of the author's position (Scholes, 1979), of intention (Frye, 1957), of will (Hirsch, 1976), and of authorial privilege (Fowler, 1979). In these works there is an attempt to locate the reader as an "intended audience," yet as any semiotician will say, the intended audience needs to be differentiated from the actual (Hall, 1980; Lotman, 1983). On the other hand, the semioticians in reader-response theory have a tendency to conflate the writer with the text (e.g., Freund, 1987), so that we find comments about the "imbalance" between implied reader and historical reader because "the text does not talk back to correct one's misinterpretations; it cannot adapt, assert, defend itself or supplement its fragmented codes" (p. 145). Of course, these approaches are extreme, but they do indicate some of the drawbacks of commentary on the strategies for communication of ideology.

Work from each direction toward the other has proved more fruitful. For example, M. Rifaterre concentrates on the semantic overload of textual interpretants that leave the reader "under strict guidance and control as he [sic] fills the gaps and solves the puzzles" (1978, p. 165) but also points out the concurrent instability of the reader. A study of the fluctuation between the two positions does, however, need to be extended into the historical before Rifaterre's concept of the hypogram becomes useful. The necessary displacement of this shuttle into the material is underlined if we look at J. Culler's rather plaintive description of the signification of the metaphor, which is at the same time "a radical or inaugural act" and "a manifestation of a preexistent connection" (1981, p. 39). Culler goes on to say that "any figure can be read referentially or rhetorically" (p. 78), indicating that he limits the rhe-torical to the technical and strategic, for an historical concept of rheto-ric gained through an understanding of stance would position the figure.

Debate about metaphor, particularly in partner with metonymy, illus-trates some of the areas in which concern with strategy alone always contains the potential for a reversal into the restrictions on the technical. The metaphor/metonymy discussion derives its current impetus from Jakobson's use of it to describe specific kinds of communication— Jakobson himself based the separation on different types of *aphasia*, thus linking the written implicitly with the oral. By assigning each term to resemblance and contiguity at either end of "the fundamental polarity within the field of figurative language" (Thompson, 1987, p. 89), he restricts their use to a prescriptive grammar and a technical rhetoric that many critics have followed. It allows, for example, spec-ulation upon the "propositional" effect of metaphor as the reason for its widespread study, because its presentation of human experience makes it more "responsible" than assonance, metonymy, or hendiadys (Culler, 1981). The concept of metaphor as inherently propositional raises the problem of how the same metaphor can communicate com-pletely different propositions, as well as avoiding the firmly entrenched historical stance of propositions themselves. Given the means or will any figure can be treated as propositional, even assonance (Kaferly & Creik, 1987) or hendiadys (Wright, 1981). More complicated is the need strictly to define metaphor, a pursuit often treated as analogous to searching for the Holy Grail of literacy theory. The technical assign-ment of definition by Jakobson also permits a futile, isolated wrangling over which figure—metaphor or metonymy—is the figure of figures. Various writers have inverted the direction of focus by looking at the incessant movement between the two figures (Culler, 1981; Eco, 1976; de Man, 1979), which is prefigured by Coleridge's discussion of meta-phor and synecdoche in *Aids to Reflection* (Hodgson, 1981). But this, too, devolves into technical acrobatics. Neither approach addresses itself to value, to the social implications of the activity rather than the isolated meaning of the device.

There have been some efforts to halt the shuttle, however, and they have—without exception—turned to the ideological. Eco uses the movement metaphor/metonymy to present the heart of his semiotics: that it is both a "theory of codes and a theory of sign production" whose rhetoric describes how one changes the world and is therefore a form of "social criticism" (1976, p. 298). To arrive at this conclusion, he re-rehearses the position of rhetorical argumentation, unwittingly reinforcing the oral/written myth and reintroducing the shuttle between the referential and the structural. In a semiotics of conversational interaction the important rule is to recognize the "one-sidedness of the premises" (p. 278); however, ideological discourse consciously (cynically) or unconsciously (ignorantly) "pretends to develop a 'true' argument presenting its own point of view as the only possible conclusion" (p. 278). Here the ideological behaves as if it were axiomatic, when it is only probable; just such a distinction leading to the corrupt/correct division. Eco later suggests that a "non-ideological statement would be a meta-semiotic one that showed the contradictory nature of its semantic space" (p. 293). The implication here is that the audience must be passive if a statement is to be ideological; indeed, Eco takes up Engels's definition of ideology as "false consciousness."

In a rather more flexible manner, C. Brooke-Rose (1981) looks at the way that communication relates from specific devices that encode the reader, and that these same devices may either overcode or undercode toward "readable" or "writerly" texts, the informative and the poetic. She concludes that the transforming semiotic criterion "must be ideological" (p. 97) and goes on to examine how certain genres, especially the fantastic, depend upon the degree of coding for their effect. This at least opens up the possibility that in different historical situations, a work may generate different textual relations and values; that is not inherently correct or corrupt or pure.

In pursuit of genre theory, the writer F. Jameson (1981) proposed three levels of communication: the first subjective and symbolic, open to rhetorical (technical) study; the second social and ideological, to do with oppositions; and the third historical and generic, to do with the ideology of form that makes explicit dialogical contradictions in the conjuncture of its own formal processes and other "coexisting modes of production" (p. 99). But these are "sedimented content" that is detectable and hence bound up into fixed kind in a manner not made plain. Jameson also sees the ideological as negative, operating through the media to manipulate the audience by offering "specific gratifications in return for his or her consent to passivity" (p. 287). He splits the generic definition between conventional acceptance of gratification in romance, and the need to secure acceptance in the novel, but notes that any manipulation is dangerous because the very things that the ideological attempts to exclude, or divert the audience from, are implicitly present by their absence and can challenge consent.[8] In a contrasting movement he proposes the positive action of utopia that conveys "the anticipation of the logic of a collectivity which has not yet come into being" (p. 286). The ideological is a "negative hermeneutic" which is yet instrumental and functional; the utopia is a "positive hermeneutic," collective and anticipatory. The apocalyptic version being offered combines the ideological and utopian into truth, admitting that this can only be possible at the end of "prehistory" (p. 293).

Jameson (1981), Eco (1976), and Brooke-Rose (1981) do together provide a helpful vocabulary for looking at written, ideological communication to large audiences. Running throughout their work is the insistence on education in terms of understanding the premises of coding. For each of these writers ideological communication occurs when the premises are hidden, the information overcoded, the gratification conventionally accepted. Eco sees the alternative as non-ideological, showing its own semiotic construction. For Jameson the opposition of conventional acceptance is the securing of acceptance; and he also provides an alternative to acceptance, which is the utopian or collective anticipatory action that becomes ideological as it becomes accepted. But for Brooke-Rose, the ideological is the means by which information is both overcoded and undercoded; the sharing of semiotic construction, and its transformation from hidden premise to overt premise, is ideological in itself. Jameson may be getting at this when he speaks of his own critical practice being part of a dominant ideology.

By drawing attention to ideology these writers are pointing out that the media pursuit of correct or pure communication is a dead end, just as the Frankfurt School sought futilely for purity in music (Negt, 1980). Whether it be scientific, journalistic, or instructional writing, or any other of the written mass communications, the dream has been to find a way: a new technical rhetoric that will not corrupt, will be able to deal with the problem of the absent audience. The result of recent work in semiotics and genre theory has been increasing awareness of the role of strategy, of *ethos* and *pathos*, the position of the writer and of the reader which is underlined by various understandings of ideology. But to varying extents this work leaves itself open to devolve once more into the pursuit of correct or pure. Jameson, for example, discusses the ideological in literary works as emerging from a conflict between "older deep-structural form" and "contemporaneous materials," while genre combines the manifest text with deep-structural origins and "history" (1981, p. 141). Text, deep structure, and history are closely analogous to the technique, strategy, and stance offered by rhetoric. But whereas rhetoric suggests that the same technique and strategy will at different historical moments generate different stances and values, Jameson clearly allocates ideology to the genres of romance and the novel, evaluating them according to a specific standard. Just so, rhetorical stance insists on specific value as part of the activity arising in an historical or material event, whereas Jameson proposes a history and a value as both "absent" in ceaseless process. The claim to an "imma- nent or antitranscendant hermeneutic model" (p. 23), that will walk quietly between totalization and absence toward a collective utopia, splits apart.

   Possibly, one of the problems is that there is no clear role for a physical ideology, and here a look at romance and utopia can be helpful. Certainly these genres address the problem of mass communi- cation as directly as some of the more obvious writings already dis- cussed: the circulation of this literature is enormous (Radway, 1984), and its structure is very similar. Recent work in literary narrative has described a heavy dependence on apparent verisimilitude, in terms of immense visual detail and description of expected action, which sets the basis for a common ground with the reader. The use of language is supposedly either strongly denotative or filled with neologism, allow- ing for little deviation in interpretation. Broad schemes such as the location of the narrative on an island, in an isolated place or carefully delimited situation, are important because they allow the writer to control the context more precisely. And the organization around sequential, rational development is a further strategy for authority (Hunter, 1989). Just as with journalism, instructional writing, and scientific reports, the reader is asked to consent to a set of standards and to information, and the process of that consent depends on an understanding of the *ethos*.

If the reader does understand, then the strategy can be seen for the isolated controlled interpretation that it is, and becomes a pragmatic directive to a possible activity; in the same manner, utopias read with understanding rarely propose the perfect alternative but rather suggest comment upon the present. But if the reader is unaware of the construction, the strategy simply imposes its version in the manner of a benevolent dictator, a paternalistic benefactor denying its own power and appearing inevitable or "natural." In effect, the contextualization necessary for this kind of strategy limits it closely to the time contemporaneous with the writing. As time moves on the contexts change and the readers are left with grounds that are either unfamiliar or different in semantic meaning to their original purpose. The work "dates," and the readers lose touch with its construction. This process may explain why later readers find utopias from the past tedious and perfectionist, and romances simply naive—they no longer appreciate the commentary (Hunter, 1989; Williams, 1978). As a corollary, works written to evade this awareness in the first place, such as scientific treatises or modern newspaper reports, become doubly unreadable—not only are the common grounds no longer apparent, but also their presence at the time is hidden.

CONCLUSION

Communication of ideology implies a corporate stance which is both a pragmatic directive for short-term action and at the same time holds out the possibility of submissive acceptance. The communication achieves these ends because it depends upon a set of literary expectations which derive from post-Renaissance education. They are not inherent to writing, nor to writing within forms of mass communication.

The construction of a courtly love romance from the medieval period, although asking for similar consent, uses different techniques. Nor is this communication inherently correct, corrupt, or pure. Sequential syllogistic action will provide most control primarily within a society trained to argue through the rational analysis it needs; other readers may well be stimulated to ask about concurrent orderings, using the sequential to foreground their absence. Nor, indeed, are these genres inherently corporate or collective in Jameson's (1981) sense. As the grounds for their arguments date they need not become tedious or naive, but through the realization of those grounds involve us into a collective stance which does not convey information or pragmatic directives, but enacts immediate practical activity. The inaction is also there for the reader contemporary with the writer. Orwell's *Animal Farm* may have pragmatic things to say about one's response to the bureaucracies of both fascist and Stalinist kinds, but it also enacts the necessary involvement in politics that human beings—as opposed to animals—have because of their communicative abilities. This latter is not directive, but an invitation to engage. A similar invitation may be found alongside the pragmatic guide to contemporary feminisms in Margaret Atwood's *The Handmaid's Tale*. The extent to which the collective or corporate stance emerges is not inherent to technique, genre ideology, or medium, but is an action within history.

Debate about the differences between the oral and the written, whether refracted through essentialist or sociological concepts of literacy, has infused the study of mass communications with the idea that the absent audience is a problem generating inherently corrupt communication. Although this has largely been redefined by researchers in terms of the ideological, it is still a commonly held attitude and, more important, ideological studies rarely address the practical problems it raises in terms of day-to-day action. It is helpful to remember that it is not the oral or written as such, nor the presence or absence of an audience in itself that Plato found worth commenting on, but the encouraging or discouraging of reasoning and participation. Further, Plato was writing at a time when writing was not a common skill, and he was writing specifically about oratory for an audience he knew would be well-drilled in its principles. He uses the faults of oratory, which he can expect his audience to comprehend, as an analogy for writing and its potential pitfalls. Both media address large numbers of people, and both media can seek to persuade of ideological norms. The distinction for Plato lies in the relative lack of education surrounding the medium of writing compared with that around oratory, and the resultant necessary lack of comprehension and participation. As for Plato, so perhaps for us. Our criticisms of writing indicate by analogy pitfalls in the new media, and we need, as he needed, the renewal of a critical education.

NOTES

1. Adopting this view, George Kennedy, has been able to unravel a number of snarled lines in the history of the topic (Kennedy, 1980).

2. I am indebted to John O. Thompson for this wording of the correct/corrupt dyad.

3. Most of G. K. Chesterton's comments on journalese may be found in issues of *G. K. Weekly*, (1925-36). George Orwell's remarks are scattered throughout his essays, especially in "Politics and the English Language".

4. See *G. K.'s Weekly*, issue 40 (1925); and *Homage to Catalonia* (1973).

5. N. Davis (1975), quoted in B. Stock (1983).

6. R. Thomson, quoted in Spufford (1983), p. 9.

7. D. MacDonald (1957), quoted in Swingewood (1985), p. 94.

8. For a discretely opposite analysis see J. Dupry in Woodward (1980), p. 14.

REFERENCES

Altick, R. (1957). *The English common reader.* Chicago: Chicago University Press.

Baudrillard, J. (1985). The masses: The implosion of the social in the media. *New Literary History, 14,* 1984-1985.

Beetham, M. (1987). *The new women.* Unpublished Ph.D. thesis, University of Manchester.

Bennett, T. (1982). Theories of the media, theories of society. In M. Gurevitch et al. (Eds.), *Culture, society and the media.* London: Methuen.

Berlin, B. (1977). Speculations of the growth of ethnobotanic nomenclature. In B. Blount & M. Sanches, *Sociocultural dimensions of language change.* London: Academic Press.

Blount, B., & Sanches, M. (1977). *Sociocultural dimensions of language change.* London: Academic Press.

Brandt, W. (1970). *The rhetoric of argumentation.* Indianapolis: Bobbs-Merrill.

Brewer, W. (1985). "The story schema: Universal and culture-specific properties." In D. Olson, N. Torrance, & A. Hildyard (Eds.), *Literacy, language and learning: The nature and consequences of reading and writing*. Cambridge: Cambridge University Press.

Brooke-Rose, C. (1981). *A rhetoric of the unreal. Studies in narrative and structure, especially of the fantastic*. London: Cambridge University Press.

Chafe, W. (1985). "Linguistic differences produced by differences between speaking and writing." In D. Olson, N. Torrance, & A. Hildyard (Eds.), *Literacy, language and learning: The nature and consequences of reading and writing*. Cambridge: Cambridge University Press.

Clanchy, W. (1979). *From memory to written record: England 1066-1307*. London: Edward Arnold.

Cole, M., & Scribner, S. (1974). *Culture and thought, a psychological introduction*. London: John Wiley.

Collins, J., & Michaels, S. (1986). Speaking and writing: Discourse strategies and the acquisition of literacy. In J. Cook-Gumperz (Ed.), *The social construction of literacy*. London: Cambridge University Press.

Cook-Gumperz, J. (Ed.). (1986). *The social construction of literacy*. London: Cambridge University Press.

Cooper, C. & Matsuhashi, A. (1983). "A theory of the writing process." In M. Martlew (Ed.), *The psychology of written language, developmental and educational perspectives*. Chichester: John Wiley.

Corbett, E. P. J. (1982). John Locke's contributions to rhetoric. In J. Murphy (Ed.), *The rhetorical tradition and modern writing*. New York: Modern Languages Association.

Croll, M. (1966). *Style, rhetoric, and rhythm*. Princeton, NJ: Princeton University Press.

Culler, J. (1981). *In pursuit of signs*. London: Routledge & Kegan Paul.

Derrida, J. (1974). *Of grammatology*. (G. Spivak, Trans.). London: The Johns Hopkins University Press.

Duggan, J. (Ed.). (1975). *Oral literature, seven essays*. Edinburgh: Scottish Academic Press.

Eco, U. (1976). *A theory of semiotics*. London: Indiana University Press.

Fowler, A. (1982). *Kinds of literature: An introduction to the theory of genres and modes*. Oxford: Clarendon Press.

Freund, E. (1987). *The return of the reader, reader-response criticism*. London: Methuen.

Frye, N. (1957). *Anatomy of criticism*. Princeton, NJ: Princeton University Press.

Frye, N. (1982). *The great code: The Bible and literature*. Toronto: Academic Press.

Goody, J. (1973). Literacy and the non-literate in Ghana. In R. Disch (Ed.), *The future of literacy*. Englewood Cliffs, NJ: Prentice-Hall.

Goody, J., & Watt, I. (1968). *Literacy in traditional societies*. New York: Cambridge University Press.

Graff, H. (1987). *The labyrinths of literacy, reflections on literacy past and present*. London: Falmer.

Hall, S. (1982). "The rediscovery of ideology: Return of the repressed in media studies. In M. Gurevitch et al. (Eds.), *Culture, society and the media*. London: Methuen.

Hall, S., et al. (Eds.). (1980). *Culture, media, language: Working papers in cultural studies 1972-79*. London: Hutchinson.

Halliday, M., & Hasan, R. (1976). *Cohesion in English*. New York: Longman.

Hauser, G. (1986). *Introduction to rhetorical theory*. New York: Harper & Row.

Hirsch, E. (1967). *Validity in interpretation.* New Haven: Yale University Press.

Hirsch, E. (1976). *The aims of interpretation.* Chicago: University of Chicago Press.

Havelock, E. (1963). *Preface to Plato.* Cambridge, MA: Harvard University Press.

Hodgson, J. (1981). Transcendental topic. In M. Bloomfield (Ed.), *Allegory, myth and symbol.* London: Harvard University Press.

Hunter, L. (1984a). *Rhetorical stance in modern literature.* London: Macmillan.

Hunter, L. (1984b). *George Orwell, the search for a voice.* Oxford: Open University Press.

Hunter, L. (1987). *Bibliography of household books published in Britain, 1800-1914.* London: Prospect Books.

Hunter, L. (1989). *Modern allegory and fantasy.* London: Macmillan.

Jameson, F. (1981). *The political unconscious.* London: Methuen.

Johnson, N. (1982). Three nineteenth-century rhetoricians: The humanist alternative to rhetoric as skills management. In J. Murphy (Ed.), *The rhetorical tradition and modern writing.* New York: Modern Languages Association.

Kaferly, D. & Creik, E. (1987). "The computer and Sophocles." *Trachiniae, Literary and Linguistic Computing, 2.*

Kennedy, G. (1980). *Classical rhetoric and its Christian and secular tradition from ancient to modern times.* Chapel Hill: University of North Carolina Press.

Lee, A. (1978). "The structure, ownership and control of the press, 1855-1914." In G. Boyce et al. (Eds.), *Newspaper history from the 17th century to the present day.* London: Constable.

Leed, E. (1980). "Voice" and "print": Master symbols in the history of communication. In K. Woodward, *The myths of information: Technology and postindustrial culture.* London: Routledge & Kegan Paul.

Lotman, Y. (1983). Text and the structure of its audience. In *New Literary History, 14.*

de Man, P. (1979). *Allegories of reading.* London: Yale University Press.

Marcie, P. (1983). Writing disorders associated with focal cortical lesions. In M. Martlew (Ed.), *The psychology of written language, developmental and educational perspectives.* Chichester: John Wiley.

Martlew, M. (Ed.). (1983). *The psychology of written language, developmental and educational perspectives.* Chichester: John Wiley.

McLuhan, M. (1951). *The Mechanical Bride.* London: Routledge & Kegan Paul.

McLuhan, M. (1962). *The Gutenberg Glaxy.* Toronto: University of Toronto Press.

McQuail, D. (1983). *Mass communication theory: An introduction.* London: Sage.

Miller, S. (1982). Classical practice and contemporary basics. In J. Murphy (Ed.), *The rhetorical tradition and modern writing.* New York: Modern Languages Association.

Murdock, G. (1982). "Large corporations and the control of the communications industries." In M. Gurevitch et al. (Eds.), *Culture, society and the media.* London: Methuen.

Murphy, J. (Ed.). (1982). *The rhetorical tradition and modern writing.* New York: Modern Languages Association.

Negt, O. (1980). Mass media: Tools of domination or instruments of liberation. In K. Woodward, *The myths of information: Technology and postindustrial culture.* London: Routledge & Kegan Paul.

Olson, D. (1977). "From utterance to text." *Harvard Educational Review, 47.*

Olson, D. (1982). McLuhan on literacy. *Working Paper 1.* Toronto.

Olson, D., Torrance, N. & Hildyard, A. (Eds.). (1985). *Literacy, language and learning: The nature of consequences of reading and writing.* Cambridge: Cambridge University Press.

Olson, D. & Hildyard, A. (1983). "Writing and literal meaning." In M. Martlew (Ed.), *The psychology of written languages, developmental and educational perspectives.* Chichester: John Wiley.

Ong, W. (1982). *Orality and literacy: The technologizing of the word.* London: Methuen.

Ong, W. (1984). Orality, literacy and medieval textualization. *New Literary History, 16,* 1984-1985.

Parkes, M. (1976). Influence of concepts of *Ordinatio* and *Compilatio* in the development of the book. In J. Alexander & M. Gibson (Eds.), *Medieval learning.* Oxford: Oxford University Press.

Pattison, R. (1982). *On literacy: The politics of the word from Homer to the age of rock.* Oxford: Oxford University Press.

Plato (1983). "Phaedrus." (W. Hamilton, Trans.). Middlesex: Penguin.

Plato (1973). "The Republic." (D. Lee, Trans.). Middlesex: Penguin.

Platt, H. (1982). The place and function of style in Renaissance poetics. In J. Murphy (Ed.), *The rhetorical tradition and modern writing.* New York: Modern Languages Association.

Radway, J. (1984). *Reading and romance: Women, patriarchy and popular literature.* London: University of California Press.

Rifaterre, M. (1978). *Semiotics of poetry.* London: Indiana University Press.

Scardamalia, M., & Bereiter, C. (1985). Development of dialectical processes in composition. In D. Olson, N. Torrance, & A. Hildyard (Eds.), *Literacy, language and learning: The nature of consequences of reading and writing.* Cambridge: Cambridge University Press.

Scholes, R. (1979). *Fabulation and metafiction.* London: University of Illinois Press.

Scribner, S., & Cole, M. (1981). *The psychology of literature.* London: Harvard University Press.

Sloan, T. O. (1974). The crossing of rhetoric and poetry in the English renaissance. In T. O. Sloan & C. B. Waddington (Eds.), *The rhetoric of Renaissance poetry from Wyatt to Milton.* London: University of California Press.

Smith, A. (1978). The long road to objectivity and back again: The kinds of truth we get in journalism. In G. Boyce et al. (Eds.), *Newspaper history from the 17th century to the present day.* London: Constable.

Spufford, M. (1981). *Small books and pleasant histories.* Cambridge: Cambridge University Press.

Stock, B. (1983). *The implications of literacy: Written language and models of interpretation in the eleventh and twelfth centuries.* Princeton, NJ: Princeton University Press.

Stock, B. (1984). Medieval literacy, linguistic theory, and social organization. *New Literary History, 16,* 1984-1985.

Street, B. (1984). *Literacy in theory and practice.* Cambridge: Cambridge University Press.

Streuver, N. (1982). Lorenzo Valla: Humanist rhetoric and the critique of the classical language of morality. In J. Murphy (Ed.), *The rhetorical tradition and modern writing.* New York: Modern Languages Association.

Swingewood, A. (1985). *The myth of mass culture.* London: Macmillan.

Tannen, D. (1985). Relative focus on involvement in oral and written discourse. In D. Olson, N. Torrance, & A. Hildyard (Eds.), *Literacy, language and learning: The nature and consequences of reading and writing.* Cambridge: Cambridge University Press.

Thompson, A., & Thompson, J. O. (1987). *Shakespeare: Meaning and metaphor*. Brighton: Harvester Press.

Tulviste, P. (1979). "On the origins of theoristic syllogistic reasoning in culture and the child." *Quarterly Newsletter of Comprehensive Human Cognition, 1*.

Vickers, B. (1982). The power of persuasion: Images of the orators, Elyot to Shakespeare. In J. Murphy (Ed.), *The rhetorical tradition and modern writing*. New York: Modern Languages Association.

Vgotsky, J. (1983). The prehistory of written language. In M. Martlew (Ed.), *The psychology of written language, developmental and educational perspectives*. Chichester: John Wiley.

Watson, C. (1983). Syntactic change: Writing development and rhetorical context. In M. Martlew (Ed.), *The psychology of written language, developmental and educational perspectives*. Chichester: John Wiley.

Wendell, M. (1982). *Bootstrap literature: Preliterate societies do it themselves*. Delaware: International Reading Association.

Williams, R. (1961). *The long revolution*. London: Chatto and Windns.

Williams, R. (1978). Forms of English fiction in 1848. In F. Barker et al. (Eds.), *1848: The sociology of literature*. Essex: University of Essex.

Winckler, A. & McCuen, J. (1978). *Rhetoric made plain*. New York: Harcourt Brace Jovanovich.

Whorf, B. L. (1956). In J. Carroll (Ed.), *Language, thought and reality*. Cambridge: MIT Press.

Woodward, K. (1980). *The myths of information: Technology and postindustrial culture*. London: Routledge & Kegan Paul.

Woolley, H. (1670). *The queen-like closet*. London.

Wright, G. (1981). "Hendiadys and 'Hamlet.'" *PMLA, 96*.

Zipes, J. (1980). The instrumentalization of fantasy: Fairytales and the mass media. In K Woodward, *The myths of information: Technology and postindustrial culture*. London: Routledge & Kegan Paul.

About the Authors

Edward P. J. Corbett (Ph.D., Loyola University, Chicago, 1956) is a Professor of English and a 1986 recipient of the Distinguished Scholar Award at Ohio State University. He was Director of Freshman English at Creighton University, Omaha, Nebraska, (1953-1966) and at Ohio State University (1966-1970). He served as the Chair of the Conference on College Composition and Communication in 1971 and as the Editor of the organization's journal, *College Composition and Communication*, from 1974 to 1979. He is the author of *Classical Rhetoric for the Modern Student* (3rd ed.) and of *The Little English Handbook* (5th ed.), and coeditor with Gary Tate of *The Writing Teacher's Sourcebook* (2nd ed.).

Richard Leo Enos (Ph.D., Indiana University, 1973) is Associate Professor of Rhetoric in the English Department at Carnegie Mellon University. His research emphasis is in the history of rhetoric with a specialization in classical rhetoric. Much of his work deals with understanding the relationship between thought and expression in antiquity. He has studied in Italy and Greece, and has done research through the American School of Classical Studies at Athens under the auspices of the Greek Ministry of Science and Culture. He has received support for the study of ancient rhetoric from the National Endowment for the Humanities and is the recipient of the Karl R. Wallace Award for his research in Greek rhetoric. His most recent major work, *The Literate Mode of Cicero's Legal Rhetoric* (1988), is published by Southern Illinois University Press.

William M. A. Grimaldi, S. J. is Professor of Classical Languages at Fordham University. He took his doctorate at Princeton University where he was the John Harding Page Fellow and spent a year as a Fulbright Fellow at the American School of Classical Studies at Athens studying archaeology. One of his interests has been in Greek rhetoric. Here his work on Aristotle's *Rhetoric* led to an interest in Aristotle's theory. The results of this research were published in *Studies in the Philosophy of Aristotle's Rhetoric* (1972). Then at the request of the American Philological Association he did a commentary on Book I titled *Aristotle's Rhetoric I: A Commentary* (1980). His commentary on the second book (research on which was partly assisted by a Senior Fellowship from the NEH) was published in 1988.

Lynette Hunter (Ph.D., Edinburgh University, 1978) is the lecturer in the Institute for Bibliography and Textual Criticism at the University of Leeds. Her research areas focus on bibliography, publishing history, and post-Renaissance rhetoric. She has held research Fellowships at the universities of Edinburgh, Liverpool, and Wales. Publications in the field of rhetoric have taken two directions. The first direction is close rhetorical analysis of nineteenth- and twentieth-century writers, the most recent on George Orwell (1984); the second is a study of the theory and practice of rhetoric in language and literature: *Modern Allegory and Fantasy.*

James L. Kinneavy (Ph.D., Catholic University of America, 1956) is a Professor of English and Rhetoric at the University of Texas at Austin. His volume *A Theory of Discourse* (1971) articulated a view of the field that has become the standard for organizing and classifying areas of study. He is a frequent contributor to journals that are concerned with the pedagogy of writing. His recent coauthored text, *Writing in the Liberal Arts Tradition* (1985) has emerged as one of the standard texts of the field. He has also earned national recognition for his scholarship on the history of rhetoric. His most recent contribution, *Greek Rhetorical Origins of Christian Faith* (1987), has already received praise from scholars in the field.

James J. Murphy (Ph.D., Stanford University, 1957) is Professor of Rhetoric and Professor of English at the University of California at Davis. He teaches courses in history of rhetoric, especially ancient, medieval, and Renaissance periods, as well as courses in medieval literature in the Department of English. He was one of the four founders of the International Society for the History of Rhetoric, and founding editor of its journal, *Rhetorica*. His book, *Rhetoric in the Middle Ages*, won the Annual Book Award of the Speech Communication association in 1975, and has been translated into Spanish and Italian. Among his 15 books are *Quintilian on the Teaching of Speaking and Writing* (1987) and *Arguments in Rhetoric Against Quintilian: Translation of Peter Ramus's* Rhetoricae distinctiones in Quintilianum (with Carole Newlands, 1986). His latest edited volume is *A Short History of Writing Instruction* (1990).

Walter J. Ong, S. J. (Ph.D., Harvard) is Emeritus University Professor of Humanities, William E. Haren Professor of English, and Professor of Humanities in Psychiatry at Saint Louis University. His books include *The Presence of the Word* (1967), *Interfaces of the Word* (1977), and *Hopkins, the Self, and God* (1986). His *Orality and Literacy: The Technologizing of the Word* (1982) has appeared in translation in German, Spanish, and Italian, and is forthcoming in Japanese, Polish, Swedish, and Korean. He has lectured widely in the United States, Canada, Europe, North Africa, West and Central Africa, the Middle East, and East Asia, and has been a visiting professor at New York University, the

University of California, University of Chicago, and elsewhere. He holds honorary doctorates from many universities, including Carnegie Mellon University.

Denise Schmandt-Besserat (Ecole du Louvre, 1964) is a Professor of Middle Eastern Studies at the University of Texas at Austin. Her field is the archaeology of the Middle East. In the last decade she has worked on clay counters, which are the precursor of writing and abstract numerals. She has published the results of her research in scholarly journals including: *American Journal of Archaeology* (1979), *Science* (1981), *American Anthropologist* (1982), *Visible Language* (1984), and *Archaeology* (1986).

Robert W. Smith (Ph.D., University of Wisconsin, 1957), Professor and Chairperson of Speech Communication, Alma College, is interested in the history and criticism of oral rhetoric. Partially funded by Virginia's Old Dominion Fund, his *Art of Rhetoric in Alexandria* (1974) pioneered the use of papyri in its booklength description of public oral communication in that Greco-Roman Mediterranean outpost. Currently, he is pursuing work on a descriptive catalog of French rhetorics from the beginning of printing to the present.

Denise A. Troll (M.A., Carnegie Mellon, 1984) is a doctoral candidate in Rhetoric and a researcher for the Mercury Electronic Library project at Carnegie Mellon. Her emphasis is the historical connection between technology and literacy, with a specialization in medieval manuscript and computer technologies. Much of her work deals with understanding the dimensions and interactions of oral and literate habits as these are constrained by technology. She has published and given talks on computer and medieval manuscript technology. Her dissertation addresses the role of medieval manuscript technology and monastic silence in the development of literate habits.

John O. Ward is a Senior Lecturer in History at the University of Sydney, N.S.W., Australia, where he has taught medieval history since 1967. He received his Ph.D. from the University of Toronto where he completed a dissertation on the study of the art of rhetoric in the Middle Ages and Renaissance, under the direction of Nikolaus Haring S.A.C. His special interest is the use made of Ciceronian rhetoric in Medieval and Renaissance cultures, and his publications lie mainly in this field. He has lectured at universities in the United States and Italy, taught classical and medieval Latin, and spent much time examining the manuscript history of Cicero's *Rhetorica* in English, European, and U.S. libraries.